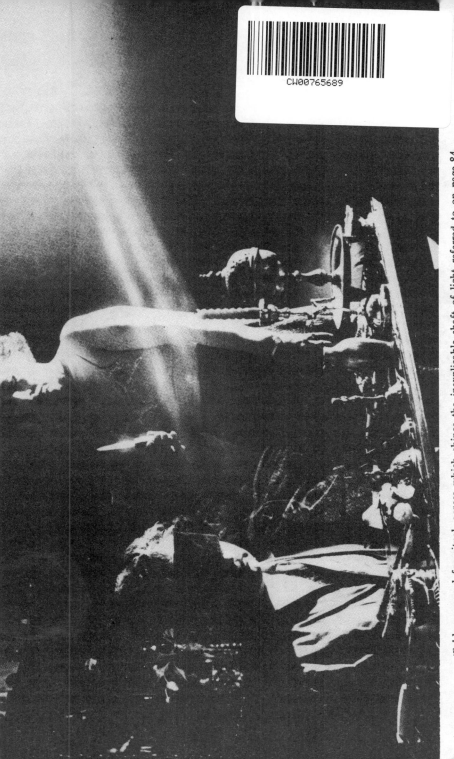

Table prepared for ritual, across which shines the inexplicable shaft of light referred to on page 84.

This copper platter, known in the Old Religion as a graal, has been in the possession of the owner's family for several hundred years (he is an hereditary witch). It has never been photographed before. It is considered to be of the Tudor period; the digits 1724 which appear on it do not represent a date, they are part of the symbolic system, which relates to that on the menhir at St. Duzec (a photograph of which faces page 65), interpreted by the Magister in Chapter XI. The number of bosses on the rim of the platter have symbolic significance, as well as the engravings in its centre. It is a ritual dish, used in celebration of the sacred meal, which forms part of the rites of most religions, including the Christian.

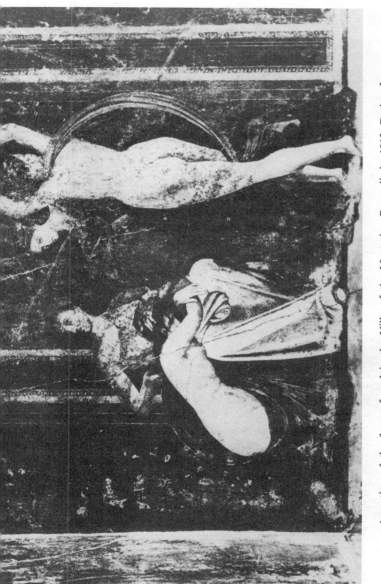

A section of the fresco found in the Villa of the Mysteries, Pompeii, in 1910. Dating from the first century A.D., it represents a stage in initiation into the Orphic-Eleusinian Mysteries, which has features in common with rites of some witch groups. The Mysteries flourished between the 8th century B.C. and A.D. 376, when the Sanctuary of the Mysteries was destroyed by Alaric's monks. Celebration of the Mysteries was forbidden by the Roman Senate, but is thought to have continued in secret.

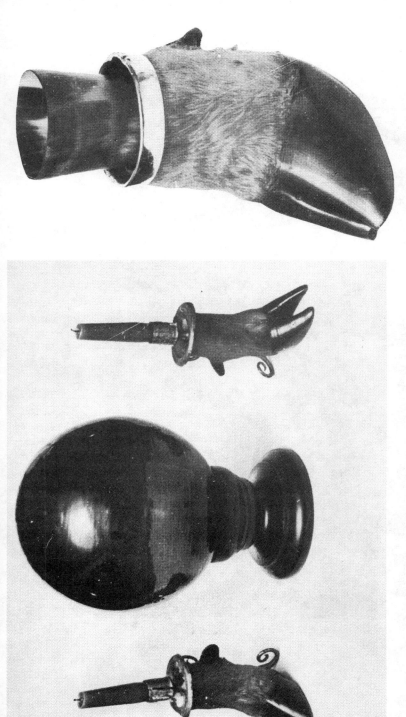

Left: Green glass fishing-float, of exceptional size. Fishing-floats are still used often as scrying-balls by witches, a custom dating back to the days of the persecutions, when, having no obvious connection with magic, a witch could safely own one, whereas possession of a crystal scrying-ball or dark mirror could be a hanging matter. Scrying is often practised during rituals, always by candle-light

Right: Sabbat wine-cup of horn in a bull's hoof holder, on the rim of which is engraved a pentagram. This would be among the

First century Bacchanalian dance, from a picture found in the columbarium of the Villa Pamphili, Rome, in 1789, now in the British Museum. Hereditary members of the Old Religion say it is likely that this form of dance derived from the witch ring dance, but that in fundamentals (such as nudity) it is not an expression of witch beliefs.

Menhir at St. Duzec, Brittany, dating from 17th or 18th century. The symbols carved on the monolith have been supposed to relate to the Christian faith, but a Magister of the Old Religion interprets them as a recapitulation of witch theology. (See Chapter XI).

Dual silver drinking-cup, which has also belonged to the owner's family for generations, though its date is believed to be later than that of the platter. It is considered to be a copy of a mediaeval vessel; its use is to measure the sacred potion in ceremonies. On the smaller cup, apart from witch sigils, is a basic design which breaks down into runic writing. The larger cup is engraved with ritual flowers; periwinkles, lime-flowers, roses, peonies and poppies.

stemming from a very ancient ritual, connected with archery. The shooting of arrows through garlands is frequently referred to in old stories about Robin Hood. The disc in the centre is engraved with the cross of the four elements. The fourth item

Left: Ritual dish, with drinking horns.

Right: Ceremonial garland, composed of nine flowers (indicat-

WITCHCRAFT, THE SIXTH SENSE

JUSTINE GLASS

Melvin Powers
Wilshire Book Company

12015 Sherman Road, No. Hollywood, CA 91605

For a great psychic

WILLIAM S. KING

PRINTED IN THE UNITED STATES OF AMERICA

ISBN 0-87980-174-3

Contents

Author's Foreword

WITHOUT acknowledgement of the invaluable co-operation of clairvoyants, witches and all those who, by allowing me to draw upon their 'extra-sensory' experiences, made possible the writing of this book, it could not be complete.

Among those in the last category are (in alphabetical order) Mr Cottie Burland, Mr Gerald Gough, Mr Gerard Noel (Editor of *Pentagram*) Mr Gerald Yorke, for whose generously-given help I am most grateful, as I am to the clairvoyants, who are mentioned in the text.

Because so much of my material came from the witches, (who prefer to remain anonymous,) I especially record my appreciation of their kindness, hospitality and patience under my questioning, for the time they gave and the trouble they took on my behalf— and I salute the qualities of mind and spirit I have found in them.

CHAPTER I

The Living Cult

WITCHCRAFT is claimed to be the oldest religion in the world; the cradle of all sects and cults and theologies of mankind. It has survived millennia of persecution, misunderstanding and misrepresentation. Probably more nonsense has been written about witchcraft through the centuries down to the present time than about any other subject.

What is witchcraft?

The real meaning of the word is the 'Craft of the Wise'. The Anglo-Saxon word 'wicca', or wise one, changed during the centuries—which is the natural fate of words—and become 'witch'. And with the change of the word, the popular conception of witchcraft changed also, so that a witch, once a respected and esteemed member of the community, became a near-outcast, from whom respectable men and women shuddered away.

Nowadays the attitude to the Craft is beginning to change once more, as it is to the metaphysical generally. Looking back in history, we can see that the most terrible persecutions of witches was an admission of the strength of belief in their powers. With the advance of what some would call materialism and some common-sense, witchcraft was taken less and less seriously, and as this happened, measures in force against it became less and less stringent. In 1735, under George II, the Witchcraft Act was passed. Its essence was that witchcraft did not exist, and that anyone who pretended to possess supernatural powers should be prosecuted. Finally, in 1951, the last of the Witchcraft Acts was taken off the Statute Book.

I am not saying that the only factor producing this altered attitude was disbelief in the powers of the witch. When public opinion changes it must be the result of many developments, and

13

in this case toleration, born of greater knowledge and understanding, played its part.

The curious thing is that today the disbelief which could be said to be the beginning of the decrease of witch persecution, is also on the wane. Within the last, say thirty years, so much supra-physical phenomena—discredited formerly as superstitious nonsense—has been established as scientific fact, that the claims of witch-powers no longer can be laughed out of court.

This feeling that witchcraft is a reality may be one reason for the undeniable upsurge of interest concerning it. Newspapers and magazines carry interviews with witches and resumés of rituals; a course of lectures upon witchcraft was given by an extended study institute, B.B.C. talks and television programmes feature it.

The inaugural dinner of the Witchcraft Research Association in October 1964, was besieged by pressmen hoping, but not permitted, to report it. Some of them managed to get a brief glimpse of the room and the guests; they must have been disappointed to see not a tall hat nor a broomstick, but only apparently unexceptional, well-dressed men and woman, enjoying an apparently unexceptional social occasion.

Yet fifty per cent of the people there were witches, who had travelled from all over England to celebrate the formation of an association, through which scattered covens, cut off from contact with colleagues through centuries of persecution, may achieve a coherence benefitting themselves and the Craft in general.

The other guests were interested, for one reason or another, in witchcraft. Some of them were professional men and women; some were artists, some worked in the business world; they were a cross section of society and of types and characters.

I have mentioned the Witchcraft Research Association because its formation is important as an indication of a new attitude not only to witchcraft but in the Craft itself.

When 'witchery' and wickedness became more or less synonymous and to be a witch was a capital crime, contact between covens was a danger to be risked rarely. Covens developed into enclaves, in which some aspects of the old lore and tradition were developed, others ignored or forgotten. Because of the nature of its history, witchcraft has no archives; there were no hiding-places for written records which could be relied on as being safe from discovery. And the consequence of discovery was death for the owner either by burning at the stake, or by hanging; often preceded by what was euphemistically known as 'questioning', in other words torture.

Father von Spee, a Jesuit Father of the seventeenth century, and one of the few men who was horrified by and protested against the cruelties and injustices of witch persecution (during which nine million men and women were executed) gives a picture of this 'questioning'. In his book, *Cautio Criminalis, seu de processibus contra Sagas,* he says: 'There is a frequent phrase used by judges that the accused has confessed without torture, and thus is undeniably guilty. I wondered at this and made inquiry and learned that in reality they were tortured, but only in an iron press, with sharp-edged channels over the shins, in which they were pressed like a cake, bringing blood and causing intolerable pain, and this is technically called without torture, deceiving those who do not understand the phrases of the inquisitors.'

I think it would be no exaggeration to say that at witch trials in general ninety-nine percent of the 'questioning' was carried out not to discover the truth of the case against the accused, but to make sure of a verdict of guilty 'as charged'.

On the mere whisper of suspicion of connexion with the Craft houses were searched and arrests made. Nothing which could possibly be construed as belonging to a witch could be stored on the premises of anyone who wanted to stay alive. The ceremonial pole was either hidden in a hollow broomstick, or the broomstick itself was used. The Athame (the sacred knife) was disguised. A present-day witch suggested to me that the continuing of ceremonial nudity into the times of persecution might have been a matter of expediency rather than of ritual—it solved the question of concealing robes.

And if, as I have said, there were no books or manuscripts concerning the Craft, incriminating evidence was reduced to a minimum . . . not that that meant a great deal in those days. There is on record a case of a woman who, watched whilst washing a dress in a river, was seen to turn the pockets inside out and clean them too. The neighbour who informed against her claimed that she must be a witch, since 'no good Christian would wash what was not visible'. She was burnt at the stake for an act which must have been done to please the Devil, it was said.

The terrors and perils of belonging to the Craft were such that its whole structure of tradition has been consistently (if one can use the term in this connexion) oral, for millennia. The lore, the ceremonials, the secrets, the 'know-how', were passed on by word of mouth, from woman to man or man to woman, for that is the way in which it should be done, except in emergencies when mother instructed daughter, or father, son.

At one time the knowledge was passed on by parents to children, who often were initiated into covens at the age of five or even younger. But this became too dangerous a practice as persecution grew more severe. Children do not realise the need for secrecy; coven meetings or rituals in which they took part were exciting, interesting matters to be discussed with their friends. And so, through children's chatter, it became known that So-and-so was a witch.

Often, one could say almost always, as a result not only the witch herself, but her whole family, young children as well, was arrested, 'tried', and executed, so that 'witch-blood' should not be passed on. The number of witches dwindled as a result of this measure: inevitably also it created gaps in the continuity of the tradition of the Craft. Some witch families were custodians of secrets which might be unknown to, or forgotten by other covens.

Covens always have been completely autonomous; it has been said that witchcraft was 'organised like Congregational Churches', in that each coven, as in each church, is an independent entity, not bound to any other, but in a sense affiliated.

In this system covens could be repositories of valuable lore or tradition, but since the laws of life, which operate at all levels, demand as the price of survival an outgoing and an incoming, a group too closely confined within its own circle of secrets, tends to atrophy, weaken and eventually to die.

This is what could be called the 'progressive' members of the Craft think may be happening today, and what they hope may be avoided, if witches can become aware of the danger. *Pentagram*, the organ of the Witchcraft Research Association, carried an article recently in which the need for co-operation between covens was urged. 'Witchcraft, however, has no . . . universally-available store of teaching on which to draw, on which to depend for continuity of tradition, or purpose or belief. The craft in Britain is fragmented into many sections . . . but there is no way in which the tradition and practice of every 'sect' can be examined, far less co-ordinated. . . . In several separate localities there are associated covens which have no contact with others; their membership may or may not be almost exclusively on a hereditary basis. Then there are several known covens which are entirely 'independent' and which have no contact—and seek none—with others.

'Such reluctant attitudes towards inter-communication may be in the short term explicable by expediency and the danger of betrayal. But is there not a far greater "betrayal" inherent in this situation? 'The historical view is that what is now known as Witchcraft was the Old Religion, embracing presumably theology, occult powers, and ceremonial rituals . . . and which was driven underground by the onslaught of the emergent Church and associated power politics. . . .

'It follows logically that during the past five hundred years or so those small and independent groups practising the Old Religion should have departed somewhat from the original and universal practice. In one part of the country the theology may have survived more strongly than elsewhere, yet much of the ritual and occult technique may have been lost or forgotten. . . .

'. . . Circumstances of the day make it imperative that something be done, and soon, to ensure that several remnants be brought together. Those who know must come forward; those who would learn, await. . . .

'. . . If the opportunities which now exist, and are so vital, are neglected, the Craft—in every section—will have only itself to blame for its own extinction. The heritage is endangered, and time is running out.'

This point of view is strongly held by those of its members who see the Craft as a living cult with a function in the modern world.

Witchcraft has evolved, they say, with the evolution of human consciousness, from a simple fertility cult, the tenets and deities of which were based upon observable natural phenomena, into a creed which could offer its followers a means to a full and satisfying life and of coming to terms with the problems which bedevil the majority of us.

Robert Cochrane, descendant of an hereditary witch family, is one of those who believe that witchcraft, if it will reorientate itself in the light of its inherent possibilities, has a useful function today. But in order that this may happen, he believes that 'radical rethinking' is necessary. In an article in *Pentagram*, he says:

'The value of the Old Craft today is that in it lie the seeds of the old mystery tradition. Through this the witch may perceive the beginnings of that ultimate in wisdom, knowledge of themselves and of their motives. The genuine Mysteries are open to all, because anyone having experience enough can understand that basic Message. To close the human mind, in order to protect it from outside circumstances that are hostile, is not a way to discover that within oneself which is most profound, but a return to the claustrophobic mother who will eventually smother the child. . . . In fossilised superstitious tradtion there are profound secrets hidden, secrets folded within the most mediocre belief and action. These great secrets, secrets of the soul and destiny, are only apparent in the open light, not in the illusionary world of Ye Olde English Wiccen. If the witches are to survive, then the religion must undergo some violent and radical changes. Changes that will open the ritual for examination, so that the spiritual content may be clearly seen. Changes that must kick over many sacred cows to see whether these old cows still give milk.

'The inherent philosophy of the Craft was always fluid, and fluid it must become again before it gasps its last breath under a heap of musty nonsense, half-baked theology and philosophy . . . there is no room for us in this society unless we have something valid to offer it, and participate in its social evolution.'

New concepts, the urge to grow and change and progress are signs of life in individual, species, movement. These are manifestations of the principle which drove our earliest ancestor, unicellular protoplasm, to seek better living conditions, the fish out of the sea to grow wings, our simian forbears down from the trees to leave behind forever the comparative bliss of unselfconsciousness and take up the cross of involution.

It seems that the working of this onward-driving principle is beyond the control of man's mind, so it is likely that the 'wind of change' will gradually bring about a reconstitution of the Craft on new, constructive lines, and that it will then, as Robert Cochrane suggests, have 'something valid' to offer society.

'The value of the Old Craft today is that in it lie the seeds of the Old Mystery tradition', he says. I think that here we have a key to the new interest in and attitude to witchcraft which I mentioned earlier in this chapter.

History seems to be repeating itself, as is its habit. Millennia ago, the witch, as I said, was a respected member of the community, valued, not feared, for possession of powers to help and heal. Treading the spiral path which returns to the same point but on a higher level, we seem to be more and more taking this view of witches and their Craft.

That there is power in witchcraft only those who know nothing of it or who cling to an outdated materialism would deny. I do not say all witches have it, but they are likely to have it, because only people whose psychic faculties are awakening are drawn to the cult, generally-speaking. I do not say that this power is good or bad. Like electricity, or any other form of power, it can be used constructively or destructively.

But it exists. Today science is discovering that many of the supraphysical activities of witches, dismissed for centuries as hysteria or gimcrack fantasy, have a solid, factual basis. Research in extra-sensory perception in this way has been the witch's best friend.

In the light of these findings of science, witchcraft has a new look. It is possible now to get some idea of what witchcraft really is and why it has survived for at least four thousand years, during about half of which it was villified and its members persecuted.

What was behind this persevering persecution? There was of course more than one reason, but one relevant to the present theme was fear. Witches were feared because they could do things that the majority of other people could not do—(and the Church taught that such powers could only come from the Devil). When the exaggeration, the dramatisation and distortion are discounted, the fact remains that if witches did not get results they and their Craft would soon have been forgotten.

Witches and witchcraft have been dissected by anthropologists, archaeologists, historians, sociologists—and by writers on magic and devil-worship. But witchcraft has not yet been evaluated in terms of extra-sensory perception and as the reservoir of 'know-how' of the psychic faculties, which it undoubtedly is.

Centuries before Dr James Braid 'discovered' medical hypnosis in the eighteen hundreds, witches were procuring painless child-birth and relieving many physical troubles by putting their patients into a hypnotic sleep. In the Compendium of the Laws of England, compiled in the thirteenth century, is a clause condemning as a 'practice of enchantment, those who send people to sleep'. Dr.

Braid's method of inducing trance was to make patients gaze steadily at a shining object; the witches set up a bright-bladed sword, at which the sufferer had to stare.

Witch-history is full of documented instances of what we now know as telepathy, faith-healing, pre-cognition, clairvoyance, astral-travelling. Witchcraft teaches the development and use of these powers—and has had more than four thousand years of practice in these techniques.

Witches who believe in the future of their cult consider that development of these powers is not only important as an end in itself, but as a means of creating a link between material and non-material worlds. To be assured of an existence on levels other than the physical can be a reassuring and stimulating experience, if brought about in the right way. This is how a witch of my acquaintance puts it:

'Once a person has had even one of these experiences of contacting forces beyond the world of form, he or she is no longer in bondage to that world.'

That this is so is confirmed by a story told to me by a woman member of the B.B.C. She has travelled widely and her life has been full of incident and interest, but she said that her most wonderful experience happened in her own home. She always left her keys on a chest in her bedroom; one night she discovered they were not there. She hunted through the bedroom without finding them; switching off the light, she was going out of the room, when a circular glow of light rather above eye level appeared, moving towards her. As it came nearer, she saw that in the centre were her keys. The light hovered over the chest, settled on it, then faded. And there were her keys.

This may seem a trivial experience of no great value but I can understand just what that woman meant when she said it was the most thrilling and satisfying of her life. She was not interested in spiritualistic phenomena, nor religious aspects. To her it was evidence of the existence of a world other than the world of matter and she felt a sense of freedom and security because of it which has never since left her.

I think that this sense of contact with invisible forces is what most of the men and women are seeking who are drawn to the Craft of the Wise. Orthodox religions do not supply the need. In them the 'seeds of the Mysteries' are so deeply buried under mounds of doctrine, intellectual concepts and complex teachings that they are unavailable to the majority.

That the need is widespread and general is shown by the number of inquiries received by *Pentagram* alone, which come from doctors, barristers, solicitors, osteopaths, housewives, artists, writers, men and women in business and commerce.

The great majority of them are looking for the 'missing factor' in their lives; a way of relating the invisible forces to themselves so that they can become complete, integrated human beings.

CHAPTER II

The Long Shadows of the Past

THE story of witchcraft, most anthropologists think, is as old as the human race itself. It goes back to the dawning of consciousness when man began to realise the existence of forces outside himself and in the first primitive conception, personalised their manifestations.

Its twin deities are the two main concepts of male and female deities which are found in the pantheons of all religions; which Jung calls 'the archetypes of the collective unconscious', the Wise Old Man, and the Great Mother. They are the personifications of the pairs of opposites, which manifest in the world of form, or appearance; light and dark, spring and winter, life and death, seed-time and harvest.

The Great Mother, the goddess of fertility, the priestess, the sibyl, was the dominant figure in the days before copulation had been related to procreation. The female produced—presumably by magic —children; without her the tribe would cease to exist. The female principle was therefore to be worshipped, and matriarchy was the order of the day. The cults of the Great Mother spanned the world, and her names are as innumerable as are the aspects under which she was adored—Hecate, Artemis, Isis, Brigid, Diana, the Virgin Mary, Cailleach, Prosperpina, Luna, Cybele, Selene and so on. She was Trivia, goddess of the three ways, and as Hecate, cross-roads were sacred to her. In some countries she was believed to be three persons (the recurrent triad motif), Hecate, Diana, Prosperina, and in this guise she was called Triformis. As Hecate, she was goddess of magic, sometimes depicted with three heads, that of a dog, a horse and a boar. Through mythology, there are identifications of gods and goddesses with animals (Thoth, the hawk-headed, Bubas-

22

tis, patroness of cats, and the hippotamus goddess of Egypt, Taueret, are examples) which perhaps are survivals of or amalgamations with totemism.

Totemism could be defined as a magico-religious idea, based on belief in a mystical relationship between a tribe or group of men and a species of animal. The belief was widespread according to anthropologists, at least 12,000 years ago. The totem animal was worshipped and in some degree held sacred, but this apparently did not secure it immunity from appearing on the tribal menu, if need arose. The theory was that the totem animal must not be killed without its permission—as to how and why this would be given were nice questions. Some formula must have existed to deal with them, otherwise the tribe could have starved to death while they were being debated.

As the god and goddess idea developed, we find marriages between them and the totem animal. Sometimes the totem animal left, as it were, his stamp upon the deity—for instance Demeter, with her horse's head. Hecate's three animal heads indicated identification with a trinity of totems, each totem belonging to a separate group.

The marriage of the totem animal with the Great Mother was a rite to ensure fertility of the tribe and of the crops. The totem animal came to be represented by a male priest, wearing the skin of the totem animal, performing the ritual marriage with the priestess, as representative of the Mother Goddess.

The Great Mother was still the dominant figure for some time after the man's part in procreation was recognised. The king was the consort of the queen. He held office, so to speak for a period of time which varied between one year and several, at the end of which he was sacrificed, to ensure the productivity and prosperity of the land and its inhabitants. In this conception of the expendability of the male there seems to be something more basic than a primitive 'gooseberry bush' motion of generation and fertility insurance. Nature worked out the idea chiefly in the bee and the spider. The drone dies while consummating the mating; the male spider becomes the main dish of his wife's wedding feast.

Apparently, as the habit never became widespread, Nature did not think much of it. Yet however indefinable there seems to be in the 'collective subconscious' a connexion between the male principle and death; perhaps stemming from the instinctive realisation of the ruthlessness of natural selection, which expresses as the urge to fight—for the female or, as in human animals, on any excuse.

The witch cult, it is thought, probably came into existence during the Great Mother stage of the development of human consciousness.

No one can put even an approximate date to its emergence, and in such a vast time-scale, a few hundred or even a thousand years here or there are not of vital significance. At any rate, it seems that witchcraft belongs to a matriarchal period, when the female principle was the dominant.

There is a passage in the Bardic Triads quoted by Lewis Spence in *The Mysteries of Britain*, which indicates that the Craft was the first religion of this country. It runs: 'There are three special doctrines that have been obtained by the nation of the Cymry; the first, from the age of ages was that of the Gwyddoniaid, prior to the time of Prydain son of Aedd the Great; the second was Bardism, as taught by the Bards, after they had been instituted; the third was the Faith in Christ. . . .'

The word Gwyddoniaid is the masculine plural form; its meaning is given in Spurrell's Welsh-English dictionary as 'Wizards or Scientists'. 'Gwiddon', a word of feminine gender, is translated by Thomas Jones, in his dictionary of Welsh words, *The British Language in its Lustre* (1688), as 'witch'. Gwyddon and gwiddon must be therefore masculine and feminine forms respectively of the same root word, and Gwyddoniaid the noun used collectively to describe the religion or cult practised by gwyddon and gwiddon.

It seems likely, though Spence does not make this clear, that the Bardic Triad he quotes comes from the Barddas, a collection of Bardic literature compiled by Llewellyn Sion of Glamorgan, in the sixteenth century, which had been copied by Edward Williams in the eighteenth century, translated by the Rev. J. Williams ap Ithel in 1862, and published by the Welsh Manuscript Society in that year.

The unknown Druid writer of the Triad is telling us that before this country was even known as Britain—a name said to be derived from the name 'Prydain' (son of Aedd)—the witch-cult was old; 'from the age of ages . . . the Gwyddoniaid'. No one can say how it originated, but the preponderance of what can be called educated guessing by anthropologists and archaeologists adds up to the theory that it grew out of the practice of hunting magic, three or four thousand years ago.

Certain methods were believed to bring about certain results; for instance, that concentration on a particular species of animal made it more vulnerable to the huntsman. Cave paintings of stags, boars and so on are thought to have been executed as a means of focussing the attention, in this way.

No doubt then, as now, there were people who were able to use and project the powers of the mind more strongly and easily than others; the psychically-gifted, in fact. And as word of their abilities got around, their prestige would grow until they became important members of the tribe.

Somewhere in the Neolithic period it is thought that the cult developed into a religion, which worshipped two deities, the Mother Goddess and the Horned God (possibly a descendant of the totem animal). He was the god of hunting, magic—and death; another example of the identification of the male principle with dissolution. In the cave of the Trois Fréres at Ariége, France, there is a recognisable painting of him dating from prehistoric times, dressed in an animal's skin, masked, with a horned frontlet on his head.

At Cogul, there is another cave painting, of probably about the same age, in which there are certain features which seem to identify it with the Craft. In the centre of a circle of dancing women, stands a man—possibly the priest—naked, except for garters. Garters are still worn by witches today, not to keep their stockings up (and this obviously was not the purpose for which the priest in the painting wore them), but as a badge of rank. One of the women carries a knife, which looks like the ritual knife of the witches.

The whole disposition of the group is virtually the same as in the ring dance of today; at least in many respects. Since earliest days of human history, the circle has been considered a means of raising and of conserving power. The circular form was used in constructions of places of worship, such as Stonehenge; which is said to symbolise the womb. And most likely that is the origin of the belief in the potency of the circle; power (in a sense) and life are generated in the womb, power and life are conservd by the womb.

Some archaeologists and psychologists, such as Erich Neuman, who was a student of Jung's, carry the interpretation of the symbology of Stonehenge still further in terms of these concepts. Neuman points out in his book *The Great Mother: An exploration of the Archetype*, that in ancient times the trilithon, or gateway, symbolised the Great Mother, from whom the sun-god is reborn; the trilithon could be taken as representing the entrance to the womb. At the winter solstice, the setting winter sun (or dying god) appears framed in the mighty trilithon (or what is left of it). The red sphere, glowing between the great stones, was a testimony to the worshippers of four thousand years or so ago, not only that man must die, but that he, like the sun, is reborn, from the Great Mother's womb.

We find in the study of our long-ago past that a solid substratum of symbology was sexual. Centuries of repression and unrealistic thought have conditioned us so that although today the attitude towards sex is becoming a little more mature, some people are still inclined to wince away from it, feeling that our ancestors must have had rather nasty minds.

But we have to remember that sex did not become a dirty word until what is called civilisation was in full swing, and man, with his genius for complication, dreamed up taboos and restrictions to make what was a simple, natural and sacred function into an exciting—perhaps because forbidden, pleasure.

To go back to the Winter Solstice, it was celebrated as a most important period of the year in ancient times, even more important, some authorities suggest, than the Summer Solstice. The Hon. John Abercrombie, in his book *Bronze Age Pottery* (1912), mentions that the entrance to Stonehenge is at the north-east. It was supposed that worship at Stonehenge was centred on the rising sun at the summer solstice, in which case, as Mr Abercrombie points out, it would be necessary to turn one's back to the south-west—where the alter is—in order to face it. In no religious rite or temple, he argues, does one enter a building and then turn round in order to confront the object of worship. Therefore he believes that the great day of the year was not the summer but the winter solstice, when the symbolically dying sun was framed in the trilithon, over the high altar.

It would be surprising, remembering the antiquity of the cult, if the witches did not celebrate the important Winter Solstice. And, of course they do, in a rite based on the same concept; the death and rebirth of the sun—or life. The priestess or coven leader, stands behind a cauldron, under which a fire is lit. The cauldron symbolises the womb, the fire represents the life force.

Round her, the coven members dance in a circle, deosil, carrying lighted torches. This is the Yule Dance, or Dance of the Wheel, 'which causes the sun to be re-born'. In primitive days, this may have been literally accepted as the purpose of the rite; for a long time witches have realised its symbolical meaning, and keep the festival much in the same spirit as Christmas is celebrated. The fundamental concept underlying both is the same; like a recurrent decimal, it appears in many creeds and cults, including Druidism.

The Druids celebrate Yule—the death of the sun and its re-birth—with rites which have a family resemblance to those of the witchcult. The light of the Old Year, burning as lamp or candle, is extinguished. Then, one by one in the darkness, points of flame appear, as candles are lit, symbolising the birth of the new light, or New Year.

Witchcraft and Druidry, although in many ways divergent in ideaology, share certain beliefs. Reincarnation is one of these, the importance of the stone circle as a place of worship is another. Both cults believed in the power of the 'magic' circle as a means of generating and conserving forces and for protection, and in the practice of what we now call extra-sensory perception. The four great Sabbats were common to both cults.

Stonehenge is orientated to the sun; Druidism is a cult of sun-worship. These facts were added up by early archaeologists to form the theory that the Druids built Stonehenge. Later investigations put the date of the earliest parts of Stonehenge at 1800 B.C. The Druids do not come into the picture until about the fifth century B.C.; they were the priests of the Celts who invaded Britain then, and occupied the south-east of the country—so whoever built Stonehenge it could not have been the Druids. The witches believe that the early Stonehenge, symbolic of the female principle, was the temple of their goddess, the Great Mother, worshipped under one of her countless names; as Albina, the Barley Goddess, who gave her name to Britain in the form Albion, or perhaps as Cerridwen from 'cerdd', meaning creative art, especially poetry, and 'wen', or white. The Druids called Stonehenge the 'Cauldron of Cerridwen' (or Cauldron of Inspiration); so very likely that was how she was known.

For a time Druidism was the official religion of this country. With the Druids the witches could be said to work hand-in-hand; each cult different from, but complementing and not interfering with the other. For about two thousand years the witches were the priestesses of the community, or village; performing rites for bringing prosperity to the land and to the people; acting as seers, healing men and animals in return for food and shelter. The witchcult seems to have been the forerunner of the National Health Service—but a more comprehensive and perhaps more effective service. . .

The position for the witches probably did not change very much during the Roman occupation of this country, which lasted about four centuries, from A.D. 43 to A.D. 410. Mention of witches during this time is sparse: the Romans do not seem to have considered witches a threat to their security. The case of the Druids was a different story; Druids impinged on the political situation. The Romans believed them to be a potential danger to the *Pax Romana* and persecuted them as such.

In A.D. 324, the collapse of the Roman Empire and of the old Roman way of life began when the first Christian Emperor of Rome, Constantine, instituted Christianity as the official religion of his regnancies. The weakening of authority caused by resultant political upheavals made the Empire vulnerable to barbarian attacks; finally Constantine had to retire to Byzantium, which was renamed Constantinople as a delicate tribute to him.

Constantine's elder son remained in nominal control at least in Rome, but not for long. The western regions of the Empire gradually fell into the hands of Goths, Huns and Vandals; in 410, the Emperor Honorius recalled the legions from Britain to help bolster up home defences.

And now clouds began to darken the witches' skies. Christianity had been in existence long enough for man to get to work on its teachings; distorting interpretations, entombing its spirit under the debris of dogma. The Church Councils were busy acquiring power in secular as well as ecclesiastical spheres, denouncing this and that and forbidding the other. In A.D. 314, at the Council of Ancyra, a batch of bishops, including the Bishop of Antioch, Vitalis, and the Bishop of Caesarea, St Leontius, issued a *caveat* against pacts with the devil.

The 24th canon of what would be called today the recommendations of the Council (equivalent to our Royal Commissions) enjoined five years' penance for soothsaying or witchcraft to cure diseases, or for following customs of the Gentiles. Another canon (the 4th) sentences to deprivation clergy who would not abstain from intercourse with 'strange women', a term which is usually taken to mean witches. Also the Council was anti-vegetarian. The 14th canon states that 'clergy shall be deprived if they obstinately refuse to eat meat or vegetables cooked with meat'.

But as yet the storm which was to burst so terribly upon the Cult was only rumbling in the distance. In 785 the Holy Synod of Paderborn enounced that 'Whoever, being fooled by the devil, maintains in accordance with pagan beliefs, that witches exist and causes them to be burned at the stake, shall be punished with death'.

Under the Saxons, things worsened for the witches. The Saxon gods were gods of war and violence, Odin and Thor—although Odin had a Wild Hunt, similar to that of Herne, or the Horned God, and though the Valkyries had a good deal in common with legendary witches, the Saxons feared witchcraft and hated magic. When they became Christianised, they made life even more unpleasant for members of the Craft. They and the subsequently-invading Danes, who also in time became Christianised, formulated laws against the common enemy, the wicca, as by then witches were known. Roughly translated, the name meant 'learned' or 'wise'. Interchangeable for a time with wicca, were the terms scin-laeca, or one able to project the astral body, and galdor-craftig, or spell-maker.

The laws were framed so as to prohibit any known form of witchcraft and traffic with witches. 'If any wicca . . . or any foul, contaminated, manifest horcwenan (whore or leman) be anywhere in the land, man shall drive them out . . .' '. . . every priest shall extinguish all heathendom, and forbid WILWEARTHUNGA (fountain worship), and LICWIGLUNGA (incantations used to raise the dead), HWATA (prophesying or precognition in any form) and GALDRA (magic) and man-worship, and the abominations that men use in the various craft of the Wicca . . .' This included WIGLIAN (divining by the moon), destroying anyone by witcraft, healing the sick (men or animals), by this means, making spells to gain a lover, 'loving wicca crafte', or worshiping sun, moon, trees, wells or stones. A curious phrase crops up at this period, unlybban wyrce, which was used to describe lethal forms of magic, which became known as black witchcraft. So far as I can trace, this is the first mention of the practice of using psychic force destructively as if it were a cult. This seems to be confirmation, however shadowy, of a point made by a modern witch when we were discussing the origins of black magic. She said that broadly-speaking it came into being when persecution of the Craft began and some of its members used 'unlawful magic' to protect themselves.

Not surprisingly, the witches did not love the Saxons, and after 1066 and all that, it is said that Norman troops sent to quash Saxon risings, were often led by witches who knew the local hideouts. One of the witches who was helping to hunt Hereward the Wake in the Fens was caught and killed by him.

By and large, the Craft seems to have fared better under the Normans than during the previous occupation, perhaps because many of the Normans had a leaning towards it, or were members themselves. The father of Duke William (The Conqueror) was known as 'Robert the Devil', and he (Duke William) had little sympathy with the Church's claims of authority. When the Pope, Gregory VII demanded William's homage as King of England, William said: 'Fealty I have never willed to do, nor will I do it now. I have never promised it nor do I find that my predecessors did it to yours.' His son, William Rufus who succeeded him, was a member of a witch cult, as were many of our early kings, including, according to Margaret Murray, all the Plantagenets. His death is supposed to have been a ritual killing. Witch marks (or signs) can be found carved into various parts including the north door of All Saints the church near the Rufus Stone in the New Forest, in the church-yard of which is buried Purkess, the man who wheeled Rufus' body to the church on a hand-cart, 'so that he would get a decent burial', and who complained that he never got his hand-cart back.

After this comparatively brief period of near-calm under the Normans, enactments against and active persecution of the witches were stepped up. What they called the 'burning time' began somewhere about A.D. 1300, and continued with varying intensity until the seventeenth century. The Craft, as a whole, went underground, but contemporary churches and cathedrals all over the country are evidence that they were still active.

The early churches were usually built upon sites of pagan worship. Pope Gregory had the commonsense to make an edict that when places or concepts were associated with beliefs too strong to be uprooted, they should be given a veneer of Christianity.

This process opened the gates of Christian sainthood to many aspects of the Great Mother and her consort of which St Bridget and St Michael are two examples. The origin of St Michael is thought by most anthropologists and archaeologists to be Lucifer (or Lugh), the god of light; Bride, or Brigid was translated into Brigit.

And in these churches, all over the country are 'witch marks'; pentacies and pentagrams, and others, carved figures of the Great Mother and masks of the Horned God, usually called the Green Man, because he is represented surrounded with scrolls of oak leaves or acorns, or with leaves seemingly growing from mouth, ears, hair.

The Great Mother usually is symbolised by what is called a sheila-na-gig, a word of doubtful origin. Sheila-na-gigs represent the female principle of fertility; they depict a woman squatting in a position which emphasises the sexual organs. They are included deliberately in the design of the church; there is a good example of a sheila-na-gig at Whittlesford, Cambs.

Sheila-na-gigs have been called 'gross obscenities' by some historians and archaeologists, but I think we have to remember that in the days when these carvings were made, sex was not obscene. The figures are an attempt, crude by our standards, to express veneration for the female principle of fertility.

In most cases, no attempt has been made to conceal the presence of the Green Man or the sheila-na-gig. The clerical authorities may not actually have commissioned the inclusion of the witches' deities in churches, but the priests must have known they were there. They were complaisant probably for two reasons. One was that Christianity and the old cult existed side by side, at least until the end of the Plantagenet period. In the Bishop's Register at Exeter, it is recorded that the monks of Frithelstock Priory were found by the bishop in the woods worshipping a statue of the 'unchaste Diana' (the Mother Goddess). Priests of all ranks from parish incumbent to bishop, took part in 'pagan' rites, for which they were, if this was discovered, 'put on the mat' in a half-hearted way; the purpose seems to have been chiefly a warning to be more careful next time not to be found out.

The other reason was that skilled labour for church (or any other) building was not easy to come by. If clerical employers had made 100 per cent Christian belief a condition of employment, they would have been unlikely to get their churches built at all. Most of the workmen would be members of the Old Faith (as well as the new), though they would not advertise it. Then as now, they reacted against any form of regimentation in religion or any other matter. Probably for this reason, as well as a desire to have the old gods around, they carved their symbols on boss and pillar and window. The Horned One and Great Mother must not be forgotten even though the place of their worship had become a church dedicated to the Christian God. . . .

Where churches had been built on the sites of traditional meeting-places, the witches went further afield for their gatherings, which became more and more secret as time went on. The erstwhile witch 'centres' are scattered all over the British Isles; if a catalogue of them were to be made, I think one, or more likely two or three, would be found in every county. Many of them are still used by modern witches, as for example Chanctonbury Ring in Sussex, which has a reputation (nothing to do with the witches) of being the most haunted place in England. Among its legends are that a horned man (the Horned God?) rides over it on horseback, and that fauns and creatures with gargoyle faces appear. Not long ago a party of thirty students decided to spend a night there to investigate the 'goings on'. Apparently they got their money's worth; manifestations occurred on a scale which sent the whole company rushing down the knoll of Chanctonbury in a panic, leaving all their goods and chattels behind, except a tape-recorder, which one student had the presence of mind to grab as he fled.

Then there is the Major Oak in Sherwood Forest, which is at least 1,500 years old. Inside its trunk thirty-two people can stand; its girth is sixty-four feet—and of course Robin Hood and Maid Marian used to foregather there.

Gorse hill, near Swindon, was another 'witch centre'; a coven which I am told is called the 'Moonrakers', meets there still. Avebury, the Rufus Stone is in the New Forest, the Stype Stones in Shropshire (which include the Devil's Seat), Toothill, outside Southampton are others. And then there are the Rollright Stones, near Long Compton in Warwickshire, which is among the oldest, if not the oldest, of such circles in this country.

Between two and three thousand years ago, possibly while our climate was still Mediterranean, the stones were put up, either by the Beaker people or by their predecessors, Neolithic man . . . and no doubt the witches danced there, as they still do. I have seen traces of ritual witch fires, roughly in the centre of the circle.

Very little is known about the Rollright Stones. They have never been excavated with modern resources; the only attempt to discover what, if any, secrets they are hiding was made by an antiquary called Sheldon in the seventeenth century. Sheldon, apparently 'was at some charge to digge within this circle to try to see if he could find any bones', but he found none, and does not mention having discovered anything else.

The stones, which are of oolitic limestone must have formed a circular wall since some of the standing stones overlap. Its diameter is about 100 feet, which approximates to that of Stonehenge's outer circle. The height of the tallest stone is seven feet, its original measurements can only be guessed at. Two thousand years of wear and tear working on friable stone such as oolitic limestone could easily reduce them by half.

The number of stones in the circle; is given as between seventy-two and seventy-eight. One of the legends about the circle is that no one ever has been able to count the stones correctly. The story goes that a local baker, determined to get the better of the hoodoo, laid a loaf on each of the stones. But when he collected the loafs he found that several were missing. He tried again and again, always the same thing happened.

When I went to the place, a vicious wind, which bit its way over the ridge on which the circle stands, discouraged me from trying to succeed where the baker failed, and also from testing the truth of another legend, concerning the King Stone. This is a monolith eight feet high, seven feet broad, and weathered, or carved, there is no means of knowing which, into an interrupted curve. It stands about 100 yards from the circle; near by are alder trees which are said to 'bleed' profusely if cut, and when the knife rips the wood, the King Stone moves. . . .

No archaeologist has been able to solve satisfactorily the riddle of the purpose which brought the Rollright Stones into place, or to offer anything but a guess as to the reason why the King Stone *should be where it is, or why it should be there at all.* There are probably as many theories as there are stones in the ring.

About the five large stones called the Whispering Knights, which stand—or, to be accurate, four stand, one is fallen—close together, as if in conclave, about 390 yards from the Rollright circle, there is what amounts virtually to certainty as to their age and purpose. They are recognisable as a dolmen, a chamber which usually forms part of a long barrow burial, though some may have been separate structures, rather of the same nature as the family vaults in churches, which still exist today. This was the way in which the pre-Beaker, or Long Barrow men, buried their dead, to which the Whispering Knights remain as witness. Of the bodies they guarded only a cheek-bone fragment was found, the age of which Sir Arthur Keith gave as approximating to the age of the dolmen.

The Wise Ones—the Wicca—no doubt assisted in the rites of the dolmen and the Rollright circle. The Old Religion has left its mark in the place-names of the country round about the Stones; Shipton-under-Wychwood—where the famous wise woman, Mother Shipton, lived—and the forest of Wychwood. 'Wych' is a modified form of spelling of 'witch' or 'Wicca'; the long, long history of the cult, echoes in these names as well as in the tradition of the meeting-places, all over the country.

CHAPTER III

The Dark Side of the Moon

BLACK MAGIC could be called a modern innovation in witchcraft —modern that is to say, in relation to the immense age of the Craft. For millennia, as we have seen, witches were respected, valued members of the community. The tool of their trade— the wand—which degenerated in later centuries into a broomstick, was a status symbol, then, not incriminating evidence or the bad joke it became afterwards.

Even in the early halcyon days, no doubt a blot or two appeared in the witches' copybook, but I think if these had been more serious than the occasional blasting of a cow belonging to a tiresome man, or causing a treasured dress of a trouble-making woman to become moth-fodder, the general attitude to witches would have changed in their disfavour, as with the arising of black magic it eventually did.

How and when and why black magic came into the picture is to a great extent a matter of guesswork. Witches (white) of whom I have asked these questions have no traditional knowledge of the answers. But they agree with T. C. Lethbridge, who says in his book *Witches*, 'It was only later (i.e. in mediaeval times) when the religion was facing dangerous enemies, that its devotees turned to the use of black magic against them'.

Stringent persecution of the witches began, as I have said, at the beginning of the fourteenth century. Open war upon them was declared by a Bull issued by Pope Innocent VIII, 1484, which reads 'It has come to our ears that numbers of both sexes do not avoid to have intercourse with demons, Incubi and Succubi; and that by their sorceries, and by their incantations, charms and conjurations, they suffocate, extinguish and cause to perish the births of women, the increase of animals, the corn in the ground, the grapes in the vineyard and the fruit of the trees, as well as men, women, flocks, herds and various kinds of animals, vines and apple trees, grass, corn, and other fruits of the earth; making and procuring that men and women, flocks and herds and other animals shall suffer, and be tormented both from within and without, so that men beget not, nor women conceive; and they impede the conjugal action of men and women.'

The Bull was intended as an enactment against witchcraft generally, but as the points made in the indictment are in exact opposition to the tenets and purposes of the original or white cult it seems to indicate that at that time the practice of black magic had grown to a point where it was attracting to itself more notice than was the parent Craft.

Dr Margaret Murray says that the cult was originally concerned with the promotion of fertility, which is true, as far as it goes. But the witch's powers and duties, as I have said, included healing sick men and animals and an advisory service which dealt with present and future situations. Dr Murray comments that '. . . it [the cult] became gradually degraded into a method for blasting fertility, and thus the witches who had once been the means of bringing prosperity to the people and the land by driving out all evil influences, in process of time were looked upon as being themselves the evil influence, and were held in horror accordingly'.

This could be true of a section of the Craft, but that a body which had been concerned for several thousand years with the good of the community should as a whole in the course of a relatively few years, perform a complete volte-face by working destructively instead of constructively, seems to be unworthy of serious consideration. It is against the law of probability, and against it also there is a good deal of historical evidence. But in spite of this, the point of view that all witches were black witches, grew to be more or less generally accepted. The word witchcraft became synonymous with the powers of darkness, with all the horrors man's mind could think up to scare itself into idiocy.

The Horned God, who was really much more nearly related to Pan, 'lover of noise, who goeth upon the hilltops', Faunus and Sylvanus, the nature gods, became the Devil.

It has been said that the Devil's reign of terror, which was to last for several hundred years, came into being because the Church had reached a stage when it needed a focus for justifiable hate, a fulcrum, in a way, to aid its progress. It could not, must not hate its persecutors, but against a postulated evil force, working to overthrow the divinely revealed and instituted form of religion by which alone men could be saved, all the considerable, ever-increasing power of the Church could be unleashed destructively.

The devil idea seems to have been at its peak in the Middle Ages, the Kali Yuga (or dark era). The graph of its violence shows a gradual decrease during succeeding centuries but even today in some degree it is with us.

The concept of duality—the belief in two powers, good and evil—which is the Devil's cradle, seems to have originated in Persia. It found expression in the sect of the Manichees, founded somewhere about the third century by Manii Khaios, who believed Satan to be co-existent and co-eternal with God. It grew and developed; Plutarch contributed his mite in the shape of an evil world-soul. Creation itself was evil, according to the Gnostics. And so the crescendo rose until it seems that Church and people were giving more attention to the Devil than to God, whom they professed to believe was omnipotent, omniscient and omnipresent.

According to the Church, it was evil which was omnipresent. Beauty was evil; happiness and pleasure were sins. Ugliness, pain and dirt were apparently approved by God. The Christian dictum was: 'Dirt is holy, cleanliness is of the witch and the Devil'. To expose one's naked body (as in washing) even in privacy where it could be seen only by its Creator was sinful; apparently God would be shocked beyond bearing by what He had made.

The cult of dirt as an expression of godliness reached such a pitch that when, after his murder, Thomas a Becket's body linen could hardly be removed, because it was so caked with filth and lice that it fell to pieces, it was said that judging by its condition England had lost the holiest of her priests.

Even more terrible than cleanliness, was sex. Sex was virtually synonymous with wickedness; it was the bonne bouche used by the Devil to lure men into sin. But the Devil had an active partner in his work of corruption—women. From her high position as the giver and keeper of life and good, women was degraded to the level of a social evil; an impure creature with whom man had to associate in order to perpetuate the race. The whole business of procreation was regarded as distasteful; disgusting even. It was increasingly clear to the Church that God could not really have known what he was doing when he organised it.

St Augustine considered the facts of life obscene; some of his followers went so far as to blame God for instructing Adam to be 'fruitful and multiply', since that entailed carnal cohabitation. The strictures extended to Adam; he should have known better than to obey God, who then would have had to think up some other way of populating the earth.

A fear of women was bred of this unhealthy attitude to sex. Simon de Beauvoir analyses it in his book, *The Second Sex*. He says: 'It is Christianity which invests woman anew with frightening prestige; fear of the other sex is one of the forms assumed by the anguish of man's uneasy conscience. . . . Evil is an absolute reality and flesh is sin. And, of course, since woman remains always the "Other", it is not held that reciprocally male and female are both flesh; flesh is for the Christian, the hostile "other" is—precisely Woman. In her the Christian finds incarnated the temptation of the world, the flesh and the devil. All the Fathers of the Church insist on the idea that she led Adam into sin. We must quote Tertullian (end of the second century A.D.): "Woman: You are the gateway of the devil. You persuaded him whom the devil dared not attack directly. Because of you the Son of God had to die. You should always go dressed in mourning and in rags" . . . Christian literature strives to enhance the disgust that man can feel for woman. . . .'

This attitude could be in part reaction from millennia of female dominance; the compensatory swing of the pendulum. But it would hardly account for the preoccupation with all manifestations of evil, with cruelty and dirt which characterises this period, although G. Rattray Taylor believes that the perverted concept of sex was a major factor in the psychological debacle. He says: 'The Church never succeeded in obtaining universal acceptance of its sexual regulations but in time it became able to enforce sexual abstinence on a scale sufficient to produce a rich crop of mental disease. It is hardly too much to say that mediaeval Europe came to resemble a vast insane asylum'.

Esoterically the period has been interpreted as a phase through which human consciousness had to pass in its development; the

Piscean Age of deification of denial and pain, when mortification of the flesh was the highest service one could offer its Creator. In what unlit corner of the human subconscious can have spawned the idea that the chief pleasure of the Universal Principle of Love lies in the sight and sound of suffering?

Symptomatic of the masochistic obsession which resulted from general psychological trauma; in this climate devil-worship and black magic could flourish naturally—perhaps 'naturally' is not the word to use in this connexion. . . .

These two forms of the black arts which are so closely related that the term black magic covers both adequately, were to be met everywhere; people from the highest to the lowest ranks were accused of its practice. In 1232 Hubert de Burgh was put on trial; it was said that he had become the favourite of King John by using spells and incantations. Then there is the case of Lady Alice Kyteler, which is quoted in almost every book written about witchcraft, black or white. In 1324, Lady Alice, who lived near Kilkenny, Ireland, was accused by the Bishop of Ossory of most malpractices attributed to the black arts. The charges including heresy and sacrilege, sacrifice of living creatures to demons, tearing their bodies apart and scattering the limbs at the crossroads, boiling in the skull of a robber, who had been beheaded, an abominable brew, some of the ingredients of which were intestines of cocks, worms, finger or toe-nails from corpses, hairs and brains of boy children who had died unbaptised, to which a seasoning of herbs was added. It is hard to see how a skull could ever be made into an efficient cooking-pot, but I suppose Lady Alice had her methods. At any rate, the results seem to have been successful; from the compound she made powders and unguents for causing love or hate, according to requirement, and for 'killing or harming the bodies of faithful Christians'. She is said to have killed off three husbands with their help, and to have enfeebled and caused impotency in the one current at the time of her trial. No accusations of black magic would be complete unless a 'familiar' figured in it; Lady Alice had an incubus, a demon called Robin Artisson, who is referred to rather snobbishly as 'expauperioribus inferni', or one of the vulgar herd of Hell.

The Lady Alice escaped to England and we hear no more of her. Her unfortunate confederate and maidservant, Petronilla de Mida, was arrested and questioned (we can guess in what manner).

As was to be expected she 'confessed' to all the accusations, and, as also was to be expected, she was burnt.

In 1324, an equally celebrated case was brought and tried before a King's Bench jury in 1325. The facts are set down in a legal deposition made by Robert de Mareschal of Leicester before the Coroner of our Lord the King, Edward II. In his statement Robert says that in 1323 he was lodging in Coventry with a Master John de Notingham, who had a reputation as a necromancer. In the November of 1324, 'on the Wednesday before the feast of St Nicholas', twenty-seven men, led by a certain Richard de Latoner, came to de Notingham's house. They offered him £20, and maintenance in any English house of religion he chose (surely under the circumstances of somewhat inapposite selection), if he would use his arts to kill the King, the King's much hated favourites, the two brothers Despenser, one of whom was the prior of Coventry, and several others whom Richard Latoner and his party found redundant. Robert le Mareschal, who it seems worked on the same lines as John de Notingham, was to get £15 for his trouble and for keeping quiet.

A deposit was paid a few days after the visit, and the payees, who seem to have been respectable local merchants, also delivered seven pounds of wax, for the making of the images, essential in this type of death ritual, of the persons whom it was desired to kill. Two ells of canvas were brought also.

In an old house, about three miles outside Coventry, the two men John and Robert began to work on the Monday after the feast of St Nicholas. As it has been described to me, the casting of spells, calling up of spirits and magic-making generally is a lengthy business. It can be done only at the right hour of the right day under the right astrological sign, which spins out the performance almost indefinitely, making necromancy no hobby for a busy wage-earner. It was not until the Monday after the Ascension that John and Robert completed their labours.

Just before the end of this time, they made what seems to have been a specimen model, the image of a man called Richard de Sowe, on which, in the spirit of scientific experiment, they tested their work. According to Robert, at John's instruction he drove a sharp-pointed piece of lead into the forehead of the image. Next day Robert went to de Sowe's house to discover if the image had been identified correctly with its human original; he found de Sowe in a crazed condition, recognising nobody, screaming and crying out one identifiable word—'Harrow'. This went on for three weeks. Then John de Notingham took out the lead from the image's forehead and stuck in into the heart. De Sowe died a few days afterwards.

This account of the affair is in the legal disposition made by Robert de Mareschal supported by 'the assent of the aforesaid Richard (le Latoner), and others and those knowing the facts.'

The end of the story is that John de Notingham died in prison while awaiting trial. The Coventry merchants left the Court without a stain on their characters; no one was executed, no one was burned. It may have been that the jury could not credit the story (but in those days there was nothing incredible about it), or that the Despensers were so much hated that the jury would have passed a vote of thanks rather than a punitive verdict on anyone who had tried to destroy them.

At any rate, it seems clear that the wretched Richard de Sowe did have an inexplicable seizure, and that he died in curious circumstances. His sufferings and death may have had nothing to do with John and Robert but there is too much evidence of the success of certain rituals which really do 'turn the power on' to make it possible to dismiss the probabilty that the two men murdered de Sowe as certainly as if they had knifed his physical body.

Accusations of practising necromancy were becoming the order of the day. King Henry V of England publicly denounced his stepmother Joan of Navarre for attempting to kill him by means of spells and incantations. That was in 1419; in 1441, the Duchess of Gloucester, wife of the Regent of England, was found guilty of using the magical arts.

The charge against Queen Joan was that she 'compassed and imagined the death of our Lord the King in the most horrible manner that could be imagined'. Her lands and her possessions were confiscated, and she was banished to Leeds Castle. Later, King Henry restored her lands.

The Duchess of Gloucester, wife of Humphrey, Duke of Gloucester, who was Regent during the minority of his nephew, Henry VI, was accused during the trial of having used magic to make the duke fall in love with her. Later, through the agency of magic rites performed by two priests, Robert Bolingbroke and Thomas Southwell, aided by a wise woman, or witch, Margery Jourdemayn, the duchess was said to have attempted to bewitch her husband to come back to her bed so that she might have a child by him, and to have abetted in the practice of necromancy, so that the future might be revealed to her. The questions to which she wanted an answer were whether she would be queen—in which case the young king would die—and whether she would have a child.

Waxen images were among the paraphernalia found in possession of the priests; a verdict of guilty was given against all the accused. Canon Southwell died in prison, Bolingbroke was 'drawn from the Tower of London to Tyburn, and there hanged, headed and quartered, and the head set upon London Bridge, and his one quarter at Hereford, another at York, and another at Cambridge'. The duchess was sentenced to walk three times through the streets of London, barefoot, white-clad, her hair hanging loose, carrying a candle weighing two pounds. After this, she was sent to life imprisonment, first in Chester, then to Peel Castle, in the Isle of Man.

At the end of the next year, 1432, the name Gilles de Rais, one of the most notorious necromancers in history, began to be mentioned. He was then twenty-eight years old; enormously wealthy, he lived in almost royal state, and for the most part, alone. He had married an heiress because she was an heiress: he was bored with her; she was unhappy with him. He had fought on behalf of the Duke of Brittany with Joan of Arc outside Paris.

When his relative the Lord of Suze died, he inherited the castle which had a library of rare books, among which Gilles de Rais found a beautifully illustrated account of the lives and habits of the Roman Emperors by Suetonius. In the confession he finally made, he said: 'I read in this fine history how Tiberius, Caracalla and other Caesars sported with children and took singular pleasure in martyring them. Upon which I desired to imitate the said Caesars, and the same evening I began to do so following the pictures in the book'. This was the beginning of a phase in his life during which he slaughtered and then burned children of all ages up to puberty; he says: 'Now I cannot say exactly how many were thus burned and killed but they were certainly to the number of six score per year'.

After a time, the satisfaction which the torture and death of young boys gave him began to wear off. He found a new means of release in the practice of diabolism, in which he was instructed by a Florentine priest, Francesco Prelati.

De Rais and Francesco Prelati with the help, no doubt, of the select group which had formed round De Rais, proceeded with the invocation of the devil using the full ritual, including human sacrifice. Judging from his confession, the idea seems to have been constant among the distortions of his mind that in spite of, or rather because of his perversions, he would achieve ultimate salvation.

Eventually the hushing up of suspicion by bribes became less effective. Rumours reached the Bishop of Nantes; evidence was collected. In July 1440, after an accusation of sacrilege had been sent to the Duke of Brittany and to the King of France, Gilles de Rais was arrested at Machecoul.

The trial which followed is probably unparalled in history for the number of crimes with which the accused was charged, and for the obsessive cruelty of their performance.

To his judges and to the assembly in the open court, before which Gilles de Rais, dressed in black, read his confession, the recital must have seemed endless; torture and murder and obscenity repeated again and again. Once, from the body of the Court someone screamed. The Bishop of Nantes rose, took up a cloth, veiled the crucifix which hung over the judges's seats.

The prisoner broke down, crying out his repentance, begging for forgiveness from God and from the parents of his victims. The Bishop of Nantes went to him and embraced him, praying for his deliverance from his sins.

On 26th October 1440, Giles de Rais was hanged. He spent the time before execution in begging two members of his group who were condemned with him to repent and to have faith in God. And for the soul of this mass murderer, after his death, the mass of the people fasted and made intercession.

Between the fifteenth century and our own, the story of the practice of black magic varies very little. The names of its practitioners change, and the ends for which the magic means are used. The basic principle has been, is and always will be the same; the use of the power of man's mind to gain illicitly something he has no right to possess and which causes harm to others.

In the black witch or the black magician, the confirmed evil-lover, there is something of the mentality of Gilles de Rais, a fantastic egotism, a form of paranoia, which stops at nothing in order to satisfy itself. It is a key to the make-up of the murderer.

Some of the black covens which exist today probably only dabble in diabolism; there is a mentality which plays about with black magic 'for kicks'. There are others which take it more seriously.

In London, several covens meet; there is one in Sherwood Forest and at Brockenhurst. At Anderwood, near Brockenhurst, there is another which uses a Mother Goddess cult and could be black in nature. There are others scattered all over the country, including the Merry Order of St. Brigid and the Order of Cybele in Hove, both of which are flagellant orders. A black coven in Brighton has doctors, accountants and solicitors among its members; the women of the coven all have floral 'witch' or coven-names.

How do people become black witches? First of all, of course, they must have the type of mentality which turns naturally to black witchcraft. The preliminary contacts are usually made by questioning friends and acquaintances who may be able to provide contacts.

After introduction to members of a coven would come questioning as to the applicant's reason for wishing to join it. If the answers were satisfactory a probationary period of thirteen months would follow, during which there would be instruction in what could be called 'outer' teachings of the cult, and a series of tests.

These vary with the order concerned, but in many cases vandalism in churches and churchyards, pillaging of graves and other such apparently senseless acts of sabotage can be traced to neophytes trying to make the grade of a black order. Sometimes the cost of admission—which is usually between £50 and £100—is waived if a probationer shows outstanding abilty in some such practice as grave-robbing.

A few years ago, in 1932 or 1933, a Catholic Youth Organisation put up a Christian cross made from telegraph poles thirty-two feet high on Marling Down, overlooking Lewes. Two days afterwards, on 21st March, which is the Spring equinox and was also that year the time of the full moon, the cross disappeared. It was found thrown into a nearby quarry. For some reason this occurrence was hushed up; there was no word of it in the local paper. I have been told reliably that this was the work of black coven probationers. It certainly would seem inexplicable that a group of people (the cross was too heavy and cumbersome to be moved otherwise) would go to so much trouble unless there were some such motive behind the act. The theft of a baby's body from its coffin, reported in the

London *Daily Sketch* in October 1962, and never recovered, probably also comes in the same category.

One evenng in December 1963, Walter Binsted, one of the bell-ringers of the village of Westham, Sussex, noticed a light in the belfry of the church. Knowing there was no reason why anyone should be in the church at that hour, he went to investigate. At the far end of the church, which was lit dimly by candles, placed in the shape of a cross on the chancel floor near the altar, he saw four men. One of them standing a little apart from the rest, was chanting, in Latin, Binsted thought, certainly not in English. The men genuflected, then began to dance, slowly to begin with, gradually increasing the tempo till, as Walter Binsted said 'they seemed to be dancing round those candles like creatures from hell itself'.

As Binsted switched on the light; the men turned and rushed towards him. Binsted ran to the Parish Hall, where he knew he would find the vicar, the Rev. Harold Coulthurst. A small party of volunteers, including the vicar, went back with Binsted to the church, which they reached just as the four men were hurrying out of it. The strangers knocked down one man who was standing beside the vicar, scattered the rest of the group, piled into a car and drove off before anyone could stop them.

The candles in the church were still burning when the police arrived, ten minutes later. Nothing had been stolen, nothing on this occasion had been damaged—unless sacrilege comes under the heading. Apparently someone had spat copiously upon the cross standing on the altar.

Within a month of this incident, a stone cross weighing five hundredweight was dislodged from a grave in the churchyard of St Nicholas, Bramber, near Brighton. Carved figures of angels on other graves were damaged; black magic marks were chalked on the chaurch-doors, which were locked.

The vicar, the Rev. Ernest Streets, carried the war into the enemies' camp by solemnly calling down the Church's curse upon them according to ecclesiastical—though now almost forgotten—usage. There was a good deal of crticism of this action, both in clerical circles and outside them. The Rev. John C. King, who edits one of the Church of England newspapers, thought to put a curse on anyone was 'positively mediaeval—it does not make sense in the twentieth century'.

Judged by these standards, neither does black magic. But whether it makes sense or no, it exists, and on occasions challanges the Church, its historic opponent, in terms of blasphemy or sacrilegeous outrage.

Within the framework of ecclesiastical procedure, provision existed and still exists for dealing with such challenges on their own grounds, rites of exorcism; formulations of curses in the Comitations. As these methods were devised to deal with a type of situation such as arose at Bramber—why not use them? No doubt the vicar of Bramber recognised that they are much more likely to be effective in these cases than 'modern' forms of deterrent, which perhaps some of his critics would have advised.

To go back to the grades of the black orders, at the end of the probationary period, if the applicant has proved a satisfactory candidate for admission to the order, he (or she) is admitted as a neophyte. Next comes the degree of Zelator; after working through a number of degrees, the student may become a Magus, or achieve the highest rank, Ipsissimus.

What the functions and responsibilities are of these various ranks, I doubt if anyone outside a black order knows. The white witches say that they can only guess; just as they say that they do not know what the Black Mass really is, nor how it is celebrated.

They know what they have read of course, in historical descriptions, from which the Mass seems to be complicated, messy and unpleasant. They think that the basic ritual is much the same now as it was in the old days; perhaps modified in some ways. Nowadays if unbaptised babies disappeared, there would be so much hue by the police and authorities and cry by the press, that the game would not be worth even a black candle and it is less trouble to use a cat, a dog or black cock in the blood sacrifice rites.

I have been assured that a good deal of animal sacrifice does still take place. And examination of press cuttings and other information show that, particularly at the times of the four Sabbats—which black witches celebrate—there is usually a spate of unexplained animal mutilations and killings. Not long ago, a chalice was missing from an old church in Dorsetshire. Eventually it re-appeared on the altar, stained with blood, which was thought to have come from a black cock, found in the graveyard with its throat cut. On Tooting Bec Common a pig's head was placed between three wooden crosses, one five feet high. Many churches have received the attentions of black magic practitioners; among them the church at Alfriston, Sussex, where 'black' signs were found, at Appleton in Berkshire, where one Allhallows' Eve the tombstone of a former rector and of a bellringer had been torn down. A stone cross six inches square which marked the grave of a twelve-year old boy, was broken in half. At St Clement's Church, Leigh-on-Sea, a sheep's heart, pierced with thirteen pieces of thorn, was found on a tomb in the graveyard.

The same symbol—a thorn-pierced sheep's heart—appeared nailed to a door of ruined Castle Rising in Norfolk, which belongs to a branch of the Norfolk family. The pierced heart of an animal is often used in the death-wish ritual, with or without an image of the person it aims to destroy.

There are so many authenticated instances from all over the world of the effectiveness of the death-wish that it and its rites cannot be dismissed as hysteria or mumbo-jumbo. The kahunas (priests) of Hawaii, who must not be confused with members of the Voodoo, or black cult, used the death-wish to punish evil-doers. They taught that it is a dangerous mechanism for any but the highly-trained occultist to work. If the sender of the wish does not know enough, or if the intended victim has learned the art of self-protection, the death-wish returns, boomerang fashion, to destroy its maker.

Only a few years ago, the majority of us would have labelled such things as superstitious nonsense. But today, although even now only the surface has been scratched of the subject of para-physical powers, it is realised that the scope of concentrated or trained thought force, so far as can be judged, is limitless, and can produce modifications in so-called matter.

The operative word is 'concentrated'. Any form of power—for example, the rays of the sun—must be focused in order to produce appreciable results. So it is with thought, and for most of us the mastery of the techniques necessary means a long period of hard work and discipline, for which few have the inclination or the time.

The object of ritual, including the Black Mass, is to raise power (paraphyscical power) to implement and strengthen the mental force of its practitioners. Some form of measurable energy is given off by intensely-experienced emotion, the exact character of which is not known—but then neither is the exact character of electricity; and there is no doubt that the emotions generated by the Black Mass constitute a considerable energy potential. I don't think anything would be gained by a detailed rehash of what purports to be eye-witnesses' descriptions of Black Mass celebrations. We all know that the basic idea of black magic is to destroy any object or principle rated as 'good' or 'holy', to profane it or blaspheme against it in every way suggested by a perverted mind. There are the denials of ethical concepts; there are the prayers repeated in reverse; there is the altar, which is in many cases apparently, the body of a nude woman, the black candles, the blood, the desecration of 'sacred' objects. A member of a black cult told Gerald Yorke, the author and eminent authority on Oriental studies, who has done valuable research into occult matters, that the custom was to keep a consecrated wafer in the vagina of a prostitute for a week before using it in the Black Mass.

If anyone felt able to make a list of practices such as these, I think that finally the conclusion would be unavoidable that black magicians believe more wholeheartedly in the Creator and his powers than do many of his professed followers. Otherwise there would be no point in the immense trouble they take, the vast ingenuity they display in refuting him, and in desecration or destruction of his symbols.

Eliphas Levi said in his book *Dogme et Rituel de la Haute Magique* that the 'pre-condition of success in black magic was to profane the cult in which we believe.'

Now and again there is an outcry that devil-worship and black magic are on the increase . . . as at the moment. From time to time these practices flare up, as in the Middle Ages. Then they die down again; the average remains fairly steady. But we shall never get rid of black magic and its 'sins of the mindless' until the sickness within the human psyche, which is its source, is healed.

CHAPTER IV

Structure of the Craft of the Wise

WITCHCRAFT, as we have to remember when considering any aspect of it, is primarily a religion. It has its creed, its system of ethics, its rituals. What we also have to remember is that it is considered to be probably the oldest of all religions, as I said in Chapter I, a pre-Druidic cult; therefore in its early phases it was, as one would expect, a primitive form of belief which lingered until gradually crude concepts were interpreted in terms of the truths they symbolised.

The story of the beginnings of witchcraft may be the story of the involution of the concept of spirit—non-material power—in human consciousness. Our ancestors' ability to think would develop in much the same way as a baby's develops today. Recognition would grow of the powers of nature, over which men had no control; they would be personalised, or deified. With the coming of the Ice Age, men would tend to become cave-dwellers. Our teeth indicated that once we were frugivorous, anthropologists say; then, as fruit became scarce, we turned carnivorous. Someone discovered how to make fire, and the art of cooking was born.

Perhaps more than cooking-fires were kindled; in the flames perhaps was the beginning of magic rites.

The earliest rites to evolve probably would concern hunting and fertility. As centuries passed the rituals and the concepts and deities would become more complicated, until at last they would split into different sections as do amoebae. And men would feel it their duty to kill and torture other men whose ideas of worship did not quite coincide with their own. The time came when witchcraft, which is thought to be the parent stock of these multifarious beliefs, was labelled pagan and heathen. And so it is, if these terms are used to describe it as being outside the limitations of the orthodox churches. Witchcraft is not antipathetic to Christianity. There is nothing to preclude a witch from being also a member of the Christian faith; the idea, which is quite prevalent, that on initiation a witch must abjure Christianity, is untrue.

The witches' attitude to Jesus is that taught by many world religions. They do not believe the he was literally begotten by the Supreme Spirit, but they accept him as a great teacher; one of the adepts or Great Ones sent to lead mankind onwards. They think that some of the old sun-god myths have been incorporated into Christianity, as do many anthropologists; they see the Virgin Mary as another aspect of their own goddess of heaven, symbolised by moon.

The early Christian concepts of the Virgin have a strong family resemblance to the witches' goddess, the Great Mother, or White Goddess. The version of Christ's coming given in a quotation surviving from the lost Gospel to the Hebrews is that a mighty power called Michal, or Mary, was sent to earth by God with Christ in her womb. This concept is allied to the Middle Ages' belief of certain mystical sects, who taught that the Holy Ghost was female. Christ was born of the Father, conceived by the Holy Ghost, they said, who therefore must be female.

This is a representation of the ancient, timeless doctrine of the Trinity, the mystical Mother-father-son relationship, which has been the doctrinal basis of most religions, since early days, when it was worshipped as Ma-ab-ben. When patriarchy was supplanting the matriarchal system, Christianity tried to institute an all-male Trinity, Father, Son and (male) Holy Ghost. But it takes more than ecclesiastical or any other form of legislation to depose an archetypal idea from the race unconscious; the Church found it necessary to bring the Virgin Mary into the picture so that the basic need of a mother goddess aspect in worship could be satisfied. And apart from names—which as we have seen have in such a context little significance since the same principle or deity is venerated in different parts of the world under a hundred different designations —there is not much real diverence betwen the beliefs of the witches and those of the Christian church.

If we believe in the existence of a spiritual source (and science nowadays tells us we are unenlightened if we do not), we must believe also that this source is universal, not the particular property of any particular sect—Jew or Roman Catholic, Church of England, Orthodox Greek, Mahommedan, Buddhist or what have you. And so long as the worship is whole-hearted (if worship is the right word for the raising of consciousness and communion of spirit) can we imagine that the Cosmic Being could concern Itself as to the form used?

The idea of a Supreme divinity—which is found, as we would expect, in witchcraft, because of its ancient origin—is of immense antiquity. It did not come into being, as I think is or used to be a fairly prevalent idea, at the period of the writing of the Old Testament. We cannot know when it arose, but we find traces of it in the oldest teachings, in the Vedas of India, the Persians Scripts or Zenoi, the writings of Thoth, the Hawkheaded, the Wise One of Egypt. High spiritual truths of contemporary religions were stated millennia ago by adepts, or Magi, whom we could call the priests of esoteric wisdom, in Chaldea, India, Egypt, Persia. St. Paul's inspired phrase: 'In Him we live and move and have our being', is an echo of a truth perceived three thousand years earlier; God is because He is, and nothing can be, except in Him and for Him.

The Magi taught that the centre of the universe was everywhere, and its circumference nowhere, because it was boundless. They taught that the physical and mental worlds existed in a continuum of spirit, which was the eternal source and sustainer of everything on all levels, the Absolute of Knowledge and wisdom. But they, themselves having some wisdom, did nᵣt attempt to explain the inexplicable. They said that the presence of God was made known to man through unfolding of perception of truth, of spiritual values, and the creative will in his consciousness; that God was perfection, love, light, beyond all human knowing, Mystery. Carved on the pediments of their temples has been found this sentence: 'I am all that is; all that has been, all that shall be, and none may lift my veil'.

One day the truth of these tremendous words will thunder in human consciousness; the petty tumult of dissentient creed and dogma will be silenced at last.

Belief in the One God was an article of the faith of many so-called pagan philosophers. In the fourth century A.D., Sallustius, a close friend of that Emperor of Rome, Julian, who was known as 'the Apostate' (because he wanted to restore the Old Religion) wrote a dissertation on the gods of the world. In this Sallustius says: 'It is proper to the First Cause to be One, for unity precedes multitude—and to surpass all things in power and goodness. Consequently all things must partake of it. For, owing to its power nothing else can hinder it and owing to its goodness it will not hold itself apart. . . . After this inexpressible Power come the orders of the Gods. . . .'

Sallustius also believed in reincarnation, a teaching of the Mysteries of which there is evidence that he was an initiate, and also of witchcraft. Which cult borrowed the tenet from which, we cannot say, but if we accept the theory that witchcraft is the older teaching, then the probability is that it originated, in however primitive a form, within the Craft.

Sallustius argues for reincarnation that: 'The transmigration of souls can be proved from the congenital afflictions of persons. For why are some born blind, others paralytic, others with some sickness in the soul itself? Again, it is the natural duty of souls to do their work in the body; are we to suppose that when once they leave the body they spend all eternity in idleness?'

Sallustius' statement is logical, but though we may be in agreement with it, we have to admit that its terms hardly constitute proof. However, that is beside the point, which is that there was a firmly-established belief in reincarnation—and therefore in survival after death—at that time, among so-called pagans. The Christian church also taught reincarnation for a while but when the doctrine of original sin was accepted, the two concepts conflicted and that of reincarnation was dropped.

But witches have always believed in it. After death, they think, the soul rests in some place of harmony and happiness, waiting to be born again on earth. They believe that the goddess, if they deserve well of her while alive allows them to be born again among their own people with whom they have ties of affection. Witchcraft has been always to a great extent hereditary; witches think that it is not only passed on within the family in each generation, but that the keepers of the tradition are reincarnate witches.

Just as there is similarity between some Christian articles of belief and some of those of the Craft, so there are correspondences between the ancient Jewish Qabbalah and the traditions of witch lore.

The Qabbalah has been regarded as a great source of mystical knowledge for centuries, upon which most systems of mediaeval magic were founded. During periodic massacres, and when Edward I banished the Jews from England, many of them escaped to the wilder, less inhabited parts of the countryside, which were strongholds of the witches; and the witches, who sheltered them, learned from these Jews something of the mysteries and magical traditions of the Qabbalah.

In the old religion of Israel the dual principle, the male and female, mother and father was worshipped. The Twin Pillars of Solomon's temple, Jachin and Boaz were symbols of its deities, the Elohim, who were Gods of Love

From them emanated the Sephiroth, the ten personalised aspects of God, some of which were male, some female.

After Solomon's death, the wind of change blew upon the Elohim who were translated by the teachings of the priests into one God, a God of wrath and retribution. The priests set to work to remove any mention of the female element in the Elohim, it has been suggested, for reasons of personal gain. But comparing this with similar forgeries and falsifications of history, when, after the swing from matriarchy to patriarchy all references to female dominance or partnership were erased, (as in one such period in Ancient Egypt), it seems more likely that the same principle was operating here. S. L. Macgregor Mathers in *The Kabbalah Unveiled*, says: '. . . for some reason or other best known to themselves, the translators of the Bible have carefully crowded out of existence and smothered up every reference to the fact that the Deity is both masculine and feminine. They have translated a feminine plural by a masculine singular in the case of the word of Elohim. They have, however, left an inadvertent admission of the knowledge that it was plural in Genesis i. 26,' And Elohim said: 'Let Us make man'. Again, (27) how could Adam be made in the image of the Elohim, male and female, unless the Elohim were male and female also. The word Elohim is a plural formed from the feminine singular ALH, Eloh, by adding IM to the word. But inasmuch as IM is usually the termination of the masculine plural, and is here added to the feminine noun, it gives to the word Elohim, the sense of the female potency united to a masculine idea, and thereby capable of producing an offspring. Now, we hear much of the Father and the Son, but we hear nothing of the Mother in the ordinary religions of the day. But in the Qabbalah we find that the Ancient of Days conforms Himself simultaneously into the

Father and Mother, and thus begets the Son. And this Mother is Elohim . . . 'One is She, the Spirit of the Elohim of Life'.

The belief in the Two, the pairs of opposites, as manifestation of the Unity, the Life Force, which is One, is the thread upon which multifarious doctrines and tenets, like beads, are strung. The Two may divide and sub-divide into innumerable personalised aspects; this again is the eternal law of the world of form.

The two deities of the witches are the Horned God and the Moon Goddess—their version of the Elohim. As we have seen, the Horned God was the personification of Nature; of something the same character as Pan. He was also the God of hunting; he was master of an After World, he had attributes in common with Osiris, the Father God of Egypt. He was the God of Death, but because he symbolised the fertility-creating phallus, he was also the Lord of Life.

In Rome we meet him as Janus, with his two faces (life and death). What he never was, was the Devil, in whom witches do not believe.

The female principle, the Moon Goddess, is the Queen of Heaven, the Great Mother. As I have said already, her names are legion.

A stone statuette of her was found in a temple of Jehovah, *circa* 1750 B.C., uncovered during the excavation of the city of Lachish on the seashore of Western Galilee. She is horned, her hair is long and she wears a high conical cap and a provocative look. Her name we do not know; she could have been Astarte, or Ashera, or Ishtar. That, as queen of heaven, the early Jews considered her a powerful deity is shown in Jeremiah, xliv 15-19, which reads '. . . even all the people that dwelt in the land of Egypt, in Pathros, answered Jeremiah, saying: "As for the word that thou hast spoken to us in the name of the Lord, we will not hearken unto thee, but we will certainly do whatsoever thing goeth forth out of our own mouth, to burn incense unto the queen of heaven and to pour out drink offerings to her, as we have done, we and our fathers, our kings and our princes in the cities of Judah and in the streets of Jerusalem; for then we had plenty of victuals, and were well, and saw no evil. But since we left off to burn incense to the queen of heaven, and to pour out drink offerings to her, we have wanted all things, and have been consumed by the sword and by the famine."'

But however the people might and did protest, and continue to honour the goddess, eventually all mention of Jehovah's consort, the queen of heaven, was painstakingly cut out of the Scriptures.

Another of her names is Cybele, the crescent moon, or in this guise she might also be called Artemis. The full moon was the symbol of Selene; the waning, or dark moon, of Hecate. She is the goddess of magic and inspiration. Jason was told by his mother, Aphrodite, to invoke Hecate, 'to draw down the dark moon', since she herself could not work magic.

Sometime Hecate is identified with all phases of the moon. She is shown in some ancient pictures as the three goddesses Artemis, Selene and Hecate, in one; each carries the ritual knife (the witches' Athame), a scourge, and a torch. Hecate was the most powerful of the three in magic. Her rites were held at night; one of their purposes was to avert evil. She was Dea Triformis, the Goddess of the Cross-roads—traditional meeting-place of witches.

The moon was thought to govern fertility; her light was the creative agent. At her festivals, fire and torches flared, candles were lit, a form of sympathetic magic to reinforce her light and persuade the fertilising force to do its work. Diana, another aspect of the lunar principle, usually is pictured wearing a crescent headdress, carrying a lighted torch.

The fire, the torch, the candle symbolised the flame of the life-force; Candlemas could be called the Feast of the Flame. This day, 2nd February, was a celebration in honour of Bride, Brigentis, or Bridget. The fire of the old year was ceremonially put out; new fire was kindled and blessed. It was and still is one of the witches' Sabbats, at which the ceremony of the flame is observed; Druids keep it with the same rite, although its form may differ. Later Candlemas was taken over by the Christian church as a feast-day dedicated to the Virgin Mary, the Mother aspect of Christianity.

In early days the fire sacred to the Moon Goddess—under whatever name she was worshipped—was guarded by priestesses. In Rome they were called the Vestal Virgins, but by whatever title they were known their work and its conditions were much the same. They were dedicated to the service of the Goddess; they must not live the family life of ordinary women, though often they bore children and sometimes the king married one of the priestesses in order to gain power. In some countries, they were sacred prostitutes; the money they earned went into the temple funds.

As is so often the case, the ancient institution of the temple virgins was incorporated into the new religion of Christianity. For about the last two thousand years, numbers of women in every generation have become the Brides of Christ; dedicated to lives of poverty, austerity—and virginity. The term virgin in early days was used to mean 'unmarried'; the Christian Church applied it technically.

That abstention from sexual relations, as in ritual celibacy or voluntary virginity is in itself virtuous, making the person practising it more acceptable to God and more fit for his service, is a curious idea, if taken at its face value. As I have already pointed out, it seems to imply that when God created male and female, he did not realise what he was doing and must have regretted it ever since. Therefore men and women of high principle minimise as far as possible this grievous error by dissociating themselves from it.

Something of this point of view I think influenced and still influences the concept of virginity as pleasing to God. I think the root of the custom, which offers a more logical explanation, is found if we dig deeper. The sexual drive, as we know, is a form of the general energy, of which the average man and woman has a certain amount, loosely analgous with the fuel tank of a car. If the energy is used for one purpose (again I am talking about the average person) less is available for another.

This fact, of course, was realised in very early days. And the idea grew, either that the gods were not all-powerful, or that they required from human beings some contribution towards psychic force necessary to accomplish desired ends. In convents and monasteries vast reserves of power were raised by women and men whose energies, not dissipated by sexual intercourse, were intensified by pain, such as the wearing of spiked belts or bracelets and by flagellation, whose thoughts were concentrated on the glorification of Mother Church. It is believed that the early Church drew much of its strength from these 'energy pools', although, as there seems to have been no organised method of using or containing it, much of it leaked away, producing psychic phenomena. These were an almost everyday experience in religious establishments, where they were considered to be either miracles or the work of the Devil. Only one sect, the Jesuits, apparently worked out a formula for canalising this power so successfully that in almost every country of the world, laws were made against them because of their influence on men and events.

There is an old saying that there are more ways of killing a cat than by hanging it. The idea behind this aphorism applies on many levels of activity, the raising of psychic power through the sex drive among them. At one end of the pole, continence was held to by a means of generating force, at the other, the sex act, under certain conditions, could produce it.

The Sacred Marriage, the 'hieros garnos' was an example of this belief. This was an ancient ceremony which was not for the satisfaction of those taking part in it; its purpose was to give power to the god, and also to create a contact, through this power, between the god and his worshippers.

The hieros garnos was a part of the Mysteries, esoterically it symbolised the dual aspect of the deity, male and female, which ultimately must be resolved by unity. Women, at their initiation into the Mysteries, took part in the Sacred Marriage, losing their virginity sometimes to a stranger, sometimes to a priest, sometimes to a phallic image. The male was considered to be either an incarnation of the God—or perhaps the God himself; the woman would not have met him before, it was unlikely she would ever see him again.

After the passing of centuries traces of these rites still linger. A version of the hieros garnos until recently was used (and may still be used) at some African tribal ceremonies for initiating girls into womanhood. In this country the echoes of the past are fainter but still recognisable; for instance, in the superstition that women desiring pregnancy must spend the night or a number of hours upon the phallus of the Cerne Giant at Cerne Abbas, Dorset, at certain times of the year. The story goes that a countryman told two nuns who had asked their way to the two hundred foot Giant cut out of the turf: 'It's no good you going there, missus. 'Tis the wrong time of the year for child-getting'.

The Goddess of these ceremonies of the Mysteries is, as we have seen, the goddess of the witches; she has her titular place still in the cult although the modern witch knows her as a symbol and worships not her, but the forces of which she is the symbol.

Symbolism is the language of the unconscious, through which the deep levels of the 'collective unconscious' can be contacted. The witches believe that symbolic representation of a power forms a channel between men's unconscious and the power behind the symbol, and that his awakened imagination enables him to make contact with it.

The core of the witches' faith of which all else is trappings, is this belief in the Unseen Invisible, the Supreme Cosmic Power whom they trust and worship. They are of the same mind as the Magi who taught that the world of reality is the world which lies beyond the reach of human sense, touch or sight, hearing, taste or smell. The teachings of materialism that these senses were the test of reality—'only believe in what you can see or touch or hear' —have been undermined now that science has begun to join hands with metaphysics. We know that the evidence of our sense is evidence only of illusion. The world in which they operate, melts away in the light of the discovery that matter is not solid, that it is a form of energy—as is mind—that the two interact, that nothing is *in reality* as it seems to be. The sky is not blue, roses are not red; they only appear to us to have these qualities.

The witches have never acknowledged the limitations of the sense-world; they have always lived, moved and had their being in the domain where the subtle forces now called extra-sensory perception operate. The importance they place upon a linkage with this level of consciousness is expressed in the words of a present-day witch which I have already quoted: 'Once a person has had even one of these experiences of contacting forces beyond the world of form, he or she is no longer in bondage to it'.

The other, only slightly less important belief of the witches is in hurtlessness; an article of faith also of the ancient Huna religion, which is thought to have originated in Africa and travelled across the world, by way of Egypt and India to Hawaii. The kahunas taught that the only sin was to hurt—either oneself or someone else. The Wiccan Rede (i.e. Counsel or advice of the Wise Ones) is: 'An ye harm no one, do what ye will'.

One of the rules of the Craft is that magic must not be used to hurt any person. It would be unrealistic to imagine that the rule has been kept always; witches do not pretend to be saints, and in every sect, cult or religion, there are always weaker vessels who may not be able to live up to the ethical standard required of them. The fact remains that this ethic does exist in witchcraft and that members of covens can and do act as a restraining influence when one of their number might wish to take too drastic action.

CHAPTER V

Operative Witchcraft

BROADLY speaking, witchcraft is organized to form two sections; operative and ceremonial. The first, which is here considered, covers spells, words of power incantations, the use of unguents for various purposes; in general what could be classed as activities and apparatus of a magical nature. The second is concerned with the carrying out the Craft rituals.

Magic is important to witchcraft, but not all important. The true witch considers it rather as a sideline or subsidiary activity. Primarily, as I have said, witchcraft is a religion, a way of life; to concentrate upon magic and development of 'magical' powers as an end in itself would be to put the cart before the horse for members of the Craft.

The ways in which results are brought about—what could be called modifications of matter, and conditions in the external world —are the mechanics of magic. By that phrase I mean spells, incantations and so on, of which the Craft has a vast legacy, inherited from the past, some of it from the very long ago past.

Many of these formulae are presented in words and instructions which may seem archaic nonsense today. What we have to remember is that their form was the best way of putting over an idea at the time when they were constructed. They speak in the language of their day; it may seem odd, but that does not mean that the principle set out in this way is not workable. Cookery recipes of even a few hundred years ago often read today like so much abracadabra, but if the ingredients were collected and the instructions followed they would produce the result specified.

Much of witchcraft's 'magic' dates back far longer than mediaeval cooking recipes. Some may be a relic of very early forms, preserved in the traditions of the Craft like a prehistoric fly in amber. Some no doubt were derived from Persian, Chaldean and Egyptian sources, and, as we have seen, from the great Jewish source of mysticism and magic, the Qabbalah.

Witches of course have no exclusive rights in magic, even if thousands of years ago, they were the first to use it. Magic has always attracted men and women to its study; many of its practitioners from time to time have made handsome incomes out of it, but not—or very rarely—in the Craft.

The base of all forms of magic however or by whomever used must be the same fundamentally, and that base is Mind. Mind is the instrument, the channel and perhaps in some cases the creator of the forces which produce 'magical' results. No one knows exactly what magic is, or how it works, but that there is some form of energy with which contact can be made in various ways and that it can and does produce results in the visible world, few people who have experience of research into extra-sensory perception will deny.

There are many definitions of the term magic. The O.E.D. calls it 'an inexplicable or remarkable influence producing surprising results'. Phoebe Payne, who is widely-known for her psychic gifts and researches into paranormal phenomena, and her husband, Dr Lawrence J. Bendit, M.A., M.B., B.CH., M.R.C.S., L.R.C.P., D.P.M., explain it in this way in their book *The Psychic Sense*, '. . . we can learn to observe the psychic world by using our psychic senses, and if we know how, we can produce changes in it. . . . This is called magic, for real magic is the active or willed aspect of psychic activity. . . .'

Aleister Crowley, self-styled the Great Beast, called magic 'The science and art of causing change to occur in conformity with the will'; Dr Gerald Gardner said: 'I define magic as attempting to cause the physically unusual'. The archaeologist, T. C. Lethbridge in his book *Witches*, described it as '. . . simply the use of powers of the mind which are not yet understood by science. Magic and miracle are the same thing. Telepathy is a form of magic which is becoming scientifically respectable. It was completely taboo among scientists till certain recent experiments showed that there was something in it. Scientists did not see how it could exist, therefore it did not exist, although thousands of their fellows knew that it existed and can be observed in use every day on the sea-shore among flocks of wading birds. . . . But you cannot measure human observation and therefore it is not scientific. Scientists can be pretty blind from obstinacy at times.'

Mr Lethbridge goes on to describe an experiment in dowsing on Lundy Island in which he, with a geologist named Dollar, took part. Mr Lethbridge with a twig tried to locate volcanic dykes which threaded the rocks in the southern end of the island. Blind-folded, Mr Lethbridge found every one of the dykes—although they were so thickly covered with earth and grass that they would have been indetectable if he had been able to look for them in the ordinary way. Finally his colleague said—not without some bitterness, one feels: 'You have located every one of the dykes. If I had known you could do that I should never have brought down a magnetometer from Cambridge'. Mr Lethbridge comments: 'Now this is magic, but it was also a scientific experiment'.

He adds: 'Other faculties of a magical nature are slowly becoming respectable. Faith healing and healing at a distance by resonance are being widely practised. Not long ago my mother said to me, "I don't get much rheumatism now, I go on the box". "What on earth is that?" I asked. "Oh, I gave a spot of my blood to a woman in Oxford and she puts me on the box and I am soon all right again." "But this is pure magic, Ma," I said incredulously. . . . It is magic, without a shadow of doubt, but magic conducted with an elaborate scientific apparatus. How it works, I have not the slightest idea, but it has clearly come to stay.'

The blood-spot technique of treatment and diagnosis is used quite widely although perhaps not in quite the same way outside the De La Warr centre, of which I believe Mr Lethbridge was speaking, as is radiesthesia. This could be called a form of diagnosing illness and its cause by means of a pendulum. I know a number of medical men, highly thought of in the profession, who use it, and there is a society of British Medical Radiesthetists. Two hundred years ago, these eminent men would have been denounced and probably executed, as witches. I have in mind one such doctor in particular, a highly respected and brilliant man who has achieved remarkable cures of mind and body. Some of his patients he treats according to materia medica, or he may use cones of cosmic force, or radiesthesia, the Bach flower remedies, or biochemic therapy. If he had been practising four or five centuries ago, his finish would probably have been a pile of ash in the market place of the Hampshire town near which he lives. When one realises how much knowledge and power to help suffering humanity went up in smoke or ended with the noose at the gibbet's crosspiece during the witch-persecution period, one could weep—if it were of any use. . . .

The derivation of the word magic is from the Chaldean 'maghdim', the meaning of which is wisdom allied wtih the qualities summed up in the term philosophy. The true meaning of magic itself, as implied in the words, is, I think, too vast a subject for compression into a few paragraphs; I make this brief allusion to its real character to show that not only is there no basic divergence between the highest concept of magic and religion, but that basically they are one.

In primitive times religion and magic were virtually indistinguishable from each other, conceptually and practically. The priests was a magician, and the magician a priest. He brought the needs of his flock to the attention of the deity by invoking his aid in satisfying their needs, a practice of which there are still traces in Christian Church services. As witches are fond of saying, the difference between their crop fertility rites, and the Church's prayers for rain is fundamentally non-existent—though they often add: 'Why anyone needs to pray for rain in this country is past understanding. . . .'

In later days there was a divorce between magic and the orthodox Church. For a time magic was regarded as a pursuit for hysterics and charlatans; as with witchcraft, whatever influence it might have was considered evil.

From the nineteenth century onwards what amounts to a renaissance of magic, and magical thinking, has been growing. The 'modern' Rosicrucian movement began to spread; the German Vril Society was formed; the Golden Dawn came into being, and the Theosophiscal Society, among many others. Rudolf Steiner founded his school of thought, which claimed that the cosmos is contained in the human mind, which has possibilities and activities undreamed of in the discoveries of psychology.

Rene Guenon the philosopher, saw dangers in this renaissance, teething-troubles, you might say. In his book published in 1921, *Le Theosophisme, Histoire D'une Pseudo-Religion*, he said: 'The false Messiahs we have seen so far have only performed very inferior miracles, and their disciples were probably not very difficult to convert. But . . . when you reflect that these false

Messiahs have never been anything but the more or less unconscious tools of those who conjured them up . . . one is forced to the conclusion that these were only trials, experiments as it were, which will be renewed in various forms until success is achieved, and which in the meantime produce invariably a somewhat disquieting effect. Not that we believe that the theosophists, any more than the occultists and the spiritualists, are strong enough by themselves to carry out successfully an enterprise of this nature. But might there not be, behind all these movements, something far more dangerous which their leaders perhaps know nothing about, being themselves in turn the unconscious tools of a higher power?'

Steiner seems to have thought somewhat along the same lines as Guenon. Believing in black and white magic, he thought that 'theosophism' and kindred movements originated in an underground world of evil—perhaps a dramatisation of the unsublimated unconscious. His followers were dedicated to work for the good of humanity.

The Golden Dawn society, to which I alluded a paragraph or so back, rates individual mention, I think, because it had a strong, if limited, influence on the trend of thought in the period of its heyday—of which it was also symptomatic. It was founded in 1887, by S. L. Mathers; it was supposed to be the offspring of the twenty year old English Rosicrucian society, members of which included Bulwer-Lytton, the novelist, and were for the most part Freemasons.

The purposes of the Golden Dawn were the study of ceremonial magic, the acquisition of occult knowledge and powers. It had a most distinguished list of members; they included most of the brilliant minds and pioneer-thinkers of the day. S. L. Mathers, whose wife was the daughter of the great philosopher, Henri Bergson, was succeeded as Grand Master of the Society by the poet W. B. Yeats. Algernon Blackwood, who wrote fascinating stories of the 'world beyond form' (I can never forget his *The Man Whom the Trees Loved*, which I read as a child), was a member. He was himself a fascinating person; very tall, with (when I met him) a very lined face. He had enormous almost aquamarine-coloured eyes which looked not only at but through you and beyond—to the farthermost horizons, it seemed. Several other authors belonged to the Society, among them Bram Stoker, author of *Dracula*, and Sax Rohmer, a great occult adept in his own right, so I have been told.

Then there was Sir Gerald Kelly, President of the Royal Academy, Peck, Astronomer Royal of Scotland, and finally Aleister Crowley.

Crowley was possibly one of the most controversial figures of the first half of the twentieth century. It is difficult to assess him as he really was, even from the opinions of men who knew him well. Some seem to think he was the incarnation of wickedness, others see him as a—perhaps a little chipped—plaster saint, or as a rather pathetic figure. I have been told that he had great power. Gerald Yorke, who knew him well and liked him, said that Crowley made such an impact on even highly intellectual people that the affect lasted for days afterwards. I met Crowley not long before his death; I chiefly remember that he was a yellowish, squarish face, that his eyes were like obsidian; they seemed never to move. On one occasion they were oysters with whatever we had to drink. I found a tiny pearl in one of mine which I had a feeling Crowley thought I ought to hand over to him. But I was young enough to think it a thrilling find; I tucked it away in my handbag. I must admit that the only impact Crowley made on me was the interest of meeting a man of world-wide notoriety.

There was a woman member of the Golden Dawn, Florence Farr, who was a director of the Abbey Theatre, and a great friend of Bernard Shaw. For some time Arthur Machen, a man of great occult knowledge and a great writer, whose books, to our loss, are almost forgotten today, also belonged to the Golden Dawn. To Machen, the world of the unseen was the reality. *The Secret Glory*, which he wrote when he was sixty, is considered to be his most powerful work, *The Great God Pan*, and the *Inmost Light* are other books by him. His name for a time became a household word, not because of his books, but through a short story he wrote for the London *Evening News*. The paper printed this on 29th September, 1914, which was the day after the retreat from Mons, but it must have been conceived and written at least some days earlier. It was a fantasy of St George, leading a band of the archers who fought at Agincourt to rescue the British troops at Mons. It was called *The Bowmen*.

The sequel is that letters flooded the office of the *Evening News* from soldiers saying that Arthur Machen's story was fact, not fiction. These men were ready to swear on oath that they had seen non-material forms which became known as 'angels of Mons' on the battlefield, fighting with them.

No one believed Machen when he declared again and again that his story was completely imaginary. No doubt, so far as he was aware, it was. But as science is discovering today, we do not know enough about the workings of our own minds, or about the forces which play upon them to dismiss phenomena as 'pure imagination'. In any case, when all the dialetics, psycho-analytic and psychological arguments are finished, we do not really know what imagination is. I have heard it suggested as a possibility that Arthur Machen unconsciously called up forces which manifested as the 'Angels of Mons'.

He was, as we have seen, an initiate of the Order of Golden Dawn; therefore he must have been trained to develop the powers of the mind and to use them through ceremonial magic. A powerful emotion (such as patriotism?) may have triggered off the familiar mechanism, without his conscious realisation of what was happening.

From 1943 to 1947, when he died at eighty, Machen lived in a cottage in Buckinghamshire. I was taken there to see him and I shall always regret that I did not ask him what he thought of this possibility. At that time I had only heard vaguely of the Angels and of Machen's connexion with the story; apparently no one thought of mentioning it to me.

With the passing of the years, the Golden Dawn became perhaps not quite so golden. Whether the order ever went out of business completely I have not been able to make certain, but the interest in the magic arts of which it was an indication continued to flourish. Now, after a period of quiescence, I believe the order is being reconstituted.

The renaissance of magic is being speeded up today by the—at least partial—recognition of many of its claims and powers by science. Having been dug out of the wastepaper basket of materialism into which it had been thrown as a worthless mixture of nonsense and crookery, the reputation of dubiety which still clung to it is being dusted off. Its prestige is gradually returning although perhaps it is not fashionable to describe results obtained by its powers as 'magic'.

Magic, as I said earlier in this chapter, can be very loosely described as the ability to contact and make use of forces of the invisible world. There is so much evidence for the existence of such forces that I think we will not go over the arguments for or against it. There have always been, are, and no doubt always will be people who say that what runs counter to long-accepted ideas is impossible. In the eighteenth century the scientist Lavoisier, denied that meteories could fall from the sky, because, he said, 'there are no stones in the sky'. Other scientists, among them Simon Newcomb, categorically pronounced that it was a demonstrable impossibility that a machine which was heavier than air could fly in the air. Another example of the same attitude is that of an anthropologist, Dr Fortune, towards a charm given to him by a New Guinea magician, who said that it had the power of making its owner invisible. The magician apparently had often found it a useful way when hungry and short of cash, of obtaining a joint of pork. He added that Dr Fortune could with its help, 'pinch anything you want in the shops in Sydney'. Dr Fortune's comment was that 'naturally' he never tried it out. While he may not have felt inclined to go on a shop-lifting spree, out of purely academic interest, he could have tested it in some safe and permissable way, one would think, if he had not shut his mind to the possibility that the charm might work.

The ability to make contact with supra-physical forces and to use them is developed or taught by techniques, such as those of witchcraft. T. C. Lethbridge has likened the unclassified form of energy demonstrably contained in the human body, in his book *Witches*, to the self-starter of a car. This force in the body gives the necessary impetus which sets things going. He adds: 'It is to speed up this force which is the objective of both witches and magicians. It was presumably the way to handle this force which was taught by Jesus to his disciples, and which now seems to have been either neglected or forgotten. Confidence in the use of this force was the "faith" which the disciples found it so hard to maintain.'

'Of course', continues Mr Lethbridge, discussing magic and its working, 'the greatest exponent of this kind of thing in all history was Christ. He had apparently very little difficulty in teaching other people to do it, and the process of teaching does not appear to have taken long. He used to get very angry with them when they lost confidence in themselves and failed to do it. There were no years of training in Yogi; it appears to have been no more than complete trust in your power to do it. If there was any further teaching necessary, it has been either lost or deliberately smothered. The power could be used for good or evil. St Peter's performance with Ananias and Sapphira was as perfect an example of black magic as could be found anywhere in Africa. St Paul's confidence was evidently so great that he learnt how to heal by himself'.

Mr Lethbridge does not mention Christ's constantly reiterated 'It is not I, but the Father that is within me, He doeth the works,' which could be the key to the performance of his miracles—the calling down of the invisible forces.

As he suggests, it is possible that the working of the miracles as described in the Bible was not so easy as it sounds—there may have been techniques necessary to their performance which have been deliberately or accidentally lost. At any rate, I gather from present day practitioners that to operate 'magic' is hard work, and that one would only use it to get results not obtainable by ordinary means.

To begin with, the confidence already mention is necessary and one-pointed concentration. You cannot be wondering what to buy for lunch tomorrow or whether the car needs decarbonising and hope to get results with magic. Then, if you are operating in a group (such as the witches' coven) all the members must be in complete sympathy with each other—a very important point. Applicants are often turned away because the coven leader realises that their personality would not be in accord with that of some-one else.

I can only speak from hearsay of the spells used, since I am not a member of the Craft. I am told that often a rhyming form is used—it is well known that a rhyme easily sinks into and is accepted by the subconscious, and that a spell must 'say itself', so that no conscious effort is required in repeating it. When the maximum power has been raised, the purpose for which it is intended is stated clearly and the business finishes usually with the words: 'As I will, so mote it be, chant the spell, and be it done'.

I have been told that magic cannot be used to make money, but this I think is not true in a literal sense. I have known money to be raised in this way with great success for legitimate purposes. On one occasion a witch I know needed £27 10s 0d very urgently; there simply was no channel known to the witch in the visible world through which it could come in time to save the situation. He did a 'private' ritual; a Jupiter ritual which must be carried out on a Thursday. The next day he was give £30 'out of the blue' by a friend who came unexpectedly to see him. I think the real meaning of the 'magic is not for money-making' proviso is that you must only ask for it when your need is great and that it must be used for some really necessary purpose.

The other important rule is that magic must never be used to harm or hurt. This means that before magic is 'worked', a coven 'committee' is held to make sure that it cannot result in damage to anyone. It also means that witches who belong to covens must not cast spells around indiscriminately. The procedure is to lay the case before the coven, so that the matter can be discussed and a decision made as to the proper action to be taken.

I was told (with checkable details) of the case of a witch who was being annoyed by a man who was doing all he could to make life unpleasant, not only for her, but for several other people in a certain village. After deliberation, the coven felt the man could be spared by the community and acted accordingly. Shortly afterwards, he unexpectedly sold his property, left the district and never returned.

Witches often work for 'outsiders' who need their help. Members of a coven of which I know were asked by a man to find him his ideal woman. Two days after the witches went to work for him, he made a trip to Switzerland. On the aeroplane he noticed a woman, 'just exactly my type', he said to himself. But she had a schoolboy with her—and she was not the kind of person with whom he could scrape acquaintanceship. In the dining-room of his hotel that evening, he saw the same woman sitting alone at a table near him. It seemed she was having difficulty in making herself understood by the waiter; the witches' protegé, who spoke fluent French, came to her rescue.

The sequel was that a few months after this meeting, they were married. The man wrote and thanked the coven for their work on his behalf; he said he had never believed that a woman so exactly right for him existed. After that, they never heard of him again.

A woman came to the High Priestess of another coven in great distress because her husband was having an affair with his secretary —for whom apparently he intended to leave her. The High Priestess discovered that the secretary was the gold-digger type; the affair seemed to be a case of the 'seven year itch' without real affection on either side. So the coven 'worked' for the harmonious removal of the secretary from the picture, without specifying how this was to happen. Shortly afterwards the secretary developed eye-trouble, for which the occulist said rest was the only treatment. The firm gave her leave of absence, but when after some months, there was no sign of improvement, they replaced her. Almost at once, the disorder disappeared; she was given a good post in another town, and that was the end of the wife's trouble.

You can of course say that these and innumerable similar cases are coincidences. Personally I do not believe in coincidence or in chance or in luck—but that is by the way. My point is that if you want something to happen, and ask non-material forces to make it happen, and it does—and if this series of events is repeated again and again, then if you still call it coincidence (the definition of which is a 'notable concurrence of events or circumstances without apparent causal connexion') a law governing the incidence of co-incidence must exist—and that is a contradiction in terms. Or to put it more shortly, it makes nonsense.

To produce effects of this order and in this way (i.e. by non-physical means) can be classified as 'magic'. It is a part of witch-craft, as I said, and its use is not a prerogative of witches, although probably it originated with the Craft. During the centuries witches no doubt learnt from and borrowed some of the methods of other systems—perhaps especially from Egyptian magicians.

At one time, Egypt had a very strong magical tradition which no doubt rose to power because the priests were custodians of 'pre-conscious forces'—the forces of the unconscious which act as bridges between the individual and the invisible realities. The early days, before man developed his reasoning faculties, were the heyday of the pre-conscious mind, whose faculties he used as a matter of course.

As our ancestors began to concentrate more and more upon problems of a material nature—making tools, building houses, ships and so on, the pre-conscious faculties weakened through lack of use, until about six thousand years ago, they were all but forgotten —except by priests, magicians—and witches . . . who wielded power because they still possessed these faculties.

In the Egyptian Book of the Dead which is over five thousand years old, the powers of the priests are represented as being virtu-ally limitless. They could heal wounds and illnesses, sometimes by merely looking at the sufferer; they restored sight to the blind, cast out evil spirits; they raised the dead. The priest Tchatcha-em-ankh opened a path in the sea by uttering words of power. Many scientists think that these men had forgotten more than we can rediscover for some time to come. Only fragments survive which hint at their knowledge, the range of which we may never know. Though the library at Alexandria was destroyed, from mentions in contemporary writings we realise it must have been a treasure-house of thousands of MSS., many of them of a scientific nature, as was the sanctuary of Ptah at Memphis.

The priests of ancient Egypt were skilled astronomers. They had brought the use of hypnosis and its near-relatives, all forms of suggestion (hetero and auto), to a fine art. Through hypnosis, they were able to perform the most delicate operations such as trepanning (the opening of the skull to relieve pressure on the brain), without anaesthetics.

No wonder that this priesthood had a formidable reputation as magicians all over the ancient world. You may say that some of the results they produced could not be attributed to magic if hypnosis and suggestion were the methods admittedly used. But though we are not accustomed to think of them as such—because they have been 'whitewashed' by science—hypnosis and suggestion are in the same category as magic. Through certain techniques a subtle form of energy—or force—is used to influence the brain; to modify its nervous impulses and so on. Whatever names are given to this force and however clearly the techniques for its use are formulated, still no one really knows what it is, any more than anyone knows what electricity really is. What is called magic also is the use of a subtle force to modify matter or conditions—nowadays it is known as extra-sensory perception. But basically all paranormal phenomena have the same source, whatever label is put on them.

As I mentioned earlier, long before medical hypnosis was 'discovered' by Dr James Braid, in the nineteenth century, witches were using it to cure disease and to make possible painless delivery of children. It is possible that this was one of the 'magical' secrets which the Craft borrowed from the Egyptian priesthood; after so many centuries proof is not practical one way or the other, but it is, as I said, a tradition of witchcraft that certain forms of magic derive from Egypt as well as from other ancient sources.

Another teaching which is incorporated in witchcraft is the belief taught in the Mysteries of ancient Egypt that the spoken word had power so long as the power was not dissipated by idle chatter or lying, so long as it was spoken with meaning, and that an intention, once uttered, was carried out, the promise fulfilled. This 'magical' word or 'word of truth' was called Ma'kheru; by which term witches sometimes refer to it. According to them if you say 'I will do so and so,' and then do not 'follow through', as it were, you break an occult law, which lessens the power of your word, and your ability to succeed. Men and woman whose word is their bond, in the time-worn phrase, whether they know it consciously or not, are working with the law; they put in operation the Biblical promise: 'My word shall not return unto me void'. The witches cite the case during the last war of General McArthur, who was, they say, well-versed in occult matters. He said, when forced by the enemy out of the Phillipines, on which there seemed then no possibility of making another landing: 'I shall return'. And, as we know, he did. Winston Churchill, witches say; belonged to the company of those whose word is power.

The use in ritual of words of power differs from the Ma'kheru in that they are a set form of generating or invoking power by certain sounds which traditionally have this effect. This is an aspect of magic which I will discuss in a chapter dealing with ceremonial, or ritual magic, but before passing on to this, I must mention the famous unguents of the witches, which belong to the operative side of magic.

Some were supposed to make the user invisible; the best-known are 'flying ointments', which gave to a man or woman the power to fly through air, sometimes on a broomstick, sometimes without visible means of support.

I don't think modern witches are much given to travelling by broomsticks, probably they find cars, aeroplanes or even 'buses less trouble, less messy, and probably cheaper. By the time the unguent ingredients have been hunted down (even if they could be found today), the unguent made with all the stress and strain of spell and incantation-casting; by the time the entire body of the witch had been rubbed over with the unguent, the whole process would be an uneconomic proposition. Also nowadays to fly around clad only in ointment might create difficulties.

Did witches ever fly? Some members of the Craft today think that they did. Others believe that the flying was subjective and was in fact astral travelling.

The three known formulae for 'flying ointments' among other ingredients contain alkaloids which, when rubbed into the skin, would produce symptoms of mental confusion, intense excitement, perhaps delirium. Belladonna (or deadly nightshade) which is featured in two out of the three formulae, would induce in combination with another ingredient, aconite, excitement and irregular action of the heart. This is known to produce in sleeping people the characteristic dreams of falling through the air.

Doubts have been raised as to whether the ointments could have had any effect; alkaloids, it is said, cannot be absorbed into the body via the skin, unless it is broken or scratched. But they can be taken in through the quicks of the nails, and considering the prevalence of lice, there can have been very few unscratched skins in mediaeval times.

Bat's blood—another ingredient—would have no effect, to quote a biochemical authority; no physiological effect, that is. But it may have produced some psychological reaction. . . .

A wild hypothesis . . . but so at one time was the possibility that 'magic' worked. Now Science has rationalised much of it into respectable terms; now Science is saying that since mind can interact with matter anything can happen. Matter has been deposed from its rulership of man and his affairs, as Sir Cyril Burt admitted when he said '. . . the physicist has arrived at the stage when he is ready to assure us that he has a conscious mind but doubts that he really possesses a material brain.'

CHAPTER VI

Ceremonial Magic and Ritual Witchcraft

IT really is next to impossible to draw a definite line between different aspects of 'magic' (a word I am using without prejudice, so to speak, and in the widest sense) or witchcraft; to say that this belongs to the one side of the line and that to the other, at any rate for the most part. There must be overlapping, because all activities of a psychic nature, religious or otherwise, are attempts to influence invisible forces in some way, whatever may be the method used. And that is the essence of magic. For convenience, one makes broad classifications, as I have done, between spells, charms and so on, and the more elaborate, organised formulae of ritual, and ceremonial magic, which we are now considering. There is a common denominator between the workings of charms or spells and ritual or high magic; the form of energy which operates in, through or as the sixth sense.

The names of certain men or women come automatically to mind when magic or magicians are mentioned. Some of them may have been witches, some are not known to have been initiated into the Craft. Among these latter was Solomon, who was one of the greatest practitioners of the high art. Rituals supposedly derived from his teachings are still among the classic text-books of magic; he was believed to have attained supreme wisdom; to have had revealed to him and to have understood the secrets of the universe; to be able to communicate with 'angels', with whose co-operation he performed tremendous miracles.

Solomon is supposed to have passed on his knowledge and wisdom in a document which is in two sections, translations of which have survived up to the present day. The Secretum Secretorum, is a ritual to be used for making contact with the 'angels' entrusted by God with the government of this world. The second part, the Psalterium Mirabille, is a collection of the psalms of David, with a key to their mystical and magical interpretation, explaining how they can be used to bring to the seeker wealth, power, honour, love, security, safety from all dangers.

According to the key, the 137th psalm can be used to evoke the love of a man or woman. The ritual laid down which should be carried out at dawn on the Friday following the new moon, instructs first the pouring of oil of a white lily into a crystal goblet. Over this, the 137th psalm is recited, ending by calling upon the angel who is the planetary spirit of Venus, Hamiel, Haniel or Anael (the dropping of an H would not be likely to matter here), and the name of the beloved, then, on a piece of cypress, the name Hamiel (Haniel or Anael) is written; the cypress is dipped in the lily-oil, with which the eyebrows are brushed. Then the cypress is tied to the right arm. At the first opportunity, the right hand of the person with whom you are in love should be touched; with this touch love will awaken in his or her heart.

Whether the rituals ascribed to Solomon actually are his; whether or not they were the working tools by which he achieved power, one way or another we know that he reached the pinnacles of power. And in the end, fell from them.

Tradition says that he was destroyed by his vast achievements, by wealth, and the world-wide adulation he received. He began to treat these not as the effect of his spiritual gifts, but as ends in themselves; and as a result lost little by little the qualities which made him great. His chief interest became the purchase of beautiful girls; his agents scoured countries round about for them. He is credited with having a collection of four thousand of these exquisite creatures, which one feels must have created an accommodation problem in even the roomiest Eastern palace. With the girls, perhaps because some of them brought their priests, came 'foreign' religions. Jehovah had to share the Mount of Olives with his rivals, who now had temples opposite to his—Astarte, or Venus, or Moloch, one of whose other names is Saturn. Solomon's own preference seems to have been for a goddess with a cow's head—probably Hathor, of the Egyptian hierarchy—to whom he offered flowers—the lotus and the rose—doves, horses and lobsters, symbolising the elements of earth, air and water. Moloch could be satisfied only with human sacrifice, which was not denied him. Into a vast hollow bronze statue of the god, made furnace-hot, were thrown babies and small children. Drums and cymbals were beaten during this rite so loudly that the victims' screams were not heard.

Faust (or Faustus) is another legendary figure in magic's history. The story of his pact with Mephistopheles is dramatised in the opera which is named after him. The correct version of the name of Faust's familiar is thought to be Mephistophiel, (one of the Maskim, or seven evil planetary spirits), which derives from the Hebrew word 'mephiz' or destroyer, and tophel or liar. A very ancient Chaldean conjuration of these spirits of the abyss, the Maskim, has been preserved and I quote its translation:

> A charm of awful power
> A spell that is older than the walls long buried
> Of Babylon: ere Nineveh was dreamed
> 'Twas old beyond the power of computation.
> They are seven, they are seven—Seven they are;
> They sit by the way, they sleep in the deep: down far
> Seven they are:
>
> They are Seven, they are Seven—Seven are they:
> Out of the Abyss they rise, when day
> Sinks into darkness. Seven are they:
>
> Born in the bowels of the hills,
> Evil ones, sowers of ills:
> Setters of unseen snares,
> Deaf to all pity, all prayers:
> Male they are not,
> Female they are not,
>
> No wives have they known.
> No children begot.
> The fiends, they are seven:
> Disturbers of Heaven,
> They are Seven, they are Seven—Seven they are:

Whether or not Mephistopheles and his kin are dramatisations of the subconscious mind, there is evidence that Faust or Faustus existed in the sixteenth century. He certainly was a magician, a magus primus; he taught magic as a Professor on the staff of the University of Poland, according to a mention by Johannes Wierus in *De Praestigiis Daemonum*, 1568. This was Dr Johannes Faustus, who must have had a solid reputation as an astrologer; there is an entry in the Bishop of Bamberg's accounts on 20th February 1520, which shows that the Bishop had sought his advice. It reads: 'Item, 10 gulden given and presented to Dr Faustus philosophus in honour of his having cast for my gracious master a nativity or indicium, paid on Sunday after Scholastics by the order of Reverendissimus'. He is mentioned in the Sermones Convivales of Johann Gast 1548; also in the *Locorum Communium Collectanea* of Johannes Manlius, councillor and historian to Emperor Maximilian II. He seems to have been considered to be a man of power, feared by some, and revered generally. Most of the dubious activities and characteristics of his legend seem to have been debited to him because he has been confused with a Georgius or Jorg Sabellicus, who adopted the title Magister Georgius Sabellicus; Faustus Junior, Fountain of Necromancers, astrologer, magus secundus, chiromancer, aeromancer, pyromancer, second in hydromancy. He was described as a 'charlatan and imposter', 'a mere braggart and a fool', 'a man entirely devoid of education'. The Abbot Trithemius of Wurzburg wrote to Johann Virdung, mathematician and astrologer, on 20th August 1507, warning him against this Georgius Sabellicus, 'who is an imposter, and calls himself the "prince of necromancers" Trithemius goes on to say that Sabellicus uses the title of Faustus Junior with embellishments which I have already quoted.

Georgius Faustus appears in the minutes of the Town Council of Ingoldstadt in 1528 as 'the fortune-teller who shall be ordered to leave the town. . . .' Dr Jorg Faustus figures on the list of expulsions from Heidelberg, and a Faustus, who appears to be the same person, is referred to by Dr Philipp Begardi of Worms as one of the 'wicked, cheating, useless and unlearned doctors'. Whenever Georgius or Jorg is mentioned it is as an imposter or fraud; Johannes is a 'philosophus', a powerful magician, astrologer and necromancer. It is not surprising that the wrong doings of one man should have been fathered on to the other in days when so few people were literate and news travelled to a great extent by word of mouth, becoming distorted in transit.

The story is still further complicated by a third Faust with whom

Johannes Faust, the magician, is sometimes confused. He was Johann Fust (sometime spelt Faust), the printer, who was born in Mainz, *circa* 1400. His chief work was an exquisite psalter published in 1457, the capital letters in which were printed in two colours, red and blue, from types made in two pieces. Since he died of plague in Paris in 1457, before Johannes Faust was born, a connexion between them seems unlikely.

The crux, it could be said, of the type of ceremonial magic we are considering, is that it provides a technique by which spirits can be conjured up and in some way persuaded to do what is wanted by the one who calls them.

The most powerful part of the conjuration was the name or names used in the evocation, usually the name of God or of an archangel or angel. In any form of occult practice, the name of a god or person is considered profoundly important; it is, as it were the innermost essence of individuality. Sometimes it was held so sacred that the true name was never spoken or revealed, except to initiates; the name used was nothing more than a nickname. King Solomon is supposed to have gained his enormous power because he knew the secret name of God. It has been said that 'prayers to the Christian God failed, or are answered only once in twelve times because people do not know how to pray (i.e. how to call on the name), although the right method is given in the Bible.' Isis, (the Mother Goddess of the Egyptian hierachy) according to legend, by some means unspecified, discovered the secret name of Ra, the Supreme King of Heaven, and used it to acquire power for herself. In some parts of the world, remote from industrialisation and modern ideas, there is still a belief that it is unwise to tell anyone your real name. Whoever knows it, can make magic against you.

The word of power, hekau, as it was called in ancient Egypt, is used to evoke the entity; sacred words and symbols are written around the circle in which the magician stands during the ritual to protect him from any unpleasant intentions the spirits might have towards him.

For some rites a triple circle is used, the diameter of each circle being six inches less than the one surrounding it. The floor must be scrupulously clean before the circles, drawn with the Athame and then marked with chalk or charcoal, are made. The outermost circle is divided into four points north, south, east, west. At the eastern point, the Hebrew word Agial is written at the southern, Tzabaoth, at the west, Jahveh, at the northern, Adhby. The pentacle, or five-pointed star, is drawn between each compass point.

Then, with the Athame, each word and drawing is traced over.

At the eastern point, in the smallest circle, a brazier of lighted charcoal is placed, and, with its centre plumb with the centre of the brazier, an altar or table, on which are placed the various 'tools' of the magician. A brass water sprinkler, containing salt dissolved in pure water in which nine herbs have been steeped, a censer, Athame, pentacle, a white handled knife, a burin and a sword, would be among them. Each tool is ceremonially cleansed by water sprinkling, censed and wrapped in fresh white linen. Candles burn on the altar and are set round the outermost circle.

The magician would have with him in the circle talismans, the pentacle of whatever governing spirit—Mercury, Venus, Saturn, Mars, for instance—were to be evoked, and the sigils of other spirits. Each spirit has a design peculiar to himself; knowledge of these sigils is one of the great secrets of magic.

Some rites begin with recitation of three of the psalms; then come conjurations and supplications to guardian spirits to keep the circles safe from any attack which might be made on them. Incense is thrown on the brazier, words of power which summon the spirit are spoken—if to visible appearance, a triangle will have been drawn outside the outer circle; it is here the spirit manifests.

The smoke and the heady scent of incense drifts and eddies around the circle. It may seem to condense into form . . . is it all hallucination, or are there non-physical entities with which it is possible to make contact?

The preparations for and the trappings of ceremonial magic—which have a family resemblance to ceremonial witchcraft—of which I have given a rough and broad outline only—may be offputting to minds conditioned to modern ways of life. But we have to remember that they are not fortuitous; they are designed to have certain effects, perhaps chiefly in the mind of the operator. They are a means of inducing a certain state of consciousness.

The 'entities' which manifest may be projections of the 'magician's' subconsciousness; even so, it can be argued that they have reality on some levels. To attempt to define here what reality is or is not would mean getting bogged down in a morass of metaphysics to no real purpose. At this stage of our development, I think to make a definition of reality is next door to impossibility. Between subjective and objective reality, for instance, the distinction is so fine that it could be considered non-existent.

At any rate the entities evoked by ritual magic serve a useful purpose; they enable forces to be concentrated, with which results can be produced. There is a theory that any thought-form which is strongly held over a period gathers or conserves an energy which gives it a life of its own. Again, this is a matter of opinion rather than proof—and perhaps one of experience.

Mr Gerald Yorke, whom I have already mentioned, told me of an experience he made in evocation while he was at Cambridge. He says that, being interested in occultism, and having studied this branch of it, he decided to see if ritual magic worked. When he had collected the materials necessary, and learned the procedure; he went to work to call up Thoth, the Egyptian god of wisdom and inspiration; about the safest subject, Mr Yorke thought, for an amateur to attempt, and also reputedly the easiest.

The words were spoken, the ritual performed—and perhaps to Mr Yorke's surprise—Thoth came . . . apparently objectively and inarguably. Mr Yorke, having established that the thing could be done, says that he was not interested in experimenting any further on these lines.

He used another form of ritual in order to find a cave which he felt was the kind of place where he could study undisturbed for a time. He carried out the appropriate rite, adding a request for a companion who was also interested in the occult.

He went to north Wales, where he wandered around on foot for some days without discovering any sign of a cave, suitable or otherwise. The weather turned rainy; one day, soaked to the skin, Mr Yorke sheltered in a farm-house. The ritual now seemed to have got into gear. The farmer, whom Mr Yorke told about his project, knew of a cave which sounded to be just what he was looking for; it had once housed a local saint.

And when, having taken up residence there, he went to the village shop to buy food, he noticed that the man who served him was reading the Egyptian Book of the Dead. Mr Yorke found in this man just the companion he had had in mind.

A lecturer and well-known scholar told me of an experience on the lines of Mr Yorke's evocatory adventure, also carried out while he was an undergraduate. In his case, he was persuaded to make the experiment by a friend who was sceptical but curious to see if there were 'anything in it'.

The entity they decided to call was Mars. The season was winter; the room in which the evocation was made had a coal fire burning in it. The circle was made, the ritual done. The lecturer told me that they saw nothing, but all around was a stirring, as of wind. The coals began to leap out of the fire into the circle as if propelled by a catapult. Neither man cared much for this manifestation; the coals being red hot could have caused painful burns and set the place afire. With all speed possible, they performed the banishing ritual, dismissing Mars before he could do any more mischief— and shovelled the coals back into the grate.

Mars is one of the planetary spirits, and whether he and his kind are subjective or objective, it seems wiser not to meddle with Maskim unless you are very sure of your ground. Gerald Yorke's theory is that even Aleister Crowley, who was no amateur in these matters, fell foul of them.

At a certain stage of the development of a Magus, it is required of him to take the Oath of the Abyss; an extremely dangerous step for a candidate unless he is fully prepared in every way, in character, mind and body. Aleister Crowley, apparently believed he had special qualities which made it possible for him to bypass the preliminaries. He took the Oath prematurely—and suffered for it.

After Growley's death some of his formulae figured in an incident, which has nothing to do with what I have been saying, but is so curious that it is worth mentioning. A man who had known him, bought, against Gerald Yorke's advice, a collection of Crowley's formulae which he had willed to a certain museum. Mr Yorke said that the formulae should go where Crowley had wished them to go, but the purchaser was too anxious to have the formulae to listen. Not long afterwards, he developed an obscure disease. No one seemed able to do anything to treat the illness, which got worse. Eventually he decided to see if getting rid of the MSS. would help. He handed them over to Gerald Yorke, who arranged to deliver them to the museum named in Crowley's Will. Mr Yorke says that during the time they were in his house, his wife, who never before had an abscess nor has had one since, developed a painful swelling on the neck. It disappeared at once when the MSS. were taken away, as did the disease of the man who bought them.

Incidentally, these formulae were always kept wrapped up in a clean white linen cloth, as are all the 'tools' of magic. This seems to serve the dual purpose of protecting them from damaging vibrations, and of insulating their emanations.

To go back to Crowley's formulae, were the unpleasant experiences connected with them the result of his discarnate efforts, or had he wrapped up his formulae in a thought form so to speak, to ensure that no one else but the museum should have them? Whatever the answer, the basic cause must have been the concentrated power of thought directed by a master of the art of such thinking.

And this, as I said before, is the root of all magic, black and white, ritual or operative . . . and it is not only the trained adept who possesses it. The Scottish cook (who came of an old witch family) of a friend of mine had been very much upset—I forget why—by a woman who owned a neighbouring house. This woman arranged an elaborate garden-party, and as the summer that year was good, there seemed every likelihood that the weather would be fine. The day came, with hot sun and cloudless sky, but the cook said to her mistress as she set off for the party: 'Better take your umbrella, ma'am'. Just as the garden-party began the sky suddenly darkened. Torrential rain soaked the guests, claps of thunder sent them scurrying indoors where arrangements had to be improvised for getting them dry and feeding them. The storm turned out to be local; not a drop of rain fell even a mile or two away.

After this fiasco, knowing her cook's ancestry, my friend asked her if she had worked on the weather. 'Ah, well', Cook said, 'I did my best and I prayed to the good Lord, and He helped me.'

From every ancient times, claims have been made that the weather can be controlled by ritual magic, concentrated thought or whatever you wish to call it. Witches were credited with raising storms; they were supposed also to be able to 'whistle up the winds', which farmers in certain parts of the country still do. Because sometimes high winds could be very inconvenient, this method of calling them up is thought to be the reason for the old saw: 'A whistling woman and a crowing hen, are neither good for God or men'.

In the season when rain was very likely, not a drop fell in Addis Abbaba on the day of the Queen's Birthday celebrations in 1964. The British Ambassador there, Mr John Russell, congratulated on the perfect weather, explained, according to a report in the *Evening Standard* of 3rd February 1965, that the fine day was by courtesy of a witch doctor. 'I paid him eleven dollars (something over a £1),' he said, 'to keep the rain off. It rained for two weeks before the day and two weeks after the day, but on the day itself the weather was perfect. The Foreign Office had the impertinence to query it when I put it down in my expenses, so I returned it to them under the word "insurance".'

Whatever form of ritual this witch doctor used, obviously was effective. Probably it did not differ in essentials from rites used for the same purpose by other practitioners of magic, including the kahunas (priests) of Hawaii.

The religion of this part of Polynesia, Huna, is so ancient that no one can put a date to its origin. The legend is that the race whose religion Huna was, lived somewhere in Central Africa; that they had migrated there from a 'lost continent'. In a vision, the priests were told to make the journey to Hawaii; the way they took led through Africa (in northern Africa where there is a Berber tribe which still uses certain 'secret' Huna terms), to India, where Yoga is supposed to be a bowdlerised form of the ancient teachings, thence across the Pacific, in outrigger canoes.

The word Huna means 'secret'; the kahunas were the 'keepers of the secret'. It was the secret of power to produce effects in the material world, but, like witchcraft and other ancient mysteries, not only that. The heart of the secret was a technique for resolving inner conflict, for expanding consciousness, so that life could be lived fully and happily.

The Polynesians lived in a more or less idyllic state probably for ten centuries or so. The time of their arrival in Hawaii is thought to be before the birth of Christ, because their legends contain no reference to him although they have recognisable versions of Old Testament stories, such as those of the Garden of Eden, the Flood and even Jonah and the Whale. They were highly intelligent people, whose civilisation according to Professor Toynbee, the historian, was arrested because conditions of life were so easy in Hawaii. Time stood still, until Captain Cook 'discovered' Hawaii in 1778.

In 1820, Christian missionaries arrived. The great attainment of the kahunas was their understanding of human consciousness, and the forces which work through of consciousness. It was this knowledge closely guarded by the 'keepers of the secret' which enabled them to perform miracles for the good of the tribe, but as with witchcraft, 'magic' though important was not of paramount importance.

To the missionaries, miracle-working was damning evidence of a low standard of spirituality and intelligence. They dismissed the teaching of the kahunas as primitive superstition, and their powers as fraudulent. They set to work with such energy to suppress Huna that it was driven underground; its priests gradually died out. At the end of this [19th] century when the celebrated anthropologist, Dr William Tufts Brigham, became curator of the Bishop Museum in Honolulu, and attempted to contact them there were only a handful of kahanus left in all Hawaii.

Dr Brigham became friendly with the kahunas; they let him watch while they worked their 'magic'. They could control weather, they healed by paraphysical means, they had precognitive and other recognised psychic powers, such as telepathy; they used the 'death wish' to punish evil-doers, they could walk bare-footed over red-hot lava. The kahunas even used their powers to protect Dr Brigham, so that he could experiment in fire-walking. There was not a mark nor a singe on the skin of either foot when he reached the far side of the glowing red-hot lava-bed, he records. But he says that another man whom the kahunas permitted to join him, was afraid to walk barefoot and insisted on wearing boots, although the priests warned him it was dangerous. The boots caught fire; they burnt the man's feet in several places.

But although the kahunas demonstrated their powers for Dr Brigham although he was often present at their rituals, and heard their chants and prayers, they never let him into the secret of just how they made contact with the Unseen Force which they said was the source of their powers. The greater part of the secret died with the last kahunas though fragments of it have been rediscovered by the researches of Max Freedom Long, who was a friend of and worked with Dr Brigham for some years. He founded the Huna Research Association, of which I was a member, and has done valuable and interesting work in reconstituting some of the kahunas' teachings and the 'secret science behind miracles'.

This secret science seems to be the 'know-how' which is the active principle of ritual magic—and operative, too, of course. Witches have it—some covens, I am inclined to think have a deeper knowledge of its workings than others. This probably is an inevitable result of the centuries of persecution which forced isolation and therefore a form of unrelated development on covens.

The purpose of ritual in witchcraft is not to call up spirits, according to many members of the Craft. But although not part of what could be called Craft tradition some witches may have rituals adapted to that end. In any case, the ritual performed for helping or healing, or anything else, is a means of invoking power which is directed to bring about the result in mind. The difference between invoking force qua force, and evoking a form ensouling it could be described as marginal.

Sometimes, without any conscious effort on the part of celebrants, phenomena materialise, either within or outside the circle; objective, in so far as all or most of these present see them. I have been told of blue light shining on or bathing an altar; a woman in green walked round and round the circle of another coven for five minutes or so. Again, a whole room outside a circle was brilliant with green light. There have been occasions when a room has echoed with loud knocks or walls and door; when the candles round the circle flickered, almost went out and then burnt high again while those on the altar did not, or vice versa.

I have seen a photograph of a manifestation, which so far as can be checked, is physically inexplicable, and authenticated by everyone concerned, the High Priestess of the coven, her husband (who is not a witch), a press photographer and another member of the Craft.

The photographer, who of course could not be present at the ritual had been given permission to take a picture of the preparations; the circle, the altar, and the 'tools' laid out on it. The curtains were tightly drawn; the photographer used a flash-bulb to get his picture.

When the negative was developed, a broad ray of light was clearly shown. It was about six feet long, one end apparently coming from a corner of the room, the other resting at an angle of about 45° on the 'tools'. There was nothing in his apparatus, which the photographer checked, to produce it; the curtains and room were examined, again nothing was found which could explain the manifestation.

It appears to be one of the unpremeditated manifestations which have no apparent significance that the reasoning mind can discover, but which seem particularly liable to occur as a 'bonus' to evocative ritual.

CHAPTER VII

Initiation

THE idea of initiation is an old, old idea, which has its roots in the deepest layers of human consciousness. With the formation of the tribe grew the feeling of security which comes from 'belonging'; the herd instinct, if you like. The security of the group,—its 'in-ness' can be maintained only so long as admission of 'outer' non-belonging elements is prevented or controlled. Just anyone who fancies the idea cannot be allowed to join in and enjoy all the privileges of the group until he has proved himself worthy of membership.

With the growth of the thinking processes and the ability to produce results through them, developed the idea that as certain discoveries and knowledge gave their possessors power, they should be the prerogative of a select few. The prototype of the witch cult, the Mysteries, Freemasonry, Thuggee—and the Klu Klux Klan was born. . . .

Initiation ceremonies to whatever tribe or cult, part of the world or period of time they belong, necessarily have a family resemblance; they originate from this basic trend in human consciousness. There is the preliminary preparation of the postulant, the ordeal, the acceptation, if the tests are passed successfully, into the cult or order.

Mystery cults in the ancient world not only flourished but had great power, possibly because the custodians of their secrets had wide knowledge and learning, as well as psychic abilities. They were highly literate at a time when relatively only a handful of people could read or write.

The mystery cult in ancient Egypt was probably one of the most powerful of these groups. The priests, as I have mentioned already, were considered princes of magic; they also were scientists and psychologists of a high order.

The first form of government in Egypt is said to have been theocratic—i.e. rule by the priests. Thebes was its centre, until an Army general, Menes, seizing political power from the priesthood, established himself as the first of the Pharaohs, in a new capital city, Memphis.

The priests, although no longer goverment executives, were still the spiritual rulers of the people. Thebes kept its importance; is it just coincidence that today enough of its architecture remains, even in its ruins, to tell of its greatness, while Memphis has disappeared so completely that so much as to guess its site exactly is not possible?

Even to become eligible for training in initiation to the Mysteries was not easy. The aspirant had to pass a series of tests of moral courage and intelligence; failure in one test meant total failure. No second chance was given.

If a man from another country asked for initiation, he was first 'screened' as carefully as we screen 'top secret' scientists. The assembly of one of the sacred colleges would then vote as to whether he were to be allowed to take the preliminary tests. The first of these was apparently an ordeal which only a man of exceptionally strong character could surmount. At that stage, he was allowed to retire, but if he chose to go on, and if, after the first symbols of occult knowledge had been taught to him, he failed in any test, there was no going back, nor going on. He was killed.

Plato was one of the foreigners who successfully passed through the tests. He was initiated into the mysteries of Hermes—Thoth at Memphis, after working for thirteen years, according to Proclus, under four Magi. Thales, Budoxus and Pythagorus also won initiation; Pythagorus' master was the great prophet, Sonchis.

The tests themselves are described by Iamblichus, the philosopher of the fourth century A.D. in a treatise on the Mysteries. He says that the tests were held in sacred vaults, the entrance to which was through a bronze door between the forelegs of the Sphinx at Gizeh. The door, opened by a secret spring known only to the Magi, gave on to a maze of corridors in the body of the Sphinx.

At this door, the postulant was met by two senior initiates, the Thesmothetes or guardians of the rite. He was first blindfolded, then led down a spiral staircase of twenty-two steps, through a second bronze door into a circular room.

With a deafening roar a trap door opened, to disclose a figure with a scythe, who cried: 'Woe to him who comes to disturb the peace of the dead', as the postulant's eye-bandage was torn off. On either side of him stood the Thesmothetes, who had put on white linen robes, one belted with gold, the other with silver, symbolical of the sun and the moon. One wore a monstrous mask of a lion's head, in astrology the symbol of the 'throne of the sun'. The bull's mask of the other Thesmothete symbolised Taurus, the zodiacal sign in which the moon is most powerful. The inner symbolism was that a study of the laws of nature was the first step towards the highest illumination; the laws governing each plane must be understood and complied with before they can be abrogated.

Seven times the scythe was swept over the postulant, so closely that it brushed his head. Then the figure disappeared. If the postulant were comparatively unshaken by the shock of the sudden apparition and the monstrous figures beside him, the Thesmothetes unmasked, congratulated him on possessing courage, and told him that he would now be tested for the moral quality of humility.

One of the Thesmothetes, by touching a hidden spring in the wall, opened a door to a corridor, so low and narrow that only a man crawling flat on his face could go through it. A lamp was given to the postulant, he was told that this corridor was the way to the inner sanctuary where knowledge and power were given in exchange for humility. The corridor, he was told, symbolised the tomb through which humanity must pass before awakening from the darkness of material life to the life of the spirit. 'Go, triumph over the horrors of the tomb,' they encouraged him.

If after a few minutes, the postulant could not face the test, his eyes were bandaged and he was led out by the way he entered. If he decided to go on, the Thesmothetes gave him the kiss of peace. As he entered the granite corridor, the bronze plaque clanged down behind him, cutting off retreat, and a voice in the distance cried: 'Here perish all fools who covet knowledge and power'. By some trick of acoustics, the echoes repeated these words distinctly seven times.

The hierophants who arranged this ordeal probably knew practically all there is to know about the processes of the human mind; the factors most likely to undermine control, to try the courage, the steadfastness and initiative of a man, were all there: loneliness, darkness (except for the faint light of the lamp) fears which must have been aroused by the distant voice crying that the test was really a death trap; the seven inescapable reiterations, constrictions in a narrow tube in which no movement except forward was possible —forward to what? The state of mind induced must have been comparable to the death agony.

The tunnel through which the wretched man had to crawl—and it would become a painful process before he had gone far— descended deeper and deeper—into a pit, perhaps? And what if the lamp went out? Suddenly the roof of the tunnel rose; the ground sloped to the lip of a vast crater. An iron ladder of seventy-eight rungs led down into darkness. The postulant braced himself for the descent; there was nothing else he could do.

When he reached the lowest rung, he found before him nothingness; a gaping pit of darkness. This must have been a moment of supreme terror and indecision. To go on, to annihilation, or to go back—and die in the corridor-tomb. . . .

A proportion at any rate of the postulants climbed back up the ladder, to discover on the way a crevice wide enough to admit a man, with steps inside. A spiral stairway of twenty-two steps led to a bronze grating through which could be seen a gallery, on each side of which were twelve sculptured sphinxes. Symbols and pictures of strange beings were painted on the walls; eleven bronze tripods stood in a line down its centre, each carrying a lamp in the form of a crystal sphinx, burning oil and incense.

The postulant was admitted to the gallery through the grating by a Magus, who welcoming him, told him that having passed the test of the pit, he had discovered the path to wisdom—and that very few postulants survived it. Other tests were ahead, but in the meantime he would be given the key to power through explanation of the meaning and symbolism of the hieroglyphs and paintings in the gallery.

The principle of all wisdom and the source of all power, the Magus told the postulant is contained in the twenty-two hieroglyphs, or Arcana. Letters of the sacred language and the numbers connected with them form correspondences with the arcana, and manifest a spiritual, intellectual or physical reality. The arcana expressed in visible pictorial form the formula of the law covering human activity in relationship to spiritual, mental and material forces, the sun of which is called life.

When the teachings and doctrine symbolised in the arcana had been explained to the postulant, he was led out of the gallery into a long narrow cellar, at the end of which was a blazing furnace. If he shrank back from what seemd to be certain and painful death, the Magus would say to him: 'Death frightens the imperfect only. If you are afraid, what are you doing here?'

The door to the gallery was slammed shut; the postulant stepped towards the flames. As he reached them, he would find that they were an optical illusion, created by small piles of wood placed on an iron grill. But as he passed between them, the ceiling opened and a torrent of oil, falling on the fire, sent them roaring upwards. In front, was a pool of dark water, which must be crossed. The water, as he waded through it, reached his shoulders. One step more—and it would close over him. . . .

But with the next step he found he had passed the middle of the lake. On the other side was a closed door, carved on it were a lion's jaws, holding a metal ring. There seemed to be no way in; as he hesitated, he heard a voice saying: 'If you stop, you will perish. Behind you is death, before you, salvation.'

The metal ring held by the lion, could be a door-knocker. . . . As the postulant lifted it, he released a spring. The floor under his feet gaped open over an apparently bottomless pit. In fact, in case his grip on the ring were not firm enough to save him, layers of cloths were stretched out under the pit's mouth to break his fall, and several of the Magi were ready to catch him in their arms.

Having passed through the opened bronze door, the postulant's eyes were bandaged once more. He was taken along passages which led from the Sphinx to the Great Pyramid. There in a crypt in the centre of the pyramid, the members of the College of the Magi awaited him.

The walls of the crypt were polished stone, on which were symbolic paintings of the teachings of Hermes Thoth, the Enlightened One. Above each painting was inscribed in a language known only to initiates the keys to all wisdom and all knowledge.

On a silver throne in the centre of the half-circle of white-clad Magi, was the Hierophant, or Master, purple-robed, crowned and a gold circlet set with seven stars.

Behind him towered, under a purple canopy, a gigantic statue of Isis, the Mother Goddess of Egypt, whom we have met already under some of her many other names. The figure which was made of alloy, of tin, iron, silver, lead, copper, gold and quicksilver (each metal being traditionally characteristic of one of the planets), wore a silver diadem with twelve rays rising from it. On her breast was a gold cross, its four arms indicating the four cardinal points, and the avenues of the infinite. At the centre of the cross was a gold rose, symbolising the universe.

On a great silver table in the centre of the crypt was an intricate planisphere, by means of which the postulant had to work out a horoscope given to him by the hierophant, without the smallest error.

This was the supreme test of initiation. Before reaching this stage the postulant had to take an oath never to reveal anything that had passed that night, an oath which has a family likeness to that of freemasonry. 'If ever I betray my oath', runs one part of it: 'I shall deserve to have my throat cut, my tongue and heart torn out and to be buried in the sand of the ocean that the waves of it may carry me away into an eternity of oblivion'.

When the oath was sworn the postulant's bandage was removed. The Magi stood over him with drawn swords, which the Hierophant told him, symbolised human justice, often fallible. The faith of an initiate must be guaranteed by divine justice; the last ordeal was one from which the postulant could be saved only by intervention of the Deity.

The Magi having lowered their swords, two goblets were offered to the postulant. One of them, he was told, contained wine, the other a virulent poison. 'I command you,' ordered the Hierophant, 'to seize without reflection one of them and empty it at a single draught'.

The postulant who felt unable to make the choice was bundled up in a black veil and imprisoned for seven months in a dungeon in the pyramid; lit by one lamp, on a diet of bread and water. He was given one book, a compilation of the maxims of Hermes Thoth concerning Man's obligations to the Deity, towards his fellow beings, and to himself, which would, if he studied them thoroughly enough, enable him to generate enough strength to pass the test of the goblets. If he passed the test when it was next offered to him, he was given the rank of Zealot and allowed to go free, but might never rise to a higher grade. If he refused it again, he was taken back to his dungeon for another seven months, under the same conditions. The procedure was repeated until at last he accepted the ordeal, or died.

The man who had the courage to face death by poison was told by the Hierophant when he had drained the goblet, that the only difference between contents of the two vessels was that a little myrrh had been added to one of them.

The final ordeal was the most dangerous of all. In a luxuriously furnished bedroom, the candidate was given a meal of rich foods and fine wines. As an unseen orchestra played sensuous music, diaphanous curtains were drawn to reveal a gallery where were dancing in a soft light, groups of girls. They were masked, so that candidate would not recognise them if he passed the test; apart from the mask they wore only a gauzy tunic emproidered with golden bees, and a garland of flowers.

The dancers were the daughters of the Magi, consecrated to Isis.

They beckoned the postulant to the threshold of the gallery. Two of the dancers, the rest of whom had disappeared, threw over him a chain of roses; then in provocative dance, apparently invited him to choose one of them.

Profound knowledge of human nature had reserved this as the last test. The effect of his ordeals and of the sudden relaxation on the mind and body of the candidate had been gauged to a hairsbreath. With his resistance at its lowest ebb, he must fight his hardest battle against the domination of the senses in conditions of the maximum temptation. If the man showed any signs of weakening he was considered to have profaned the Mysteries; he was killed there and then by one of the Magi who had approached unnoticed.

A candidate who stood unmoving at the gallery entrance, or who broke the garland of roses, was judged to have passed the test. The Magi congratulated him; the Hierophant addressed him, telling him that magic is composed of knowledge and strength, describing the purpose of the Mysteries and the powers that were his; offering him the choice of living among the Magi or returning to the outer world. Plato elected to stay on in Memphis after his initiation, for thirteen years.

Nine grades were open to the initiate; Zealot, Theoricus, Practicus, Philosophus, Minor Adept, Major Adept, Enfranchised Adept, Master of the Temple, and finally Magus of the Rose-Cross. Only a man of superhuman qualities and abilities could attain the ninth grade, for which a brain with computer-like scope and accuracy was necessary. He had to have at his finger tips knowledge of the hieratic sciences, not one word concerning which was, or ever must be, written down. He had to know all the arcana, and how to apply the seven keys of symbolism as given by Hermes Thoth. These Magi were the men who were the real rulers of Egypt; they attained a profundity of knowledge and a range of power at which we can only guess today; it is believed that no civilisation then—neither in India, Chaldea, Persia or China—nor since has achieved anything comparable.

As centuries passed, the Mysteries lost the strength and purity of the concepts behind symbolism, the purpose of which is, through translation of force into visible form, to enable man's mind to achieve some degree of realisation of invisible powers and to make contact with them. The glory of the high spiritual tradition of the Magi began to fade; the key to their secrets was lost—or perhaps mislaid would be the better word. Generations grew up which could not grasp the inner truths, they mistook symbols for reality, so that it seemed to the rest of the world that animal worship was the religion of the Egyptians.

And so the prophecy of Hermes Thoth was fulfilled. He had written 'O Egypt, a time shall come when, instead of a pure religion and an intelligent cult, you shall have nothing left but ridiculous fables that posterity will find incredible, and there shall be nothing left to you but words graven upon stone, dumb and almost indecipherable monuments to your ancient piety'.

In their book, *The Dawn of Science,* Louis Pauweis and Jacques Bergier have said: 'In the last resort, however, all real scientific and technical knowledge carried to its highest level implies a profound knowledge of the nature of mind and of the the resources of the psyche functioning at the highest level of consciousness.' The great purpose of all Mystery cults in all ages was to enable men to attain and to maintain those levels of consciousness. But it seems that there is a law whose terms were expressed by Solomon when he said: 'There is a time for everything'. Its operation causes even what appear to be systems embodying transcendental realisations of spiritual truth to crumble and disintegrate; perhaps because it is necessary that the truth shall be presented in a new shape once more.

The Greek Mystery School went the same way as the Egyptian, although it too had at one period a great tradition of knowledge and enlightenment. That the Orphic Mysteries infiltrated some of the Mediterranean parts of the Roman Empire, there is evidence at Pompeii. In the Villa of the Mysteries a wall-frieze depicts the stages of initiation into its rites. And if today a frieze were to be painted showing the rites of witchcraft initiation, few alterations would be necessary—one of these being that the ritual meal of the Craft is taken at a different phase of the proceedings.

It seems possible that the witchcraft ceremonies of initiation resemble the Orphic rites because Thessaly was a stronghold of the Craft; at one time it was as famous for its witches as for Thermopylae. Thessalian witches either learnt the rites from the priests of the Mysteries—or perhaps the priests learnt from the witches. At any rate, the particular form of celebration is more or less generally part of Craft ritual. That is to say, most covens would be likely to use its main features but as I have said earlier, each coven is a law unto itself, and might introduce modifications or changes.

As with selective groups of any kind—Mystery cults, Masonry, gangs, or Ascot's Royal Enclosure—there is 'screening' of the applicant for membership to the Craft. Discreet inquiries are made as to his or her background; then comes an interview with the Leader or one of the coven.

The first question is, as a rule is: 'Why do you want to become a witch?'

Sometimes the answer is along the lines of: 'It's so thrilling; so mysterious; I'd just adore to be a witch'. One woman wrote: 'There is the enticing prospect of being an accepted member of a colourful cult; a chance to participate in exciting actvities—not just being a placid spectator and member of a congregation, sitting in a hard pew being preached at'. Sometimes a whole list of reasons is given. One man said simply: 'I want to get ride of my wife.'

Covens often get applications for membership from middle-aged men. One of the first questions asked them is: 'Does your wife know and does she agree to your joining us?' If the man says she does not, he is told to talk the matter over with her, and then come back, if she agrees.

If the answers to the preliminary questions are unsatisfactory—as in the case of the dissatisfied husband—candidates are told their applications for admission to the Craft cannot be considered. One High Priestess considers the best answer to be, 'I don't know'. She believes that the man or woman who feels a strong urge to join the Craft without a clear cut reason is probably being led—or pushed—into it by the awakening sixth sense, or drawn back into it by ties from a previous incarnation. Candidates are questioned as to whether they believe in reincarnation (a teaching of the Craft), also about their habits and ambitions, recreations and principles. Their aura is analysed, their psychic powers are assessed.

After a preliminary 'screening' comes a probationary period of about thirteen months. This is a time of study. Some of the subjects 'set' are herbal laws, the Qabbalah, telepathy, archaeology, dowsing, clairvoyance, interpretation of numerology, mediumship, comparative religion.

From time to time the candidate's progress is estimated by tests. Guidance in psychic development and various forms of psychic perception is given; in strengthening intuition, in the use of hypnotism, self-induce trance, levitation, astral projection, precognition, exorcism of evil spirits, and in recalling of previous incarnations. Sometimes candidates are given objects on which to practice psychometry.

The rite of initiation is celebrated when the coven has decided that the applicant is a proper person to be admitted to the Craft, and one who will be able to work harmoniously with the other members. Sometimes the only reason for refusing entry is that the personality of the newcomer would not fit in with the coven's atmosphere.

The actual form of the rite no doubt varies, as I suggested, from coven to coven, but the broad outline of procedure is more or less similar. First, a nine foot circle is drawn with the sacred black-handled knife, and for convenience, the circle is marked out with chalk or charcoal. In the centre of the circle is the altar, upon which are placed the 'tools', varying in number according to the custom of the celebrating coven. The sacred knife, symbolising air, the cauldron symbolical of water and the Great Mother, the wand, the phallic sign of the male element and fire, and the pentacle, symbol of earth, would be there. There might also be a sword and a burin (an awl-like instrument), a white-handled knife used for making ritual instruments and talismans, and a cord the meaning of which is the unifying factor, the spirit which binds all elements together. Candles on the altar are lit, incense rises from a censer placed beside a vessel filled with salt and water, and a scourge, the symbol of purification.

After sanctification of the circle and the ritual instruments with salt and water, the circle is circumambulated while an invocation is repeated, calling upon the Mighty Ones, the Ancient Gods of the north, east, south and west to assemble.

The candidates stand outside the circle. The Coven Leader touches the breast of the candidate with the point of the black-handled knife warning that it is better to die by it than to attempt to join the Craft with fear in the heart. The candidate replies with the passwords 'Perfect love and perfect trust.'

The candidate enters the circle—which is then closed with a ritual gesture of the Athame, while the hands and feet of the postulant are ceremonially bound with cord. After presentation to the Lords of the east, south, west and north, the candidate is led back to the altar where, when in a kneeling position, the feet are firmly bound together. 'Are you ready to swear you will be true always to the Art?' the High Priestess asks. The candidate replies: 'I will'.

'First you must be purified.' As she speaks these words, she strikes the candidates with the scourge, first three times, then seven, then nine, then twenty-one. The scourge, as I mentioned, has symbolised all through the centuries the concept that pain was a purifier; that it was necessary to suffer in order to learn. The scourge was used in ritual of the Greek Mysteries, and in that of the Christian church at one time. It was also a sign of the power and domination which come through the overcoming of pain.

Apparently this part of initiation is not the terrible ordeal it once was. Today in many covens, at least, a token scourging is given, by flicks instead of strokes. It is now believed that so long as the symbolism of the ritual is fully realised, its object will be achieved. Some hereditary witches say that scourging never was part of the Craft practise and do not use it.

A witch who was initiated in the days when scourging was considered necessary by some covens, admitted that it was an experience she would not care to undergo again. 'But', she said, 'there is this to be said for it; it was at least a deterrent to any one who was not a genuine seeker from joining the Craft'.

After the scourging, if any, comes the question: 'Are you prepared always to protect, help and defend brothers and sisters of the Craft?' When assent has been given, the oath is administered. 'I, in the presence of the Mighty Ones do of my own free will most solemnly swear that I will ever keep secret and never reveal the secrets of the Art, except it be to a proper person, properly prepared, within a Circle such as I am now in, and that I will never deny the secrets to such a person if he be properly vouched for by a brother or sister of the Art. All this I swear by my hopes for a future life, mindful that my measure has been taken and may my weapons turn against me if I break my solemn oath'.

Though in this oath the blood-chilling visitations invoked by the Freemasons and other cults for apostasy are not mentioned—no talk of throats to be cut, tongues torn out burial up to the neck in sands where the tide will wash over the victim—for the witch its mild-sounding terms are as powerful a discouragement from oath-breaking as any of these. The witch is invoking the vengeance of elements on abjuration, for the weapons symbolise air, fire, earth and water. There is no hiding place for a traitor to the Craft.

Now the neophyte is consecrated with oil, wine and a ritual kiss; after this the weapons of the Craft are presented, the black-handled knife which some witches call the Athame, the white-handled knife, the censer, the sword, the cauldron, the scourge and the wand. The cord, which, as I have mentioned, symbolises the unifying power of the spirit, is given last of all.

The newly-made witch having been proclaimed an initiate to the spirits of the four cardinal points, they (the spirits) are asked to depart. Then, sitting in the circle, the ritual meal of cakes and wine is eaten. The ceremony is over.

The white cord which is given to the neophyte indicates the first degree of initiation. The red cord is the sign of the second degree. At one time a third degree existed, initiation to which was by a sex rite. Some covens may still use it, but so far as I can discover, today it is considered unnecessary by most witches. There was no oath to be taken, apparently, with this degree; its rites, according to tradition, must be carried out only by two people who loved one another. To misuse it was rated as a sin which could carry the death penalty in this world and oblivion in the next.

Many neophytes ask how long it will be before they can enter the second degree of the Craft. And to that no definite answer can be given. Sometimes years of work might be necessary to its attainment or it could be achieved in a relatively short time. Everything depends on the individual; to enter witchcraft does not confer omniscience but it opens a door to a way of life which helps to develop natural powers.

The procedure at initiation to the second degree is much the same as at the first. There is the consecration of the candidate; the invocations; but this time he or she is not blindfolded when led around the circle by the High Priestess. There may be the ritual scourging of forty strokes; after which a 'coven' name is given, chosen either by the initiate, or by the High Priestess. Names are considered most important, probably a derivation of the ancient belief that the name represented the essential reality of the person. A witch may change the coven name; as the personality develops or alters, it is thought that the first chosen name may no longer express the true qualities and character.

The next stage is the taking of the Great Oath, of which this is the form as described to me: 'I swear upon my mother's womb and by my honour among men and my brothers and sisters of the Art, that I will never reveal to any at all any of the secrets of the Art, except it be to a worthy person, properly prepared, in the centre of a Circle, such as I am now in. This I swear by my hopes of salvation, my past lives and my hopes of future ones to come, and I devote myself to utter destruction if I break my solemn oath.'

After a further consecration as initiate of the second degree, the new graduate is ritually shown the use of the tools or weapons. With the Athame, the circle is re-drawn, then with the sword. With the white-handled knife a pentacle is incised on a candle. The wand is waved to each of the four cardinal points in turn; the pentacle is presented to these four quarters. Swinging the censer, the graduate walks round the inner perimeter of the Circle.

Then returning to the altar, the cords are given to him or her, with which the High Priestess must be bound. The graduate must scourge her as he or she was scourged in a coven where this practice is observed, but with three times the number of strokes. According to the tradition of witchcraft for one must be returned three in any conditions or circumstances. This is why, I am told, the initiator in this rite was careful to be gentle with the initiated. . . .

Lastly, the graduate is proclaimed to the Mighty Ones at the four quarters; and the words of dismissal are said.

D

CHAPTER VIII

Sabbats and Esbats

THE Wheel of the Year begins to turn anew at the Winter Solstice, which is called Yule—meaning the wheel. This is the first of the sabbats in the witches' calendar, one of the four Lesser Sabbats, the other three of which are the Spring Equinox, Summer Solstice and Autumn Equinox. The four Great Sabbats are Hallowe'en, Candlemas (2nd February), May Eve, and Lammas.

Some centuries ago, before the Christian church achieved its dictatorship over man's beliefs and actions, the sabbats were something of a public holiday. The people from the surrounding countryside—most of whom probably had witch blood, anyhow—would come along, picnic, and to some extent join in the fun. Fires were lit to cook the food, which may be, some authorities think, the origin of the 'fires of Hell' reported to have been observed at witches' meetings.

Many of the picnickers might not have been fully initiated witches, but in those days, before the persecution, the Old Religion probably meant more to them than the relatively new. It was accepted as a matter of course by the great barons and knights, by bishops (who often practised it), and by kings. According to Dr Margaret Murray, all the Plantagenets were witches. Edward III, she believes, founded two covens, and in the light of her opinion, the little incident of the Countess of Salisbury's garter is significant. As we learnt at school, while dancing with the King, Lady Salisbury's garter fell off; Edward retrieved it and slipped it on to his own leg . . . and an apparently trivial event was immortalised in the founding of the Order of the Garter.

Dr Murray thinks that there was more to the garter episode than met the eye. The garter, as has been mentioned by me already, has been part of the insignia of the Craft for millennia, a point to support which Dr Murray produces copious documentation. She argues that Edward's action was meant to convey to Lady Salisbury that the secret of her witch-hood was safe with him—because he himself was the priest of a coven.

The Church's toleration of the Old Religion seems to have come to an end with the Peasants' Revolt in 1381, which in fact was directed chiefly against the Church. The archbishop of Canterbury, Simon of Sudbury, was beheaded, and the prior of Bury given a trial parodying that of Christ. The feudal lords were disorganised; their forces scattered. It seemed that nothing could hold the rebels.

Richard II, the boy king, son of the Black Prince, descended from the man who picked up Lady Salisbury's garter, saved the situation. He rode out to the rebel army alone, unsupported by any force or form of law. With authority he spoke to the men. He told them to go home—and they went—although he was only a boy of fourteen. There seems little doubt that they obeyed him not because he was the king, but because he was the accepted leader of the Old Religion. It is likely that not only the Church, but the feudal 'Establishment' had good reason to think that the serfs and labourers who had risen against Authority, were either members of the Old Religion and the new, or the Old, only. Recognising this and recognising also its strength and potential menace, Church and barons determined to cripple the power of the Old Religion once and for all. They saw that it could employ militarily-efficient force —Crecy and Poitiers had shown what English yeomen armed with the long bow could do. And then there was another factor; the magic skills possessed by its followers. They could cause crops to fail, and disaster to men and animals.

The feudal barons learnt a lesson in the Revolt. There could be no more turning a blind eye to what had seemed a harmless continuance of old practices.

Richard's promises to the rebels were permitted to have no more substance than the echo of his words; the machinery of the Church and the State began to grind away ruthlessly all possibilities of opposition. Before very long, there was no more public merry-making at the witches' sabbats. They had to be held in secret, furtively; where there had been carefree gaiety and no one had seen anything wrong in the traditional ceremonies, the interdict of the Church made the gatherings and everything to do with the Old Religion sinister and sinful.

Most of the existing descriptions of sabbats date from post-persecution times (that is after the latter half of the fourteenth century); the information in these descriptions is taken chiefly from depositions made at witch trials. This may account for lurid practices mentioned, some of which opposed to traditions of witch-craft.

Charles Leland who was President of the first English Folk-Lore Congress in 1899, and an authority on folk-lore, published in the same year (1899) *Aradia, or The Gospel of the Witches*, a trans-lation of a form of their 'gospel', apparently current in the Mediterranean parts of Europe, since it was obtained for him by an Italian witch called Maddalena. Most of the material in it is believed to date from the fourteenth century, though some of it may be older.

As set out in Leland's translation of the 'gospel', the chief deity of the witches was Diana, the Moon Goddess. She fell in love with her brother, Lucifer, the sun, who was expelled from Heaven for the sin of pride. Diana, in the shape of a cat into which she transformed herself, crept into Lucifer's bed, then, in the darkness, changed back into her own form and seduced Lucifer. Aradia was the result of the escapade; she was charged by her mother with the responsibility of descending to earth to teach to humanity the arts of increasing crop fertility or destroying it; magic powers and witchcraft generally.

Aradia was believed by earlier witches to be a flesh-and-blood person, who lived on earth for a time to give her message; one of the company of avatars among whom were Christ, Krishna, Buddha, Mohammad and Zoroaster. Her message may have had a good deal in common with theirs in its original form; there is so little to go upon that we cannot come to a definite conclusion about that or whether Aradia ever existed in time and space.

The Aradia legend follows the general avatar-pattern. When she had finished her teaching, she told her pupils that as she must return to Heaven, from then on they would be on their own. Her mother Diana, would instruct them more deeply in magic, if they called on her with the appropriate rites.

The prescribed ritual could be similar to ancient sabbat cere-monies; no one can be certain. According to Leland's 'gospel', witches were to meet at each full moon, preferably in a wood, or in some unfrequented place. They were to be naked, as a sign that all were equal, and free. In passing, let me point out that Durer's painting of the four witches symbolises this idea. The witches are from four different social classes as is shown by the way in which their hair is dressed; their nudity is a declaration that in the Craft all are equal.

The freedom symbolised by nakedness was not only physical but mental—some cults in India today still believe that mental freedom and nakedness are inseparable. After centuries of conditioning—chiefly by ecclesiastical teachings—to the idea that there is something obscene and unpleasant, not to say embarrassing, about the unclothed human body, we are apt to feel that the purposes of rites which are performed unclothed must be licentiousness and debauchery. Before the Church really got a stranglehold on people's thought-processes, the naked human body was not considered as a lust-stimulator; it was just a naked body. It was unclothed in bed because night-clothes had not then come into fashion; it was clothed in the day because it would most likely catch pneumonia if it were not.

The idea that nudity makes for licentiousness is, I think, a tribute to the quenchless optimism of man. Anyone who has visited a nudist club must realise that nakedness has the effect of damping rather than firing ardour. The only desire aroused by most of the bodies on display is that the rules of diet and muscle-control were more generally adhered to. In the early days there were the additional complications of dirt and lice.

The most compelling reason for nudity at coven meetings was no doubt the age-old belief that it is essential to the raising of the force through which magic works. Clothing, according to this idea, 'earths' the current in some way, the current being a force probably akin to electricity, inherent in the human body. This current was stepped up by the circular dance; a ring of stones served the purpose of insulation, to keep the power in the circle.

That not only the Mystery cults held this faith in the virtue of nudity, is shown by the teaching of Jesus in the Gospel of St Thomas. 'Jesus said: "When you take off your clothing without being ashamed, and take your clothes and put them under your feet as the little children, and tread on them, then shall you behold the Son of the Living One, and you shall not fear".'

Whether this belief in the effects of nudity is valid or not, the fact that it was a belief puts it on a practical rather than on a concupiscent level. The same principle applies to the sex act, which undoubtedly had its place in the early rituals, and was part of the programme Aradia outlined for his disciples.

We have to remember, I think, that the need of fertility in crops, animals and in themselves was a goad, perpetually activating the consciousness of our ancestors. Their problem was not division but multiplication—not 'divided we fall', but 'if we don't multiply, we have had it'. The sex act since the beginnings of humanity's chequered history, has been used as sympathetic magic, to illustrate to the gods the results they were being importuned to accomplish; the abundant harvest, fecundity of stock and family.

It was originally a religious rite, but there is no law against taking pleasure in a rite, and no doubt it had what might be called its secular aspect. Sexual intercourse also had significance in rituals for the raising of power; these figure in ceremonies of magic as well as of the Craft. The witches' attitude to sex is disappointing to anyone who has read the usual type of description of witch practices in the press, and in the past. It is neither prudish nor prurient; I think perhaps a good adjective with which to qualify it is 'natural'. There is in an old French book of 1731, a recapitulation by the Sieur Boissier (who, incidentally was no friend of witches, having protested to Louis XIV against his commutation of death sentences on members of the Craft to banishment) of evidence in the witch trial of 1669 at La Haye Dupuis, which shows something of how the witch regarded sex. He quotes Marguerite Marguerie, one of the witnesses in the trial as saying that when a witch was not present at a Sabbat, his or her opposite number did not join in the dance. The dance itself she described as being performed 'back to back and two by two, each witch having his wife of the Sabbat, which sometimes is his own wife, and these wives having been given to them when they were marked, they do not change them, this kind of dance being finished, they dance hand in hand like our villagers. . . .'

Sex to the witch is a natural function; neither unclean nor shameful; not to be used promiscuously. Perhaps because of witch-recognition of the great power-raising potential of sex energies, it is regarded as sacred; this attitude may stem from the ancient worship of the forces which generated new life.

Aradia also gave instructions that a ceremonial feast should be held. The ritual meal is another very ancient concept; in most religions it is found in some form; as in the Christian Communion. The main elements of the meals were flour, water, honey and salt, which in some rites were prepared with a conjuration to Diana. According to Leland, the conjuration ran: 'You shall make cakes of meal, wine, salt and honey, in the shape of the crescent moon, and say: "I do not bake the bread, nor with it salt, nor do I cook the honey with the wine. I bake the body and the blood and the soul, the soul of Diana, that she know neither rest nor peace, and ever be in cruel suffering till she will grant what I request, what I do most desire, I beg it of her from my very heart and if the grace is granted, O Diana! in honour of thee, will I hold this feast and drain the goblet deep, we will dance and wildly leap, and if thou grantest the grace when I require then when the dance is wildest, all the lamps shall be extinguished and we will freely love".'

The main facts of the Sabbat celebration, as given in Leland's translation, tie in much more nearly with the acknowledged canons of the Craft than do the accounts of it which are drawn from depositions brought forward at witch trials. The most glaring anacronism in these is the monotonous mention of the devil in the existence of whom witches do not believe, as being the chief figure at the proceedings; he is presented as the God whom the witches worship.

The sixteenth century writer Danaeus gives this summary of the proceedings: 'Satan calleth them together into a Devilish Sinagogue and that he may also understand of them howe well and diligently they have fulfilled their office of intoxicating committed unto them, and who they have slaine, wheretofore they meete togither in certain appointed places . . . he appeareth visibly unto them in sundrie fourmes, as the heade and chiefs of that congregation. . . . Then doe they all repeate the othe ehich they have geuen unto him, in acknowledging him to be their God . . . he demaundeth agayne of them what they would require of him . . . unto some he geueth poysons ready made, and others he teacheth how to make and mingle new. . . . Finally if in any thing they neede his presence and helpe, by covenant he promiseth to be present with them'.

More detailed versions describe the celebrations as beginning with homage to the Devil—which entailed a renewal of vows of obedience, and loyalty, and a ritual kiss on any indicated part of his anatomy. Cooper (1617) says that '. . . when this acknowledgment is made, in testimonial of this subjection, Satan offers his back parts to be kissed of his vassall', but that this was considered to be the invariable routine is not borne out by other descriptions. Italian witches were said, when paying reverence to the Devil, to bend backwards, lifting one foot forwards.

After the homage, came reports of magic worked by the coven members, consultations with and instructions from the Devil. This, which was the business of the meeting, was followed by the religious rites. Lastly, there was the feast and dancing, which ended at dawn.

In the Somerset witch trials, of 1664, of Anne Bishop (officer, or priestess of the coven), a description is given by Alice Duke, Anne Bishop, Elizabeth Style, Mary Penny, of how a Sabbat celebration began. 'At their first meeting, the Man in black bids them welcome, and they all make low obeysance to him.' '. . . met about nine of the Clock in the Night on the common near Trister Gate, where they met a Man in black clothes with a little Band to whom they did courtesie and due observance.' According to Mary Green, of the same coven, she went with others to Hussey's Knap in the forest during the night, where a fiend appeared in the shape of a man in black clothes with a little band, to whom they all made obeisance. 'On Thursday Night before Whitsunday last . . . being met they called out 'Robin'. Upon which instantly appeared a little Man in black clothes, to whom all made obeysance, and the little Man put his hand to his Hat, saying How do ye? speaking low but *big*. Then all made low obeysances to him again.'

The name Robin crops up several times in Somerset witch trials, as soubriquet of the Devil. Two of the coven, Elizabeth Style and Alice Duke, used this name when they called upon him privately, Elizabeth Style adding the conjuration 'Oh Sathan, give me my purpose'.

'Robin' also figures in one of the earliest known ritual witchcraft trials. In 1324, in Ireland, Lady Alice Kyteler of Kilkenny (as already mentioned) was accused, 'to haue nightlie conference with a spirit called Robin Artisson, to whom she sacrificed in the high waie .ix. red cocks.' The information about her and her trial comes from notes kept by the clerk to the Bishop of Ossory (who tried the case), Richard Ledrede. Lady Alice had had four husbands, the first of whom was the brother of the Lord Chancellor of Ireland,

Roger Outlaw. By him she had a son, William; it was for his advancement she was supposed to have become involved with 'Robin Artisson', or the Devil.

The prosecution was not by the civil Courts, but by the Bishop of Ossory, who made out his case against Lady Alice with the help of Bulls promulgated by Pope John XXII. William Outlaw was tried at Kilkenny before the Chancellor (his uncle), the Lord Treasurer and other high civil dignitaries. The verdict was he was to hear three Masses daily for twelve months, maintain poor people, and foot the bills for repairs to the Cathedral choir-stalls.

The Bishop of Ossory, foiled of his main prey, Lady Alice, who escaped to England, turned on Roger Outlaw, whom he accused of disloyalty. Roger was acquitted of the charge by a panel of ecclesiastical dignitaries, who declared him to be 'loyal and upright, zealous in the faith, and ready to die for it'.

Determined not to be baulked the Bishop seized on women in Lady Alice's household, who, he said, were members of her coven. Petronilla de Meath, and several others, were tortured, flogged and executed by burning; as I mentioned in an earlier chapter.

The 'black man' appears in a number of witch depositions, even when not called 'Robin'. A Northumberland record of 1673 describes how 'the devil' in the forme of a little black man and black cloaths, called of one Issabell Thompson, of Slealy, widdow, by name, and required of her what service she had done him. She replyd she had got power of the body of one Margaret Teasdale. And after he had danced with her, he dismissed her, and call'd of one Thomasine, wife of Edward Watson, of Slealy.'

Again, the Somerset witches claimed that 'the Man in black sometimes playes on a Pipe or Cittern, and the company dance'.

Among indictments against Aberdeen witches in 1596 is the charge that: 'upon Hallowe'en last, by pact . . . the said Thomas Leyis . . . with ane gryit number of vtheris witches, come to the mercatt and fische croce of Aberdeen, under the conduct and gyding of the Dewill present withe you, all in company, playing befoir yow on his kynd of instrumentis.' Two witches of North Berwick coven, Christen Michell and Bessie Thom admitted that they had been at this meeting, and also at another gathering, three years before, where, with 'certain vtheris witches, they devillische adherentis, coven-it upon Sainct Katcherines Hill . . . and thair, vnder the the conduct of Satan, present with yow, playing befoir yow, efter his forme, ye all dansit a devilische danse, rydand ontreis, be a lang space.' The North Berwick coven was also accused of taking bones from certain graves indicated by the Devil for the purpose of making charms with these bones. On another occasion it was said they used magic rites in order to wreck a ship.

Helen Guthrie confessed in Forfar in 1661 that at one meeting 'they all daunced together a whyle and then went to Mary Rynd's house . . . and made them selfes merrie; and the divil made much of them all, but especiallie of Mary Rynd, and he kist them all.' One of the coven, Elspeth Bruce, 'by turning the sive and sheires, reased the divell, who being werry hard to be laid againe, ther was a meiting of witches for laying of him and at thie meiting they had pipe-music and dauncing.'

Marie Lamont 1662 confessed that she was at a meeting where the 'devil sung to them, and they dancit; he gave them wine to drink, and wheat bread to eat, and they warr all very merrie . . . Shee was with Katie Scot and others at the meiting at Kempoch wher they danced and the devil kissed them when they went away.' Marie Lamont claimed that her coven 'in the lykness of kats' accompanied by the Devil as a man with cloven feet, made a charm with 'wyt sand' against two men, a Mr Blackhall and a Mr John Hamilton.

From Marie Lamont's deposition comes confirmation that meetings were held at night. 'The devil came to Kattrein Scott's house in the midst of the night . . . and when she had been at a mieting sine Zowle last with other witches, in the night, the devill convoyed her home in the dawing.'

In 1604, a coven of Ayshire witches, which included one Patrik Lowrie, was charged that 'at Hallowevin in the yeir of God foirsaid, assemblit thame selffis vpon Lowdon-hill, quhair thair appeirit to thame and devillische Spreit'.

The form in which the Devil appears at the Sabbat—or Esbat— varies as does the spelling of his name. But in one shape or another according to these depositions he is always there, a figure irreconcilable with witch beliefs.

The Horned God, who is the consort of the Moon Goddess, Diana, the Great Mother, has no link with the Church's Satan, the embodiment of evil. As the god of death he might inspire awe; he was worshipped by the Romans as Cernunnos, Lord of the Underworld. He was the god of hunting, the woods and the field were his. He ruled the horned beasts; he was the god of farmers and shepherds; he was Faunus, Sylvanus, Pan, but it is hard to see how he can be the 'black man' of the witches' depositions.

At the Sabbat, the High Priestess represented the Great Mother; the male priest personified the Horned God. Often he would wear a stag's frontlet and skin, or that of some other animal. This may have been a survival of totemism, and the concept of the marriage of the totem animal with the Great Mother, or it may simply have been considered a means of identification with the god himself.

Whatever the origin of the ritual guise, in the eyes of churchmen of the Middle Ages, it had only one interpretation. The devil was horned; ergo the Horned God was the devil. So the witches whose deity he was must be devil-worshippers; any powers which they had came from him, and must be evil.

During the Middle Ages, fear of the devil had become obsessive. Today it is difficult for us to realise the power which this belief in an ever-present threat of active evil had on the minds and lives of people in those days, and its devastating effects. Pre- and non-Christians might or might not have faith in malignant forces; among them Satan (or whatever his counterpart might be called) was never given the leading part with which the teachings of the Church at that time invested him. The devil still exists today as personalised power in the minds of primitive races; they may fear him, but he is not the terrifying figure, dread of whom drove our unfortunate ancestors to a psychotic condition in which they maimed or killed other human beings because of some imaginary link with him. Not only England, but Europe was devil-mad at this time; the result, anthropologists say, of the Church's doctrine of the time. It has been shown that only a form of religious belief which works on the minds of its followers by fear is the breeding-ground of devastating terrors. To complete the picture, to understand why such tenets were almost generally accepted, I think we have to look for the conditions which could make men ready to accept these teachings.

The devil mostly can thank the Feudal system, I think, for establishing him in his prominent position in the Middle Ages. Complete subjection to some form of dictatorship, squalor, poverty and illiteracy tend to foster the growth of irrational or distorted ideas. People who live in such circumstances are rarely normal—and these circumstances were habitual for the masses under the feudal system. Only the great barons were really free, and even they, because there was so much superstition, were to some extent dominated by the Church.

The lands of lesser nobility were held in fief to the baron; they and their families were dependent upon his humours; so far as they were concerned, he was the law. The next grade lower in the social order was that of serf—and serf was another word for slave. His life was valued at eleven farthings; anyone who happened to kill a serf could, by paying that sum, go free today the fine for damaging a farm animal would be relatively much heavier. The hovel in which he lived, its crude furniture, any farm implements he might possess, could be seized at any time by his overlord, who also could do what he liked with the man's wife and children.

It is hard to believe that the custom of *droit du seigneur* could have been taken as a matter of course by any man, however brutalised, but in this period it undoubtedly was. Theoretically if the serf paid a set sum to the overlord, his bride was his own. In practice, when the newly-married couple arrived at the castle, if the girl were at all attractive, the baron would tell his serf that the fee for marriage rights had been increased, knowing that the man would be unable to raise extra money.

While the husband was hustled with kicks and blows from the castle, the usual procedure was that the wife's dress—probably her only one—was torn off by the pages and men-at-arms. She was then carried to the Baron's bedroom and when he had finished with her, knights, squires, pages, possibly also the Baron's chaplain, each took her, and considered that they were honouring her—a mere peasant—by their attentions. Some women are said to have committed suicide after their 'wedding' night; some went mad and were kept in the castle dungeons; the majority survived, but the experience must have had a life-long effect on the mind of any woman. A child conceived during the mass-rape, and any subsequent children she might bear, would be to some degree affected by her mental state, in all probability.

It seems that there could not be any greater hell than the hopeless, pointless drudgery of a serf's life at that time—but when the Black Death, the great plague of 1348 swept Europe, conditions became so appalling that even the serfs probably would have turned back the clock, if they could. The mortality rate from the plague was ninety per cent; two thirds of Europe's population was decimated by it. Morality, principles, law, civil administration went into the discard. Cut-throat bands whose slogan was 'Enemy of God, of all mercy, all charity' terrorised the people everywhere. A contemporary playwright, Theofil, blaming the Almighty for the cataclysm, wrote: 'O Thou thoroughly wicked God, if I could but lay hands on Thee, truly I would tear Thee in pieces'.

Famine followed the plague, and according to some reports there was cannabilism among the starving peasants in France.

Some scapegoat for the visitation had to be found. The King of France, Phillip the Fair, blamed the lepers—every leper in the country was burned to death. Then it was said that Jews were responsible—ninety per cent of the Jews in Europe were massacred. The Church gave out that the plague was the work of Satan, and since it must have seemed that some active power of evil had broken loose in the world, the average person accepted this as truth.

Circumstances had conditioned them to a belief in the reality of malignant forces; mental resistance was weakened, as was physical resistance. On the physical level they fell victims to the Black Death, on the mental, to the Church's insistence on the ever-present menace of Satan . . . which was at least as potentially dangerous to the health of the mind as the plague was to the body.

Today we would call this tap-tap-tapping of an idea into people's minds a form of brain-washing; looking back three or four centuries we can see that it was successful then as it was when the Nazis used it centuries later. A very large proportion of men and women became what can be described as mad in the Middle Ages on the subject of devil-sponsored wickedness. And this, I think, is a partial explanation, at any rate, of Satan's cropping up so pertinaciously in evidence at the witch-trials.

In most cases, the witches were no better educated than anyone else; therefore their mental defences against suggestion would be vulnerable. It would have been utterly useless for them to deny belief in Satan when both Church and State were certain that they worshipped him. It is possible that through the brain-washing techniques of their questioning, they—or at least, the more illiterate among them—confused the Church's idea of the character of their god with their own concept of him. It would not be surprising if under the mental and physical torture to which they were subjected, this were so. There is also a recognisable pattern in the evidence given, which suggests almost a script prepared beforehand. I think there can be little doubt that in many cases, at least, this means that witches more or less agreed that the accusations against them of doing or believing certain things, were true, for fear of further 'questioning'. It has been said that at most English and Scottish trials 'legal torture' was not applied. This, I think, is not only casuistry; it implies that judges and officials of that time possessed objectivity and impartiality although no evidence appears to exist to show that any but the exceptional few had either.

Most members of the prosecution would consider it their duty to obtain the information required by any means possible; if suffering were the only means of making the accused speak, then that must be the method used. And what constituted torture? From what we knew of the outlook the proceedings of those times, we can be fairly certain that the meaning of the word would be 'bent' to suit the case and the questioner. I quote Father von Spee again: 'There is a frequent phrase used by judges that the accused has confessed without torture . . . in reality they were tortured but only in an iron press with sharp-edged channels over the shins, in which they were pressed like a cake, bring blood and causing intolerable pain, and this is technically called without torture. . .

Even today, horns and hooves, forked tail and brimstone still form part of the popular image of witchcraft. But here and there, there are signs of recognition that the god of the witches is not the devil. In 1959, Dr Serge Hutin, Ecole Pratique des Hautes Études (Sciences Religieuses) wrote in his *Histoire Mondiale des Societies Secrets*: '. . . Witchcraft is hereditary in certain families, guardians, in secret of the ancient Cult. It is not connected with devil-worship, nor is it an anti-Christian reaction . . . British witches do not worship Satan, for the simple reason that their god existed well before Christianity. One must not see in every horned idol a representation of the devil'.

The dances with which a Sabbat is celebrated probably have not changed much through the centuries. The principal form is the ring-dance in the circle, of which there are many variations. There is also what could be called the follow-the-leader dance; sometimes apparently both were combined in one complete dance. Dr Murray says that in the follow-my-leader form, pace was important '. . . and as it seems to have been a punishable offence to lag behind in this dance, this is possibly the origin of the expression, "The Devil take the hindmost" '.

The witches in the old days danced to the music of a pipe or cittern; in Scotland usually it was provided by a Jew's harp; in this age of automation a gramophone or tape-recorder is used for sound effects.

Aradia's original menu of cakes and wine for the ceremonial feast was widely interpreted in earlier centuries. Weather permitting it was held out-of-doors; a cloth was spread on the ground, on which the food was laid out. Roast mutton or roast ox are mentioned in several accounts of feasts as the meat course; in the *Pleasant Treatise of Witches,* it is said that: 'They sit to Table where no delicate meats are wanting to gratify their Appetite. . . .'

Sometimes the meal was very simple, when Goodwife Foster was questioned in 1692 about a meeting of the Andover coven, and the 'ritual feast', 'She answered that she carried Bread and Cheese in her pocket, and that she and the Andover Company came to the village before the Meeting began and sat down together under a tree, and ate their food, and that she drank water out of a Brook to quench her thirst.'

Nowadays the form of the ritual meal is again much the same as that in Aradia's formula—cakes and wines, or sometimes beer. Most witches do not drink more than two glasses of whichever may be available, but there is no hard-and-fast rule as to quantity. The meal is taken inside the circle.

The English climate as a general rule not being favourable to outdoor festivities, although the Druids claim that they always have fine weather for their meetings, mostly witches prefer not to risk being rained or snowed upon, or frozen, and hold their Sabbets indoors. A witch with whom I was discussing a Candlemas celebration—then a day or two ahead—emphatically said that anyone who expected her to go leaping about on a cold February night in darkness and probably rain, could think again. She found it hard to believe that the Craft had ever gone in for outdoor activities in winter, if they did, she said, that would account for the popular image of the witch as a bent old crone—'crippled with arthritis and riddled with rheumatism'.

The circle is drawn on the floor of the room where the Sabbat is held with chalk and then with the witches' knife. The altar, with its candles and ritual instruments, or tools, with water in a cauldron. and salt, with incense in a censer, stands in the circle centre. The rites are celebrated, the cakes and wine are taken. The witches talk and laugh together—to enjoy the meetings is part of the tradition of the Craft—and then they wish one-another good-bye in witch-fashion: 'Merry meet, merry part.'

This is a very rough outline of the procedure at the Sabbats of today. The phrases I have used, such as 'the rites are celebrated' of course refer to the core of the Craft, of which only initiates can be allowed to learn. The witches have their own ways of raising power, and there is a great deal of evidence to show that it works.

The esbat differs from the sabbat in that it is a less formal occasion, at which any business with which the coven needs to deal can be transacted. Or it may just be a pleasant 'get together', which serves the purpose of enabling the members to keep in close touch. It takes place at or about the time of the full moon.

Much the same preparations are made for it as for the Sabbat; cakes and wine are on the programme. In the sixteenth and seventeenth centuries, esbats, so far at least as references to the Devil go, are carbon copies of the sabbats; the routine of dancing and feasting is much the same as at the religious occasion.

CHAPTER IX

The Powers of the Witch

THE power of witchcraft is probably its most fascinating aspect to most people. They want to know if it does or does not exist. And if it does can it do anything for them?

Most of the letters which reach witches from time to time are variations on this theme, people ask if a spell can be made or power invoked; if it can bring them something they want or remove something they don't want.

This has probably been the general attitude to the Craft since first it came into being and not only to witchcraft but to all forms of magic, which is now classed as manifestation of extra-sensory perception.

The powers of witchcraft in the early days seem to have been chiefly concerned with increasing and ensuring fertility, which is what one would expect, since that was the main preoccupation of most people then. Life was dependent upon fruitfulness of earth and crop, animal and human being. Some measure of weather control, reputed or real, must have formed part of witchcraft's activities. It seems likely that a proportion, at any rate, of its practitioners of those days could influence meteorological changes . . . and that they still can.

They were, as well, acknowledged healers, by herbal and 'extra physical' methods. Their clairvoyant faculties made their advice and counsel much sought after.

The witches of those early days in fact seem to have made more or less full use of the not ungenerous range of powers with which Aradia was permitted by her mother Diana to endow her disciples. According to Leland's *Gospel of the Witches*, (mentioned in an earlier chapter), these numbered eleven. Aradia's followers could obtain success in love and all worldly matters; they could bless friends and curse enemies effectively, converse with spirits, find hidden treasure in ancient ruins, conjure the spirits of priests who had died knowing where treasure was hidden, understand the voice of the wind, change water into wine, use cards in divination, know the secrets of the hand, cure diseases, tame wild beasts—and finally, 'whatsoever was asked from the spirit of Aradia would be granted unto them that merited her favour.' This promise is repeated in another part of the *Gospel*: 'If thou adorest Luna [another of the goddess' names], what thou desirest, thou shalt obtain'.

Aradia does not specifically include flying in the list, but no doubt this could come under the heading of 'whatsoever thou desirest'. At any rate, the belief, which I have mentioned already, that witches could and did transport themselves to Sabbats and other assemblies by air, was widespread and very ancient. In the ninth century, a decree attributed to the Council of Ancyra, was made against 'Certeine wicked women following sathans prouocations, being zeduced by the illusion of diuels, beleeve and professe, that in the night times they ride abroad with Diana, the goddesse of the Pagans, or else with Herodias [believed to be identifiable with Aradia] with an innumerable multitude, vpon certeine beasts. . . .' Apparently as a rule, a 'magic' ointment had to be smeared over the whole body, as I have said, in order to make flight possible, then the witch took off, either unsupported, mounted on her familiar, or on a broomstick. What evidence there is on the subject is not entirely hearsay. There are numbers of testimonies from witches that they themselves had flown in this way or had seen others actually in the air.

In 1609, a man of twenty-five years old, Isaac de Queyran, gave evidence that witches who lived at some distance from the meeting flew home; the others walked. A Crook of Devon witch, Bessie Henderson, stated that 'ye was taken out of ye bed to that meeting in an flight.' Isabel Gowdie's description in 1662 of flying was that 'We will flie lyk strawes quhan we pleas; wild strawes and corne-strawes will be horses to ws, an we put thaim betwixt our foot and say: "Horse and Hattok, in the Divellis name" . . . Quhan we wold ryd, we tak windle-strawes, or been-stakes, and put them betwixt owr foot, and say thryse: "Horse and Hattok, horse and goe; Horse and pellattis, ho! ho!", and immediatelie we flie away euir we wold. . . . All the Coeven did fflie lyk cattis. . . .'

Joseph Glanvil in *Sadducimus Triumphatus,* 1681, quotes the testimony of Somerset witches. One of them Elizabeth Style says: '. . . they anoint their Foreheads and Hand-wrists with an Oyl the Spirit brings them (which smells raw), and then they are carried in a very short time, using these words as they pass, *Thout, tout a tout, tout, throughout and about.* And when they go off from their Meetings, they say *Rentum, Tormentum* . . . all are carried to their several homes in a short space.' Alice Duke gave the same testimony, noting beside that the oil was greenish in colour. Anne Bishop, the Officer of the Somerset Coven, confessed that 'her Forehead being first anointed with a Feather dipt in Oyl, she hath been suddenly carried to the place of their meeting. . . .'

A woman named Julian Cox was out strolling one evening when, about a mile from her house 'there came riding towards her three persons upon three broom-staves, born up about a yard and an half from the ground. Two of them she formerly knew, which was a Witch and a Wizzard. . . .' Two New England witches confessed in 1692, to rising on a pole. Reports of evidence by Goody Foster of flying from Andover to a coven meeting are identical in the important details. The first states 'One Foster confessed that the Devil carry'd them on a pole, to a Witch-meeting; but the pole broke, and she hanging about Martha Carrier's neck, they both fell down, and she then received an hurt by the Fall, whereof she is not at this very time recovered.' The second recounts: 'In particular Goody Foster said (Inter alia) that she with two others (one of whom acknowledged the same) Rode from Andover to the same Village Witch meeting upon a stick above ground and that in the way the stick brake, and gave the said F. a fall whereupon said she, I got a fall and hurt of which I am still sore.'

The evidence for witch-flying, first-hand or not, has been dismissed, at any rate in the nineteenth and twentieth centuries, as hallucination or hysteria—or as plain falsehood. But now that science is beginning to doubt the validity of its doubt, we can even dare to wonder if there were any truth in the witches' claims.

It seems improbable that the physical bodies of witches were propelled about in the air, either on broomsticks, animals, or without visible means of support, but in the light of recent discoveries— or rediscoveries—about the nature of matter it would be rash to say it was impossible. Mystics of countries such as India and Tibet with a long tradition of mind and body training, and spiritual knowledge, believe that they can, by altering the vibrations of the body, resolve it into atomic form, and reassemble the atoms in another place. Some mediums in the West claim to be able to do this; among them was the late Ronald Strong, whom I knew well. He had great reserves of 'extra-physical' power, but as to whether he could or could not dematerialise and re-materialise, I cannot say of my own knowledge. But he gave me two instances of materialisation, not of the body, but of money, both of which were confirmed by his secretary, Doris Garland Anderson. They are not scientific proof but I think are interesting enough to mention before we go back to the witches.

Ronald Strong had been holding a series of meeting in the north of England. He was extremely careless about money, and for some reason—which I forget—he found that his funds were not enough to settle his hotel bill. He decided to call for help on his 'guide', Red Eagle, and after a period of concentration Ronald told Doris the impression had come to him that Red Eagle had co-operated. The money necessary was in his bedroom . . . but he didn't know where. They hunted for it in all likely and unlikely places, without uncovering so much as a halfpenny. Ronald, undismayed, said the money must be there; Red Eagle had never let him down. As he spoke, he glanced at the ceiling, and there, tucked into the moulding was what looked like and proved to be a ten-pound note. Their gratitude to Red Eagle was not unmixed; the ceiling was high, Doris had to stand on Ronald's shoulders and then, with the ferrule of an umbrella, struggle to dislodge the note from its cache.

On the second occasion, Ronald found himself with only enough ready cash to pay for two cups of tea instead of the dinner which both he and Doris Garland Anderson urgently needed after a long hard day, before catching the London train. Ronald again asked for Red Eagle's help. The impression came to him that they were to go to a good restaurant; they were to order the good dinner they needed. The money for the bill would be forthcoming.

Ronald ate his meal with gusto, but Doris Garland Anderson was too disturbed to enjoy hers. When Ronald insisted on rounding off the dinner with liqueurs and coffee and a cigar, and there was no sign of money to pay for it all, she was really worried. The waiter brought the bill. Doris and Ronald sat in silence for a moment, then Ronald said: 'We must get up from the table.' As he did this, he felt something, he said, in his hand—and there was a five-pound note, just enough to cover the bill and a tip for the waiter.

An experience of a similar nature occurred to a woman I know who is working on research into ancient mystery cults. She received (in the presence of another person, who confirms the incident) a document of some antiquity connected with her researches. Fantastic as it may sound, these two people saw the document materialise above the table at which they were sitting, then float gently down till it rested in front of the woman who needed it. It is still in her possession; I have seen it. Both she and the man who saw the materialisation have a highly developed sixth sense, but neither practices psychic science or magic in any form.

To go back to the question of witch-flight. We know so little of what laws govern the non-physical levels that perhaps it is safer not to come to definite conclusions as to whether or not witches actually flew in their physical bodies. It could even be that sometimes some of them did, and that at other times they 'dreamed' their experiences with the aid of a 'flying ointment' which may have induced a form of trance . . . and this brings us to the almost non-existent line dividing the subjective from the objective. The more deeply this question is studied the less possible it becomes to make arbitrary distinctions between these two types of experience. It could be that the 'flying ointment' was the equivalent of a railway ticket to the physical traveller, enabling the subconscious to journey in space and time.

'Astral travelling' is the name usually given to this form of excursion. Although it is not included in Aradia's catalogue, it is one of witchcraft's traditional powers. Some covens today work for its development by training and increasing pyschic faculties, which may be a longer and harder way of getting results than the use of an ointment, but gives the satisfaction of having mastered a technique, whereas all one would be likely to get out of the experience through the short-cut would be a headache.

Some people seem to be able to go out of their bodies in this way as easily and naturally as you or I would go out of our house. A witch told me that when she was investigating astral travelling she called on a woman in a remote country district who was supposed to be expert in the art. She was asked to stay the night, which she had to spend in an enormous bed already shared by mother and daughter. After a few hours, she woke, to find the mother, who lay beside her, rigid and quite cold. The daughter, when wakened, looked at the apparent corpse. 'She'm not dead,' she said, 'She'm just out and about'.

The Council of Constance, which was in session from 1414 to 1418, apparently had no idea that witches' curricula included air-travel by any method. Otherwise it certainly would have been included in the list of their 'crimes' which the Council set down as 'Second Sight, Ability to read Secrets and Foretell Events, Power to Cause Diseases, Death by Lightning and Destructive Storms, to Transform themselves into Birds and Beasts, to Bring Illicit Love, Barreness of Living Being and Crops, and the Devouring of Children'.

The chief object for which the Council was formed by the Emperor Sigismund was to clean the Augean stables of the papal office. At that time there were three Popes, Pope John XXIII, Pope Benedict XIII, and Pope Gregory XII, all claiming to be the Vicar of God. Eventually the Council deposed all three and put Cardinal Colonna into office as Pope Martin V. In the meantime it could be said to have established by its edicts and authority a general belief in black magic with which it confused witchcraft—and, of course, omnipresence of the Devil.

This Council offered John Huss a safe conduct to come and explain his religious views to them. Huss went, and paid the penalty of his trust in the Council's bona fides by being burnt alive at their order. A colleague of Huss', Jerome of Prague, although he recanted in the hope of being spared Huss' fate, was burned alive also, after having been excommunicated and anathematised. Even the dead could not escape the Council's vigilance. They ordered John Wycliffe's bones to be dug up and desecrated.

Divination by Tarot cards came under the heading of 'Ability to read Secrets and Foretell Events', and therefore under the Council's ban. In 1423 St Bernadino of Siena preached against them, saying that they were an invention of the devil. In 1484, Antonio Cicognara, a famous artist of the period, who commissioned to paint a pack of these cards as a gift for Cardinal Ascanion Sforza. Some of the cards from this pack, which must be unique, are still in existence, or were in 1954. In that year they were on show in America.

The cards may have been used for some form of gambling, but it seems more probably that a Prince of the Church at that time, when interest in occultism, black magic and witchcraft was at peak among the nobility and in ecclesiastical circles, would put them to their real purpose of divination.

Queen Marie de Medici of France made no secret of her interest in occultism. It was said that she was a witch, and that her son, Henri III, practised black magic. He, at any rate, made a collection of magicians' tools or instruments, which were exhibited after his death . . . whether he knew how to use them is another matter.

Probably both Catherine and her son were witches, according to the definition of Sir Edward Coke (1552-1634), Lord Chief Justice of England, who enacted that 'A witch is a person who hath conference with the Devil to conspire with him or to do some act.' The act might be bad or good. Power, whether used to heal and help or to harm and destroy, Church and State agreed could come only from the devil. Therefore to use such power was a capital offence and death was the penalty.

The inexorable treatment of witches suggests that the Craft was looked upon as a grave threat to the Establishment of those days. And since witches have never been politicians or proselytisers, Church and State must have seen their powers as a potential danger to their authority. Allowing for the bias towards superstition and lack of scientific knowledge of those days, there still must have been enough credible evidence to convince men—who often had brilliant minds—of the reality of these powers.

This was the most terrible heresy conceivable—to possess powers which the Church could not claim as coming from God; powers which worked. And which if allowed to go on working, might cause the crumbling of the existing order. . . .

Fear of this debacle grew until it became maniacal. A pitch was reached when it was almost unsafe to remark that the next day was likely to be fine; this could be called fortelling the future. In 1571 a travelling conjurer performed, as part of his show, a few uncomplicated card tricks. These were denounced as witchcraft; the man was tortured and under torture 'confessed' that he had been to a witches' Sabbat. He was condemned to be burned alive; a number of people who had been named as having associated with him, were also burned at the stake. Probably none had committed any crime at all, except the crime of being alive. The majority of the judges were not concerned with whether the prisoner was guilty as accused. The charge was immaterial; everyone was guilty of the great crime of Original Sin; as Spina, Master of the Sacred Palace, wrote: 'Why does God permit the death of the innocent. He does so justly. For if they do not die by reason of the sins they have committed, yet they are guilty of death by reason of original sin'.

To bring a person to trial as a witch, all that was necessary was a denouncement to a judge, by an identified witness, or if that were not possible, an unidentified witness—or if no witness were forthcoming, report of a general rumour was enough. Jacob Sprenger, the Inquisitor General of the fifteenth century, held that '. . . the testimony of men of low repute and criminals . . . is admitted . . . so great is the plague of heresy that in an action of this kind . . . any criminal evildoer may give evidence against any person soever'. Or, if there were no other grounds of complaint, a man's face could be testimony against him. Boguet, the French civil jurist laid down that it was possible 'to draw from the repulsiveness of a man's face an indication against him sufficient to expose him to the torture'.

King James I, who feared witchcraft and worked tirelessly against it, drew up almost a manual of witch-detection methods. Among these was an instruction to attempt to make the witch weep, for, he said; 'They cannot even shed tears.' Or long pins could be stuck into the body of the suspect, as if it were a pincushion, in the hope of discovering the Devil's Mark, which was supposed to be an area insensitive to pain. Or having bound the witch's hands and feet together, she should be thrown into a pond or river. Water, being the holy baptismal fluid would reject any person in league with the devil; therefore if the woman were a witch she would float (to her execution, presumably); if she were innocent, she would drown. In any event, the case would be closed satisfactorily, except to the accused.

For a witch on trial to be found innocent was almost unheard of, even when facts proved it. In Wurzberg, a woman under torture, 'confessed' that she had dug up the corpse of a child, in order to use it in making of spells and magic. On the husband's insistence that this was not true, the Inquisitors had the grave opened. The body of the child was there; it was identified, but the Inquisitors decided that it was only an illusion created by the Devil. The woman was found guilty and burned. There are a number of instances of girls who 'confessed' that they had been deflowered by Satan at a Sabbat. Although examination proved them to be virgo intacta, they were burned.

As well as fear and sadism, there was another incentive to witch-hunting. Canon Law laid down that after a witch's death, accuser and judge might divide her property between them. As a direct result of this a new profession came into being—the profession of witch-finder. Perhaps its most notable member was Matthew Hopkins, who in 1640 toured Norfolk, Suffolk, Essex and Huntingdonshire, 'purging' villages and towns of witches for the fee of twenty shillings, plus expenses. His method was to discover who was suspected locally of witchcraft, accept any evidence or none, seize the 'witch', strip her, prick her with pins, bind her and throw her into pond or river, tie her with chains into an agonising cramped position, in which she would be left for days, or walk her up and down a room for hours between relays of jailers until she fell down.

Executioners worked overtime, but still the prisons overflowed with Hopkin's victims. Thousands of people were jailed and executed on the flimsiest evidence; motivated by spite and jealousy. Eventually people began to get frightened of each other rather than of Hopkins. And then they turned on him. Hopkins was subjected to one of his own tests; he was bound, hand and foot, and thrown into the Thames. He floated, so, as he must undoubtedly be a witch, the crowd dragged him out of the river and burned him alive.

According to evidence given during the Hopkins witch-hunts and many of their trials, among powers attributed to and often claimed by witches was the ability to change themselves and others into animal form. The belief that witches could do this was current long before the 'burning time'. Apuleius tells the story of a witch who changed her lover, because he had been unfaithful to her, into a beaver, and an innkeeper, who was jealous of her, into a frog. '. . . now in his old age, he swims about in a vessel of his own wine, and squatting in the dregs of it, greets his former customers with hoarse, servile croakings'.

The shape of a hare seems to have been the favourite choice of a witch who changed into animal form; perhaps because hares are the creatures associated with the Moon Goddess in myth and legend. Sometimes a witch would take on the appearance of a cat, or a dog, a crow, a rook or even a bee. Ann Armstrong of a Northumberland coven, gave in evidence a description of a witch meeting, when, she said: 'They stood all upon a bare spot of ground, and bid the informer sing while they danced in severall shapes, first of a haire, then in their owne, and then in a catt, sometimes in a mouse, and in severall other shapes. . . . She sees all the said persons beforementioned dancing, som in the likenesse of haires, some in the likenesse of catts, some in the likenesse of bees, and some in their own likenesse.'

When the change was made this spell or conjuration was repeated :

> I sall goe intill ane haire
> With sorrow and sych, and meikle caire,
> and I sall goe in the Divells nam,
> Ay quhill I com hom again.

with the substitution of 'crow' or 'catt' for 'haire' according to shape the witch decided to take on.

To come back into her own body, the witch said :

> Haire, haire, God send thee caire,
> I am in a haire's liknes just now,
> Bot I sal be in an womanis liknes ewin now.

Evidence given by witches of the Auldearne coven shows that the witches believed they could turn other witches into animals. 'If we in the shape of an cat, an crow, an hare, or any other likeness, etc., go to any of our neighbours' houses, being Witches, we will say I (or we) conjure thee, Go with us (or me). And presently they become as we are and go with us whither we would.'

Some of the transformations into animal, bird or insect shape no doubt were ritual, not actual, their purpose possibly originated in race beliefs of totemism. A mask or some sign of identification with the animal or other form would be worn, to show that its character had been assumed by the witch. But this explanation may not fit all the cases.

There is the possibility that some of the appearances were thought-forms—a possibility which cannot be brushed aside altogether when we remember that a mental image can be objective enough to be photographed. Hypnosis—auto and hetero—may be a clue to others.

Witches certainly understood and could use hypnosis. We have seen that long before Dr James Braid 'discovered' medical hypnosis in the mid-nineteenth century witches were using its powers to heal and to procure painless childbirth. In the thirteenth century, in the compendium of the Laws of England compiled by Britton, the 'practice of enchantment, as those who sent people to sleep', is mentioned as an offence.

Of the powers granted by Aradia, cursing has always been one of the most publicised. Blessing we do not hear so much of, although the white witch curses seldom and blesses often.

Under the heading of blessing comes healing, in which some covens specialise. I know of a number of cases in which the 'power' has been used, as Aradia promised, with success. One such was a gall-bladder condition. The patient was not himself a witch; he asked a friend, who he knew was a member of the Craft to work for him. The trouble cleared up and has not returned. Another instance was of the wife of a coven member, not herself a witch, who had severe dermatitis, which would not react to any form of medical treatment. At one Lammas celebration, the husband, without telling his wife, with the other witches 'did what was necessary', as they put it. The next day the condition began to clear and finally disappeared. A male witch who was very ill with bronchitis sent a message to his coven asking for help, with the result that he was perfectly well again the morning after the ritual had been done. He had not told his wife, who was not a member of the Craft what was afoot; when she saw his apparently miraculous recovery, she said: 'I see the witches have been at you.' An unusual blessing described in the *Evening Standard* of 15th February 1965, came fifty years ago to Mr Walter Arthur, who was then undertaker at Claygate, in those days a mere village. A gypsy woman came to the shop in Common Road where he still lives; her daughter had died; and, said Mr Arthur: 'She didn't have much money but she wanted her daughter properly buried in a churchyard'. He made a coffin for the girl and had her buried as her mother wished. In return the gypsy who had nothing else to offer, gave him a piece of paper on which two words were written, blessed it, saying: 'It is a special lotion. If you use it daily you will never go grey or bald.' Mr Arthur still has dark, plentiful hair—and he is 101 years old.

In some cases of witch-healing—or in any healing work—suggestions no doubt plays a part. In others, as for example that of the woman who did not know she was being treated, it can be discounted. Probably most cures are brought about by what is called 'resonance'—which I have mentioned already. It is thought to be the working principle of the De la Warr treatments; of 'blood spot' diagnosis and 'remote control' healing. A physical link between patient and healer seems to be an advantage, such as a lock of hair, or nail-paring, a sock or a stocking—or a blood-spot, but does not appear to be essential. Even if we say resonance is the factor involved, it is no explanation, it is only referring the question back a term, as Professor Joad used to say. No one knows exactly what resonance is.

Cursing, probably, operates by means of resonance also. Again, the physical link between the curse-maker and the cursed seems to be important but not absolutely vital. The Voodoo operator, the African witch-doctor, the magician of any part of the world, seems to like to obtain some object which he thinks establishes contact with his victim; either an article of clothing worn next to the skin, or a hair—or nail—cutting. Curses could probably be relayed efficiently via blood-spots; modern black magicians may be working on these lines already. . . .

Cursing rituals in white witchcraft, which are almost always used only to prevent someone from harming someone else, are often carried out on a Saturday which is the day for Cassiel rituals. The form they generally take is the making of some kind of replica of the person with whom the coven is dealing. The feet and hands are bound to symbolise restraint from hurtful activities, or the lips may be stitched up, if difficulty is being caused by malicious talk. I have been given innumerable well-attested instances of the success of these rituals; the trouble-maker either leaves the neighbourhood or ceases to cause unpleasantness. A scientist who had done a great deal of research into magic of many kinds told me that he carried out a 'preventive' ritual against a man whom he knew was going to be needlessly and unconstructively hampering in a conference at which they were both speaking. He said that the man behaved in unusually reasonable way and everything passed off well.

Other forms of witch-cursing were causing horses and carts to stop in their tracks; perhaps by creating some form of psychic barrier. Mrs Doreen Valiente, in her book, *Where Witchcraft Lives*, tells of a witch who lived on Ditchling Common, and who frequently inconvenienced traffic in this way, as did another witch between the Half Moon and Plumpton. I have not been able to discover whether witches find it possible to immobilise cars, or whether it works only with animals. . . .

In curse-making the time-honoured method of creating the link with the victim is the making of a wax image, mommet or poppet, as mentioned a few paragraphs back. If this link were firmly established, the man or woman was thought to suffer in the body the injuries inflicted on the image. I quote in another chapter a case which happened three centuries ago in Coventry, no doubt it could happen today, provided the link, or resonance were in being. The only ingredients needed are a small quantity of tallow and some pins for sticking into it—and trained, one-pointed concentration, tremendous thought control, vivid imagination, disciplined will, determination and faith. Very few people, fortunately, want so much to hurt others that they are willing to work hard and long enough to acquire the necessary mental powers.

Mr Cottie Burland, an eminent ethnologist, whose research into the psycho-dynamics of magic is encyclopedic, holds that there can be reality in curses and blessings, whatever 'sending' technique is used. The 'pointing bone' of Australian Aborigines or the wax 'mommet' can be equally effective media for bringing desired results provided the operator is a master of the technique.

The 'pointing bone' technique (i.e. the raising of power and directing it to the selected object) was used in an unpremeditated experiment in which Mr Burland took part. He was walking one day with some witch friends in an open part of the country where there way no shelter when a thundercloud suddenly rode up the sky, threatening an immediate deluge. There was not a macintosh nor an umbrella among the party; a soaking seemed inevitable, when one of the witches looked at the gravid cloud and said: 'Let's split it.'

So, said Mr Burland, they got to work with the technique I have just mentioned, with the remarkable result that as they watched the great cloud parted as if snipped in two by giant scissors. Each half lumbered off in different direction without spilling so much as a drop of rain. 'It is not scientific proof of weather control', Mr Burland said; 'it could have been coincidence.' If it were, it was a very convenient one. . . .

The witches claim to have raised the storms that drove off the Armada in the sixteenth century and the force that prevented Hitler's invasion in the twentieth. I asked Mr Burland if he thought that, speaking as a scientist, such things were possible. He said he thought that they were, granted the proper conditions.

Traditionally, when Phillip of Spain's battle fleet was sailing up the English channel, witch-covens went into action, the winds rose, the seas raged, and with these allies, Drake drove off the Dons. Would he have beaten them anyway, in fair or foul weather? That can only be now, a matter of opinion. Certainly, reading accounts of the battle, it seems that the storm came in the nick of time to turn events in his favour. And as to the raising of the storm . . . again, who can be certain what happened?

There are more details available as to the part the witches claimed to have played in repelling the Hitler invasion. The late Dr Gerald Gardner, anthropologist, folk-lore authority—and witch —has described what happened in the South of England, where he was then living. Gardner said that when Holland, France and Belgium fell, 'we expected Hitler on the seashore any day'. Our air and land defences were practically non-existent; the outlook was not bright.

At this stage, the old lady who had initiated Dr Gardner into the Craft, and who was an important figure in it, alerted covens, as he said, 'right and left, although by witch law, they should not be known to one another'. Then, Gardner says: 'We were taken at night to a place in the (New) Forest, where the Great Circle was erected, and that was done which may not be done except in great emergency. And the great Cone of Power was raised and slowly directed in the general direction of Hitler. The command was given: 'You cannot cross the sea. You cannot cross the sea. YOU CANNOT COME. YOU CANNOT COME.' Just as, we were told, was done to Napoleon, when he had his army ready to invade England and never came. And as was done to the Spanish Armada, mighty forces were used, of which I may not speak. Now to do this means using one's life force; and many of us died a few days after we did this. My asthma which I had never had since I first went out East, came back badly. We repeated the ritual four times; and the Elders said: 'We feel we have stopped him. We must not kill too many of our people. Keep them until we need them'.

The cone of power, of which Gardner speaks, has been known to and used by witches since time out of mind. It is an auric emanation which recently T. C. Lethbridge studied. His experiments show it to be, as he says in *Ghosts and Divining Rod,* an invisible but demonstrable cone of force, surrounding all form, animate and inanimate—and that is how the witches have always described it.

Apart from the witches' intervention, 'magic'—or the power of extra-sensory perception in various forms—is said to have a significant effect on the outcome of the last war. A powerful group of reputedly 'black' magicians was supposed to exist in Germany, the Thule Society, of which Dietrich, Eckardt and Alfred Rosenberg were founder members. In 1920, these two men met Adolf Hitler at Wagner's house in Bayreuth; and until he died a few years later, Eckhardt, as Conrad Heiden wrote in the Austrian corporal's biography, undertook the 'spiritual formation of Adolf Hitler'. Eckhardt's teachings were concerning the 'secret' doctrine, the doctrine of the Aryan myth, which had as kernel the world-over-lordship of the German race to be established by working with the invisible forces. Another powerful influence on Hitler was Karl Haushofer, whom he met just before the Nazi Party came into power. Haushofer was a General, a professor of Munich University, an initiate into an inner order of Buddhism, a disciple of Schopen-hauer, and of Ignatius de Loyala, whose aim was to govern man. Haushofer had also highly developed psychic sensitivity.

Haushofer became one of the founder members of the Nazi Party, who believed it was their destiny to change life on earth, and that they were sustained and protected and prospered in their mission by the supra-physical powers with which they were in contact. Outside Germany, three eminent writers tried to sound the alarm against what they regarded as a satanic religion. Rudyard Kipling had the swastika decoration removed from the dust-covers of his books; Saint George Saunders wrote *Seven Sleepers and the Hidden Kingdom*, which exposed Nazism, its Tibetan inspiration and its aims, as a threat to civilisation; John Buchan (Lord Tweeds-muir) in two novels, *A Prince in Captivity* and *The Judgment of Dawn*, showed the menace to the rest of the world of a nucleus of psychic, intellectually directed, forces working for evil.

If this inner circle of Nazism had made, or thought they had made, some pact with invisible forces, what could be called the protocol of the arrangement occultly-speaking, would be that the group could only invoke these forces through the agency of a magician, working via a medium. Apparently, Haushofer's role was that of magician. Hitler was the medium.

Many people who met Hitler seem to have had this impression about him. 'He entered into a sort of mediumistic trance,' says Francois-Poncet. Rauschning wrote: 'One cannot help thinking of him as a medium . . . Hitler was possessed of forces outside him-self—almost demoniacal forces of which the individual Hitler, was only the temporary vehicle. . . . It was like looking at a bizarre face whose expression seems to reflect an unbalanced state of mind, coupled with a disquieting impression of hidden power.' Dr Delmas described him as 'A powerful resonator, Hitler had always been the "sounding board" he claimed to be at the Munich trial and remained until the end . . . he only retained and used what at any given moment could satisfy his ambition and lust for power . . . and his crazy obsession: the biological selection of a species that would be half man, half god.'

Hitler's preoccupation with astrology is well-known; at one time he is supposed to have five experts in this art working for him. Probably the best-known was Ernst Kraft. After the war, the late Louis de Wohl, himself a brilliant astrologer, told me the story of an unusual episode in modern military history, which is documen-tarily confirmed.

There was a period at the beginning of the war when everything seemed to be going Hitler's way. Louis believed that this was because of the astrologic advice Hitler was getting from Kraft, whose methods—and the man himself—de Wohl knew well. He thought the only answer was to forestall these coups by working as Kraft worked. Louis believed that by casting the horoscopes of the heads of the German armed forces, and so discovering whether success in an attack by air, sea or land—for instance, on an island —were indicated in any individual's delineation, a clue would be given as to where an assault might be launched, and counteractive measures taken.

Probably one of Sir Winston Churchill's leading characteristics was his elasticity of mind, which enabled him to see that Louis' idea which was submitted to him, was worth a trial. So de Wohl was enrolled as astrologer to British High Command; what his official title was I cannot remember. To comply with regulations, he had to have Army rank, and he was made a Captain. He always said he was the only unnaturalised foreigner ever to hold rank in the British Army—later he was given British nationality.

The sequel was that Louis, feeling that from the British point of view, it would be better if Kraft were out of the picture altogether, made a plan for eliminating him. The Rumanian Minister in this country, M. Tilea (who had chosen to stay on when war broke out) was a great friend of Louis', he had showed Louis a letter from Kraft in which a few sentences, although harmless in their context, when lifted from it appeared to read as criticism of Hitler and the Nazis.

Armed with this letter, and with the blessing of the authorities, Louis went to America. He was already known over there, but he spent some weeks in recalling himself, through press mentions, to public memory. Then he gave interviews to leading papers all over the country, quoting Kraft's remarks about Adolf Hitler and the Nazis. Louis showed me his cutting book; banner headlines screamed the apparent criticisms of the Fuerher by his leading astrologer. And I saw too, the paragraphs carried by these papers within a fortnight of the 'scoop': 'Hitler's astrologer falls from power; Kraft in Buchenwald.'

Louis said that he had to do what he did; it was necessary and his duty. And whether or not it was due to the threadbare explanation coincidence, after Kraft's downfall, Hitler's timing began to go wrong; the phenomenal run of successes ended.

Hitler is said to have used witches or magicians, or both, to raise power to interfere with our aircraft's radar when they flew over Germany, so that they missed their targets, got lost, and often were shot down. Three high-ranking responsible officers told me at different times, independently of each other, that this 'psychic' warfare became such a menace that we set up our own branch of it. From a remote part of Wales, so I was told, our operatives worked to counteract the thought-forces sent out by the Germans, and generated power to their own which was used to deflect the Luftwaffe from its objective into R.A.F. ambushes. I hope it is true, because if it is, possibilities open up that the power which was used in this case to further the aims of war could equally well be used in an effort to prevent it.

E

CHAPTER X

Witchcraft Today

WHAT I may be forgiven for calling 'modern' witchcraft is almost always connected with the name of the late Dr Gerald Gardner, possibly because he brought the Craft more public notice than it has had since the 'burning time', and caused more controversy within and outside it than it has known before even in its stormy history.

Opinions about Dr Gardner are so divergent that it seems the truth must lie somewhere between the extremes. He has been described to me as a brilliant scholar, and a man with a veneer of learning; as a lovable, delightful character, and a 'messy old man'. Some say he was a master of witchcraft, others that he had no real knowledge of it—and that he did more harm to the Craft than the persecutions.

If this is true, it must have been the crowning irony of Gerald Gardner's life. Whatever else he was, he proved himself to be deeply and genuinely interested in the Craft; his chief objective was to make the image of witchcraft acceptable again in the public mind. He believed that the best way to do this was to give Press interviews, to write articles and books about the Old Religion, which horrified the hereditary witches. It has always been against their policy to advertise.

The 'old' witches claim that Dr Gardner's publicity campaign, far from helping the Craft, harmed it by cheapening it and making it a laughing stock; harm from which the more pessimistic cannot see it recovering from generations. Whether this is true or not, at least his impact on the Craft was such that it has to be considered in any assessment of witchcraft today.

He was initiated into an hereditary coven in the New Forest area,

I have been told, but after a relatively short time he and this coven parted company. The reason seems to have been his urge to publicise Craft matters.

After this split, he formed groups of his own. Eventually he established a witchcraft museum in the Isle of Man, and a reputation as an authority on witchcraft—outside the Craft.

Today, as I have said, while there are many divergent opinions and beliefs among covens, there could be said to be two broad categories into one of which any coven would fit—Gardnerian and non-Gardnerian.

Old, or hereditary witches (non-Gardnerian) have been known to describe Gardnerian initiates as 'fringe' witches. By this, they mean that they consider the Gardnerians do not know the inmost secrets of the Craft; that they have no real power; that their rituals originated with Dr Gardner; that their methods of getting results are hit-and-miss. Some of them say that scourging and nudity, which it seems are practised in some Gardnerian covens, were part of ancient mystery rituals, but not of witchcraft tradition. They consider that where scourging is used today, it is liable to degenerate from an integral part of the ceremony into a perversion. However, Gardnerian principles of witchcraft are often described by the 'old' witches as 'sweetness and light coupled with good, clean fun, all under the auspices of a Universal Auntie.'

In most Gardnerian covens, the priestess is the dominant figure, which, knowing the Craft to be a cult of the Great Mother, one would expect. But in some at least of the hereditary groups, the male, the Magister, is paramount. This is a symbolism, as explained to me, of the esoteric truth that the outer world is a world of illusion, a mirror reflection. A mirror always reflects opposites; what is seen on the external must be the opposite of the inner reality.

As an example of the gaps in Dr Gardner's knowledge of Craft practices, 'old' witches quote a statement he made to an hereditary witch concerning *Amanita Muscaria,* a mushroom, which, when chewed or brewed, can produce hallucinogenic effects. Dr Gardner said he knew nothing of its use in the Craft, and did not believe it ever had had a place in the rites of the Old Religion.

As the witch pointed out, there is proof in the form of recipes in possession of a number of covens that decoctions of *Amanita* were used in the fifteenth century. And it is only reasonable to suppose long before that time witches must have discovered the properties of the mushroom, since they have always been adepts in herbalism.

The use of hallucinogenic drugs is another instance of the 'discovery' by science of something which has been Craft knowledge for centuries. Comparatively recently, it was found in E.S.P. and psychiatric experiments that certain drugs, among them *Amanita Muscaria,* heightened awareness, or could be used in psychiatric treatments to shorten abreactive processes. In America, particularly, there has been interest in these possibilities. Dr Andrej Puharich, whom Aldous Huxley described as 'one of the most brilliant minds in parapsychology', calls *Amanita* the 'key to eternity' in his book *The Sacred Mushroom.*

Dr Puharich, as he explains in this book, was searching for a drug which could stimulate the action of E.S.P. When, he says, the properties of *Amanita,* and information about its—then—unknown use in ancient Egyptian rites were described to him by a certain Harry Stone, while in a trance condition. This man, who knew almost nothing about E.S.P., had never shown any signs of clairvoyant gifts until one day he spontaneously became entranced, controlled apparently by an entity claiming to be an Egyptian priest of royal blood, Ra Ho Tep, of the Fourth Dynasty. Puharich found that there had been a member of the royal family named Ra Ho Tep, who was a member of the priesthood at that time.

Although there had been no hint that the mushroom cult had been part of ancient Egyptian mysteries, until Ra Ho Tep— through Harry Stone—demonstrated the ceremonial use of *Amanita Muscaria* in rites performed in the year 2700 B.C., it is known to have been a feature of rituals of the old religions, and to have been used by the Aztecs in the sixteenth century. In Mexico and in Central America, *Amanita* and drugs with similar properties are, and for centuries have been employed to quicken the physical and psychic senses, and expand the range of consciousness. These also are the purposes to which E.S.P. research applies them—as witchcraft did in the past, and sometimes does today, so I am told.

Not that the mushroom cult could be said to be widespread in witchcraft; on the contrary many witches do not believe in the use of artificial (extraneous) means to induce conditions or states of consciousness which otherwise can be attained only by hard work, by mind and character-training and acquiring necessary techniques.

Hallucinogenic drugs such as *Amanita* or L.S.D. 25 (Lysergic acid diethylamide) are a short-cut, so they say; opportunities for gaining strength and knowledge are sacrificed by using them.

But to get back to the internal pattern of the Craft today, as well as the Gardnerian and hereditary groups, there are within it different ideas and opinions which correspond roughly to the right and left wings of political parties, or the High and Low sects of the Church of England. In every corporate body (if this term can be applied to witchcraft) such divergences seem inevitable.

The Old Religion is so unco-ordinated at present that no one coven could truly be said to be representative of the Craft tradition as a whole. A move towards some sort of stabilisation may be made before long, since I gather that a substantial section of the Craft regrets these schisms and the dissociation which has scattered covens like islands in an archipelago. The witches may not feel that 'united we stand, divided we fall', but a growing number of them realise that the Craft is due for an overhaul; that its practices should be examined objectively and brought into line with modern concepts. Witchcraft has survived through millennia because its philosophy was fluid, because it was able to adapt itself to changing conditions, and to make some cardinal contribution to life in varying contexts. As one of the 'old' witches says: 'I hold no brief for the modern world myself, but we have to live in it, and so we must do all we can to improve it and prevent it from becoming a radioactive cinder. The things that are being done to the natural order of things, both plant and animal in the name of the great god progress; the vast waste of armaments while millions starve—these are the sort of things that must be fought today . . . The Craft could conceivably be a force for good, or merely another of the occult curios of twentieth century Britain.' And from another traditional source: '. . . there is no room for us [witches] in this society unless we have something valid to offer it, and participate in its social evolution.' Members of the Craft who believe it has 'something valid to offer', say: 'We could all be on the verge of something great as far as the Craft is concerned'.

The effort of re-organising and co-ordinating the Craft no doubt would be a Herculean labour, but also no doubt it could be done if a general decision were taken to make the effort. The teachings of the Old Religion tend to develop strength of will and character; I doubt if weaklings could find any place in the Craft. The popular belief that it is a 'simple religion for simple people' is denied by the 'old' witches, who say that it is 'a complicated and all-embracing way of life, requiring study, determination and a rare attitude of mind and discipline of the spirit'.

Purposiveness is a key-note of the Craft. Its rites and rituals are designed to produce clearly-defined ends, and from what I have been privileged to see and hear, I think there can be no doubt that these ends are achieved.

For example, I have come across innumerable authenticated cases of healings, some of which I have mentioned already, and to which I now add another. A woman (not a witch) had an advanced cancer of the womb. Without her knowledge, her husband asked a witch-group to work for her; within twenty-four hours the growth disappeared, as X-ray tests confirmed. It did not return.

Witches will often 'buy' a minor ailment, which then leaves its victim, and, if the spell is correctly operated, does not seem to harm the purchaser. I saw this happen when a friend of mine 'sold' a streaming cold to a witch for threepence. The day before she was to give a talk at the B.B.C., she had a temperature; she felt so ill that she said she must telephone to cancel her appointment. The witch gave her three pennies, and said: 'Wait'. Next morning the cold had gone, temperature and all.

A coven which specialises in telepathy has established contact with a group in America. A request was 'beamed' to them for the return of a loaned book; it arived in this country within a week. Another coven is trying to get in touch with witches of the past; already they have had a 'visitor'. A presence in sixteenth century dress manifested at their last Sabbat.

Some groups experiment in necromancy, others in re-establishment of magical images, or in stimulating plant-growth by extra-physical means—which could be a modern version of the Craft's fertility promotion in the past. Out of thirty-three geranium cuttings taken by a witch with the white-handled knife, not one died; all were healthy and flourished. The cuttings were 'spoken over' when planted, as was a dying shrub, round which water was hosed in a circle at the same time. I have seen the shrub, which is, as the witch who treated it says, 'budding like mad'.

The witches work constructively to help and to heal, but where there is abuse or exploitation, they feel they are justified in remembering that they have the power to curse as well as to bless.

When a transistor-radio, a present she had given to her husband, was stolen from a witch I know, she had a strong urge to 'work' on the situation, which was not wholly accounted for by the fact that she felt it was a mean, unnecessary theft. It was, she thought, explained when after a week the thief was caught and twenty-two other charges of the same kind were brought against him. The police had been wanting him for some time; he got a two-year sentence—and the witch got her transistor radio back.

The witches see eventualities of this kind as the outworkings of Nemesis, or the law of come-back; it operated in the case of a girl who had asked a witch (who has the inherited power to cure warts and yelow jaundice) to remove an unsightly growth for her. The witch agree to cure the wart, saying that when it was gone, he would expect her to pay him. She was ready to pay anything he asked, she said. In fact, he told me, he meant to charge her one shilling, as 'charm' or token fee, traditionally given in these healings. A few days later, he met the girl. 'I see I have cured your wart,' he said. She could not deny that it had gone, but, she said, as there was no proof that he had had anything to do with its disappearance, she was not going to pay his fee whatever it was. Nothing more was said. Within a few days, the girl found that another, larger wart had developed.

Phenomena such as the appearance of lights—usually blue or green—candles flickering for no explicable reason, cauldrons boiling and bubbling unaided by terrestial fire or flame, are considered to be routine manifestations of the power raised at Sabbats. These, not being a member of the Craft, I have not seen, but I was given a glimpse of the ways of the witches at a May Day gathering to which I was invited.

It was to have been held, according to custom, in the open air, at a traditional Craft meeting place in the Cotswolds. About ten days beforehand, however, the Magister (roughly equivalent to High Priest) said that the weather would be unsuitable; most of the day would be wet, windy and cold. He added, not boasting, but regretfully: 'I'm afraid there's no hope it will be fine; I am never wrong about the weather'.

The B.B.C. forecast, on May Eve for May Day, fine warm weather, continuing over the week-end. Sun and blue skies on the morning of 1st May seemed to prove the B.B.C. right—for a few hours, until clouds rolled up, temperature dropped, and down came the rain. The deluge went on for the rest of the day, except for two or three short intervals.

So the meeting was held indoors, in the house of the Magister, who came into the Craft at five years old, and was a Magister at twenty-eight. He is an hereditary witch; among ritual paraphernalia which his family has used for generations is a copper dish, engraved with symbols and with figures. During ceremonies a candle is held under it; according to the position on the dish of the holder's thumb, a shadow thrown on the ceiling takes the form of the Horned God, a ram's head, or the Moon Goddess. A silver cup, chased with Craft sigils, and several ceremonial drinking-horns also have belonged to the Magister's family for generations.

As at an ordinary cocktail-party, to begin with we stood or sat around while wine, spirits or beer circulated. There was music from a tape-recorder; after a time, people began to dance, in couples, at first, then in rings of about six, three men and three women.

Later the music stopped. The witches began to sing as they danced, traditional songs, which without consciously knowing, one seemed to remember. They were mostly in a minor key, as folk songs often are; yet they did not sound sad. Somehow they were just right for the rhythm of our steps as we went round and round, faster or slower. The high boots in which some of the women arrived, has been exchanged early on in the evening for shoes; these were kicked off as the dance went on. Now and again as the tempo of movement quickened there was a faint tinkling from tiny gilt bells, sewn in pairs on black garters worn by many of the women. Now and again the circles broke up into pairs; men and women mostly dancing at arms' length, their heads on their partner's forearms.

Although the round dance was not in any way ritual, still it was a ring dance, which, since time began has been held to generate power. Certainly as the circles formed and reformed, it was as if currents of low voltage electricity were circulating; the effect was energising and exhilarating.

One of the witches had put on her robe; black, tabard-like, belted with a black cord, from which hung her black-handled knife, sometimes called the athame. She unsheathed it, as did some of the others, while dancing, holding it with the blade pointing upwards.

Now the room was lit only by pointed flames of candles, which created from darkness and movement an antic play of shadows on walls and ceiling, until, as the robed witch slid to the floor, the dance ended.

The Magister knelt beside her, shaking two small gourds over her body, from head to feet and back again. After a moment or two, she began to speak; a message of greeting—perhaps from the Old One, the Horned God.

The Magister asked for an identifying sign. With her left hand she sketched a movement; at that moment—and only for a moment —I felt as if the blood were draining out of my body.

After a few minutes, dancing began again; the party finally ended at about 3 a.m.

Some days later, the Magister, discussing the trance incident told me that it was a fake; deliberately arranged as a test to separate the sheep of the selective-minded from the goats of the ultra-credulous. Witches, he said, must be objective; they must not get bogged down by illusion; they must learn that every unusual-seeming incident is not an other-world manifestation. The witch who had worn the robe told me that at the end of her 'trance' she had meant to give an imaginary identifying sign to the Magister; instead she found herself impelled to make the correct ritual movement, with the correct hand—which then became cold and numb; a sensation which I, too, had felt at that time.

Illusion, its meaning and the part it plays in the development of understanding, in an important part of Craft teachings, as it was in those of the Mysteries; as it is in the practices of magic and of the occult sciences. The function of illusion on these levels is to create an atmosphere, rather as the music of an orchestra creates in an audience a mood receptive to the play which follows. Priests of some mystery religions—shamans of northern Asia, for example —begin their rites with what everyone knows to be a show of conjuring tricks. The purpose of this to condition the mind by the seemingly miraculous to the reality of phenomena, which also appear miraculous, because not subject to physical laws. Producing illusion is like playing a game of 'let's pretend'; acting out the existence of some condition or embodied force beyond the accepted range of reality, as if it were reality. But one must not forget that in ritual, illusion is symbolic. Under the pretence, and behind the mask, reality is there.

Illusion feeds imagination, and disciplined imagination is necessary to the opening up of new stages and degrees of experience.

The operative word here, as the Craft and all the old teachings emphasise, is discipline. Imagination and illusion are tools, not ends in themselves. Imagination must be controlled, illusion must be recognised.

Pretence and illusion have a place in the principles of sympathetic magic. In rain-making rites, water may be thrown into the air; pins may be stuck into the image of a person ill-wished in a destructive ritual. The basic idea behind these methods is that outpicturing sets in motion a force which brings what is imaged (or imagined intensely) into manifestation. One theory is that the working principle of the operation is resonance, which it well may be.

Powerful aids to the building of illusion, or inducing changes in consciousness, are rhythm, vibration as in music, or of words, and the pictures they call up in the mind, which no doubt is the reason poetry has always been associated with ritual and magic. Rituals of the old mystery schools were often framed in sentences with a regular rhythmic beat; spells are almost always formulated in rhyming verse. The Druids used poetry for magical purposes; their Bardic order was an integral part of their tradition.

Poetry has been called 'the language of the subconscious', perhaps because, since rhythm and vibration are laws of universal functioning, it is a primordial form of expression, and the subconscious operates at the natural or instinctive level. It also as we know, accepts easily suggestion given to it in rhythmic form.

Bonded as it is with the deeper layers of the mind, poetry is also the language of mystery and mysticism. Professor Neville Coghill, M.A., F.R.S.L., president of the Poetry Society of London said in his inaugural speech to the Society in April, 1965. 'Mystery cannot be demonstrated, it can be conveyed, and one way of conveying it is by poetry.'

It follows that poetry is the natural language of the Craft, which has always used it, not only in spell-making, bnt as Professor Coghill said, to convey its mysteries. I have the permission of its author, Doreen Valiente, to quote The Castle, an example of witch symbolism expressed in poetry. Though its inner meaning is secret and may mean little to the uninitiate, it illustrates the evocative power of vibration, rhythm and word-pictures, through which other dimensions may be glimpsed. Some witches say that the five castles of the poem actually exist in these dimensions; others that they are symbolic. Perhaps they both mean the same thing . . .

Before Caer Ochran
The winding of the ways is long
Before you come to the smooth white walls
Shining like pearl in the darkness.

Before the Glass Castle
Are the spirals of the maze,
The lifting veils and the closing shadows
And the murk of night upon all.

Before the Castle of Sorrows,
Is drowning in the sea of darkness
The last light of the Moon, with her sharp sickle,
The toothed portcullis and the quaking drawbridge.

Before Caer Arianrhod
Are the Gate and the Guardian,
The armoured rider with the naked sword.
Cold is the air as he passes by.

Red and flaming is the fire
Within the hall of that high queen.
Filled with bright wine is the bowl in her hand.
Her eyes are blue and shining as the sea.
How many shall go therein and return?

Her vesture, half of blue and half of red
Life and death are in her two hands.
In the deeps of her bowl, the perilous vision.
How many shall enter before her and return?

Through the empty hall, a wind of laughter
Whirls us, frail straws, back across the drawbridge.
Our boldness moved the Powers to mirth and mercy.
How many shall enter the Castle and return?

Black and silver is the wood of bare trees,
Wherein by moonlight treads her unicorn's hoof.
Bare on his bare back she rides, veiled in her own bright hair,
How many shall enter the secret realms and return?

When I told Douglas Brown of the B.B.C. who had asked for my definition of the Craft during a discussion of its nature in a radio programme, that the essence of the Old Religion seemed to me to be its competence as a practical method of making contact with forces beyond the world of form, he said: 'But this is mysticism,' which of course it is. Perhaps some witches would not like to be described as mystics; perhaps some of them are not. There are, as I have said, great variations of practice and belief within the Craft. But however widely ritual and approach may differ, basically the Old Religion is a mystery religion. Its roots are entwined with mysticism and occultism; to separate one radicle system from another would be next to impossible. Fundamentally, each aims to open up new levels of experience, and to increase awareness, by raising the consciousness.

When I told Mr Brown that witchcraft was a system of practical mysticism, I had in mind its techniques for applying inner knowledge to outer problems of everyday life. The witches themselves are proof that these methods work; as an ethnologist who has studied the Craft said to me: 'Witches are psychologically sound'. He meant that they seem to be free of the fears, frustrations, lack of confidence, feelings of insecurity, which bedevil so many people today, providing full appointment-books for psychiatrists and customers for chemists.

Witches may have their financial stresses now and again (rich witches are rare), but these do not become distresses, possibly because materials possessions do not unduly interest Craft members. Traditionally they can claim, and seem to receive, what they regard as enough for anyone—'a roof over the head, clothes for the back, fodder and love.'

There has been talk in psychiatric circles of trying to discover the techniques by which the Craft builds these positive attitudes of mind, and perhaps applying them in mental treatments. It might be an excellent idea, but even if the Craft would co-operate, I doubt if it could. Witchcraft is a way of life, not a collection of methods for producing this or that result; it seems likely that it can offer little on these lines to an outsider.

But there are other possibilities. Witches are supposed to be children of the Aquarian Age; one of the characteristics of this era is the enjoyment of life, and this they might help to spread abroad. *Joie de vivre* has always been a key-note of the Craft; a 'witch' chant of the twelfth century epitomises this aspect of the Old Religion.

> Hear and answer gracious Goddess,
>   Grant us laughter, wit and wine. . .
> . . . Banish heavy-hearted hate.
> Accept our Craft, O greatest Mother
>   Let cheerful brightness be our fate.

Then there is the Craft's knowledge and uses of the forms of perception, which are just beginning to be accepted by science, and generally, by us. Fragmented though it is, the Craft has a vast store of such knowledge, accumulated through centuries. Probably even witches themselves cannot know or even guess at its extent unless or until covens are co-ordinated. If they ever are, witchcraft would be in full possession, for the first time for centuries, of its birthright, a tradition which probably is one of the richest sources of esoteric philosophy and learning in the world today, and which can be of immense value to that world. Wicca and psychic have important complementary roles to play, as the trends and pressures of the next cosmic phase grow.

CHAPTER XI

An Hereditary Witch's Revelations of Craft Symbolism

AS in all mystery cults, the doctrine of witchcraft is expressed in symbolic form; the only form in which mystery can be conveyed; by which it is safeguarded—since symbols mean nothing to the uninitiated—and preserved almost unchanged through centuries. Symbols are not easily forgotten and seldom are subject to major variation.

Until a high officer of the Craft (a Magister) interpreted many of its sigils for me, never before in the long history of the Old Religion has the inner meaning of its symbolism been revealed to 'outsiders' by an hereditary witch. The Magister chose as illustration for its exposition the carvings on the two or three hundred year old menhir at St Duzec, describing them as "a complete recapitulation of Craft theology', although the menhir has always been supposed to be a Christian monolith.

He says: 'Although the carving upon the stone (i.e., menhir) is either eighteenth or seventeenth century, and supposed by archaeologists to be a representation of the Passion of the Christian Christ, and depictions of the implements of the crucifixion, it is in all probability a depiction of basic witch theology for that area and that time. I have not gone into any great detail since the nature of my oath forbids it. However, within the structure of that oath I have done my best to explain them as I personally would interpret such symbols. It is also advisable to remember that the Catholic Church took over many pagan concepts and symbols and debased them to their own use.

'In the centre of the carvings there is a "God" figure supporting a bell-skirted "Goddess". It corresponds to the copper plate (a photograph of which faces page 64 with its bulls' horns supporting a cockatrice. As in the plate, the arms are bent to depict horns and bound with what would be in practice red and white cords made from wool. The binding forms a spiral pattern, a common magical practice among witches. The depiction of a mother, or moon goddess, supported by bulls' horns is a common motif in classical vase painting, especially amongst the Etruscans. It is usually associated with the bull God separating the heavenly twins.

'Upon the head of the bull God there is a crown comprised of a band and four spheres or representations of the physical elements, and the winds. Beneath the head and arms or horns comes a set of hammer and tongs, another indication that this figure is the God of the witches; in one of many guises the God is depicted as a blacksmith or Wayland. Apart from mythology and references in folk lore, the symbol of hammer and tongs is used to this day by some of the older cuveens.

'In the Craft, symbols are read as if the reader were wearing them. Also symbols placed upon the left are concerned with the Goddess, that is the feninine side of the mysteries, and symbols placed upon the right are concerned with the God or the masculine side of the mysteries. This placing of symbols is a common form of practice amongst other magical systems apart from the Craft. Therefore where the moon appears in the carving is the feminine mysteries, and where the sun appears upon the carving is the male mysteries. At the bottom of the carvings is a statement of ritual and practice, common to both sexes.

'Upon the left side of the carving is the moon looking rightways, usually taken to represent the Goddess in her aspect of the Virgin of the Waters. She is enclosed in a ring, which is again a Craft belief. Immediately below this comes a glove and a vase. The Glove is a symbol as potent as the ancient pentagram and often means much the same thing. Again the hand from the moon is often used in certain forms of magic. Witches also have a magical system associated with their hands, although this may not be common to all clans. The object next to the Glove, depicts a vase, which again corresponds to the Moon since it has been used in the Dionysic and Egyptian mysteries, usually associated with the ritual known as "Drawing down the Moon". Below this comes one of the major parts of the feminine mysteries, the flask, used to pour the sacred drink which is the beginning of a form of induced mysticism. Various hereditary clans have different methods, and I understand they may range from a brew made from Fly Agaric to a deadly combination of datura and belladonna or similar herbal poisons. Nearly all genuine witches used a sacred drink or food as part of certain rituals, but it cannot be stressed enough that in the hands of the ignorant or silly such methods are a quick way to the underworld of insanity. It must also be stated that these brews are usually ineffectual unless used in combination with certain other methods and practices.

'Lower down comes a linen tabard, more common on the Continent than in Britain. It has much in common with a shroud, and also possibly with a veil, and though I believe few, if any, British clans wear such a garment, it can be considered a magical garment, much as are the cloak and broad-brimmed hat worn by some English witches. On the extreme outside of these carvings there is depicted a spinner's distaff, a sword and a broom. All these instruments are used by British witches today, and very briefly can be described as follows: The distaff is used for spell-binding along with other things, the sword is a magical implement, and the broom is a very ancient and potent symbol. It is held across the shoulder when in use, and in Norfolk to this day, there is an ancient broom dance performed by *men*, in which the dancer leaps over the broom in a series of cross steps. The broom is the major magical implement of the female witch when prepared properly out of five woods and with a stone at the stake.

'Underneath the carving of the feminine mysteries comes a line of symbols connected wth ritual and practice. The three squares are usually coloured black and white, and depict the basis of witch magic, the three foundations or three moons, which means power over fate. Next to the three squares is what the archaeologists describe as three nails. They can be either nails or knives since three nails or three knives are used in certain forms of magical practice. The nail was often used in the Cotswolds as a binder to a charm, and a horseshoe nail dipped in spring water was considered a prime remedy to use against the 'little people' when they grew bothersome. Nails were often made into rings also. Their actual ritual use is of course a matter of secret. The skull is a symbol of death, and surprisingly a symbol of inspiration. With the crossed bones directly next to it, it means words, or inspiration of the spirit. If the bones had been straightened, as at Clophill, then the ritual takes on a different cast. It becomes one of death and resurrection since to cross the bones is to stop birth, to straighten them is to assist birth. The cross bones themselves are a form of blessing along with two other crosses. The whole line ends with a carving of a sacred bell, something normally used to summon spirits. The ritual becomes one of Death and Wisdom. Probably the Bretons drank a poison brew, and then with various other aids made contact with the Fathers, or those of the Craft who help us on earth.

It is interesting to note that the skull be situated directly under a pillar with the cockerel on top. This again is a witch symbol and states emphatically that from the grave comes the greatest impetus to life, and conversely that all things must eventually return to the grave. The pillar and the cockerel at its simplest interpretation (and there is more than one) is phallic.

'Upon the right side of the carvings is the masculine mysteries. The ladder, amongst other things, is a depiction of eight stages of progress, leading towards the Sun. These eight rungs are stages leading towards the unfoldment of the Horn Child within the Soul. The Horn child is the child born of the union of the masculine and feminine mysteries. The Sun is Arthur emitting twelve rays or twelve aspects of the Round Table, in which the virtues of the male pagans were depicted. The twelve rays also have another reference to certain gods or seasons. Along with the eight rungs or trials of strength, it becomes the pursuit of the Graal, and to confirm this there is the javelin on the extreme right crossed with a pilgrim's blackthorn stave. The flail or scourge also appears here. If it were depicted with shears and a sieve, the picture would be complete.

'All these carvings support a simple depiction of the Goddess, arms folded in such a fashion as to show two hearts linked together. The Great Mother brings union wth male and female, life and death; the great Rose Queen secure in her garden in the east.

'Above them all is a figure, carved in the round, of what could be Jesus. Maybe the Catholic priest who ordered this carving knew the witches and their beliefs, and said "Here is Christ conquering all", but I am more inclined to think that it does not depict Jesus. To me it is Man, half divine, half animal, pinioned on the Cross of the Elements, born of flesh, dying of flesh, going to another life.

And as such it is a description of that ancient prayer, "To Thou who hast suffered as we have suffered. . . ." In fact, the whole stone reads like a prayer to that Great Mother whose spirit is everywhere and in all things.'

With the Craft salutation, 'Motte a ye', the witch ends his interpretations of the Old Religion's symbolism. The momentarily-lifted corner of the veil which hides the mysteries falls again. . . .

CHAPTER XII

Powers of the Unseen

NOT much more than thirty years ago, a revolutionary change in world thinking began to show itself. The grip of materialism, at its most powerful in the nineteenth century, was relaxing its stranglehold on men's minds. Scientists here and there were admitting that there might be phenomena which could not be explained in terms of physical laws or formulae. The word 'psycho-somatic' echoed in even orthodox medical circles. At last a place, even if not very important one, in the scheme of things was conceded to man's mind and to his psyche.

One of the men who more or less compelled science to consider the existence of forces other than those of the physical world was Professor Joseph Banks Rhine, who holds a Chair in Parapsychology at Duke University, California. He became world-famous for his experiments which established telepathy as an acceptable scientific fact, after years of testing and checking, through the use of 'P.S.I.' (psychic or extra-sensory perception) testing cards. These consist of packs of twenty-five cards, five suits of five symbols (a cross, a square, a circle, a star and wavy lines) printed on the card-face instead of the usual hearts, diamonds, spades or clubs.

The experiments varied almost endlessly, but whatever the arrangements as to the disposition of the subject (man or woman) or the form of the test, the object was to record how many symbols the subject could 'see' correctly in, say, four runs through the pack without touching it or being shown anything but the back of the cards; in some cases the experimenter who called the cards (that is to say, took each card off the pack, either looking or not looking at it according to the nature of the test) might be in a different room from the subject or even in a different town. A high scoring rate was recorded in tests made at Duke University with a subject, Dr Carlo Marchesi, in Zagreb, Yugoslavia, four thousands miles away. Distance, Dr Rhine found, was not a relevant factor in the operative of P.S.I., which was confirmed by experiments in telepathy carried out by Dr S. C. Soal and F. Bateman, who showed that the scoring rate was not affected when subject and experimenter were 200 miles apart.

One of the first things which had to be done to establish the validity of this form of E.S.P., was to prove how many correctly 'guessed' symbols were due to chance in a given number of runs through the E.S.P. cards. Without so much as a computer to help them, Dr Rhine and his staff, checked and counter-checked and investigated results, arriving finally at an estimate that right naming of twenty symbols in four runs through the pack could be due to chance. Correct results over and above this number were attributable to the functioning of P.S.I., or extra-sensory perception.

Dr Rhine went on to demonstrate that mind, operating in some as yet unexplained way, can affect matter. In what he called P.K. (or psychokinetic) experiments with dice chiefly, he found that their trajectory could be influenced by concentrated thought, not necessarily held in the mind of the person making the throw, but in that of an observer of the experiment.

What actually is P.S.I., or extra-sensory perception? Dr Rhine thinks that a great deal more research is necessary before any conclusions are reached as to its fundamental nature or how it operates. 'Perhaps', he says in *New World of the Mind,* 'we have merely come upon a deeper-lying unconscious stratum of mental life—a stratum that has had to wait for its discovery until a sufficient interest in the operations more peculiarly psychological (i.e. non-physical) in man's personality have been awakened'.

But even if this were so—and Professor Rhine mentions it as only one of many possible theories—the reply to such an explanation could be 'So what?' It does not really explain anything; that is to say, it does not offer any clue as to the causatory factor operating in this deeper layer of mental life; nor as to the nature of this layer. As Professor Joad said of scientific expositions: 'At no point have we come within sight of a true explanation, that is, of an explanation which really does explain. We have only been pushed back to an earlier point in time, the phenomenon which is to be explained.

All scientific so-called explanations are of this type. We are only given a slightly more complex and technical account of the fact to be explained.'

The tremendous value of investigations such as Professor Rhine's are not so much in their indications as to *what* E.S.P. is as in establishing *that* it is. The card tests demonstrated that we have powers of perception which have a range beyond those of the five senses; even though as yet the nature of the faculty involved is not fully known. Some of the results of the tests were due to what is called telepathy—names are convenient labels only. We do not know what telepathy really is but few people would deny today that it exists. In 1949, Professor A. C. Harcy told a meeting of the British Association at Newcastle-on-Tyne that 'in his belief, the communication of one mind with another, other than through the ordinary sense, has been established and that it has passed scientific tests.'

And how does telepathy work? The usual answer is 'By some form of electricity.' But since no one knows what electricity is, this assertion only peels off another layer of the onion-skin-like problem, leaving us, as Joad said, with the 'phenomenon to be explained'. Professor Rhine believes that a plausible hypothesis of telepathic activities 'would be that the receiver mentally interacts in some way with the sender's nervous system, much as the latter himself does when he remembers something. This would be a kind of clairvoyance, though it might be of a special kind. Or the sender could be operating in some way directly on the nervous system of the receiver, something like the way he operates on his own in bringing about motor response.'

But in E.S.P. tests telepathy, whatever it is and however it works, cannot be the only form of psychic perception involved. In some cases, the results could only be obtained by precognition—which ties up with the experiences of clairvoyants and seems to rebut the arguments of those who claim the causatory factor of all E.S.P. is a physical mechanism. Professor Rhine says: 'No one has ever produced a plausible explanation of precognition based on established theory. This has not been done even for the short-term precognition covering a few seconds of time that might be involved in the forward displacement results obtained by Soal and Goldney with their subject, B.S. It will be recalled that in this forward displacement the subject kept identifying, not the card at which he was consciously focusing but the one that was coming next, even when a ramdomising method of selecting the cards was followed, and the next card was selected *after* the subject's response was given'.

Professor Rhine in his P.K. experiments has carried out tests to establish weather or not manifestations of this faculty could be due to physical causation. He says results show, as with E.S.P. that 'physical laws do not hold'.

In fact E.S.P. tests, (in which we can include P.K.) not only demonstrating that results are obtained but that they are obtained by many different forms of extra-physical activities, open vista after vista of new possibilities. There is the subject of retrocognition, which has figured in E.S.P. experiments. 'Whether E.S.P. can reach into the traceless past as well as into the non-existent future is still an unanswered question', Rhine says of it.

Time and space, as we know them seem to have no meaning in the dimension where the sixth sense operates. Rhine observes that '. . . the person who has a clairvoyant experience often does not know whether or not the event that comes to his consciousness has happened yet. . . . There is no time arrow along with the experience to mark it as past, present or future.' He goes on to state that 'Precognitive experiences more often than not do come as dreams. Such dreams may not be exact. Often they are fragmentary, sometimes dramatised and elaborated. Sometimes they have interesting substitutions, as this one does'. He quotes the case of a woman of Youngtown U.S.A who dreamed that she had injured her right hand, how she did not know; that she was in great pain, and that though she tried to get a doctor each one she called was out. At last she made contact with one, who said: 'Don't worry, it will be all right'. In her dream—about which she told her sister—she kept repeating 'Doctor, it hurts'.

During the next day, her five year old daughter caught her hand in a mangle. The mother rang two doctors, only to find they were out; the third, when he had examined the child, said: 'Don't worry, it will be all right'. All through the day, the child kept saying, as the mother did in her dream: 'It hurts'.

This substitution mechanism and dramatisation of the main facts of an event in a precognitive dream will be familiar to anyone who has made a 'dream test' along the lines suggested by J. W. Dunne in his *Experiment With Time*. The test is a simple way of proving to oneself that dreams are approximately as often of future as of past events. If you want to try the experiment, keep a pencil and some paper beside your bed, and immediately you wake, jot down your dreams while they are still fresh in your mind. Perhaps you think you do not dream, but you do, and if you keep up this routine you will begin to remember them. Most people find at first that dreams are not easy to record; they seem to melt like mist while one looks at them; but with practice they become easier to recapture. Dunne gives a number of illustrations of the forms of subconscious embroidery which I have just mentioned from his own experience, and I found they constantly recurred in my own dream-records.

One night I dreamt that I was on board a pleasure-cruise ship sailing out of what I recognised as Plymouth Sound. Suddenly there was panic; I knew that the ship was on fire. Screams drowned the playing of the band; people milled around the decks. Then I was in the sea, with heads bobbing about all around me and I was screaming too. Two days afterwards I read a description of the facts of my dream in the morning papers; the only difference was that the experience had not actually happened to me (so far as I know . . .). Another time, I 'saw' a collision between a private car and an omnibus. I was horrified; I thought everyone in the car must be killed, to my surprise, no one was injured at all. The next day the collision was reported in the Press; the car had been wrecked but no one was hurt. This example is more or less unembroidered; more often than not, I think my precognitive dreams tend to be 'straight', but with no personal significance. The only reason for most of them seems to be that they have an element of what a journalist calls 'news'; some feature which is unusual enough for the subconscious to keep it on the menu, so to speak, and serve it up in dream form, as often happens with past incidents of similar nature. The same psychological pattern appears to operate in retrocognition and precognition, which is only to be expected if in dreams, as in psychic experience, we crash the time and space barrier.

Precognitive dreams can and often do have a specific purpose. Dr Rhine quotes the case of a woman who dreamed, during the last war, that a palm tree was falling across a tent in which her son, on active service in the Pacific area, was sleeping. She screamed out his name, and woke up. The next letter which arrived from him described a dream in which he had heard her calling him so clearly that he got up and went outside the tent to see if anyone were there. While he was walking around a tree fell, crushing the bed in which he had been sleeping. He said that his dream had saved his life; when he wrote he did not know his mother's side of the story.

In this dream there is the element of precognition—the woman 'saw' the tree falling before it fell—and what is called telepathy—the contact which her mind presumably made with her son's mind warning him of danger.

Sometimes manifestations of the sixth sense do not appear to fit into any watertight classification; they may have features characteristic of several generally-recognised forms, with added uncharacteristic variations. Mr Gerald Gough, well-known lecturer and authority on international affairs, who has done valuable research into occult matters, had an experience of this type. One morning, he felt impelled to telephone to a friend of his. After exchange of 'How are you's?' and so on, she asked Mr Gough to give a message to her boy-friend that she could not keep her appointment with him. It would be awkward for him if he turned up without her, she said.

Mr Gough asked her some question about this commission, but the line seemed to have become dead. He was still saying 'Hello—what's happened?' when the friend with whom she shared a flat spoke. She had heard the sound of a voice coming from the receiver which was dangling from its hook. He told her about the conversation which had been broken off; she said 'But it's impossible you should have been speaking to her—a dreadful thing has happened. She was killed in a car-crash about an hour ago—I've just had the message.'

When Mr Gough carried out the promise made to his dead friend he found that the details of the appointment he had been asked to cancel were just as he had been told on the telephone. In this case telepathy is the probable explanation of his urge to ring her up—it does not explain the use of a physical medium—the telephone—for a non-physical communication. This form of interaction while it has been recorded in a number of other instances, is far from general. So far no entirely acceptable hypothesis has been put forward as an explanation.

The story I am going to tell you now belongs to a wider field of psychic experience than the personal. It is the story of the psychic cleansing of what was considered to be a nucleus of negative influence—the prison camp at Belsen. So far as I am aware it is known only to the men (scientists and others) who realised not only the potential dangers of a place so charged with the dynamite of emotions—agony, terror, sadism—but the necessity for neutralising them; and the man and his colleagues who carried out this work.

We know that on the physical level the room, and everything in it, of a person who has an infectious or contagious disease, has to be decontaminated before it can be used with safety by anyone else. The only evidence of the presence of germs or virus, can be that anyone vulnerable who enters that room may develop scarlet fever, smallpox, measles or whatever disease might be transmitted by the germs.

This physical situation corresponds very much with that of Belsen camp on the psychic level. It was realised in certain centres that vibrations of hate and suffering and fear were building up there and like a river in flood, might break loose, causing serious damage.

In December 1956, a University scientist and authority on psychic research, travelled with a small party to Belsen. He described the road leading to the camp, through a desolate, larch-scattered heath past long lines of burial mounds, as a 'Via Dolorosa'.

The first of the three main centres where the cleansing ritual had to be performed was the memorial, which in his words was 'squat and ugly', to '30,000 Jews, done to death in this place by the murderous Nazis'. Here, astrally, he said, was a 'threatening star of David, glowing like a red-hot iron, threatening all who approached with a word meaning vengeance. . . . Calling on the power of the Lord God of Israel, I destroyed it utterly and it was not. Its place was taken by a radiant Star of David, wth the four lettered Names in the centre, and a symbol of reconciliation between Jew and Gentile.' One of the man's companions who also experienced this phenomenon, said: 'I saw the Star of David break into a thousand pieces, and with it went the spirit of revenge and the large part of the Jewish racial karma.'

The second centre was a rough cross further on, round which were a crowd of apparently earth-bound spirits, whose conscious-ness of suffering had created a fog around them. The figure of the Virgin of Czestow (the Polish Queen of Heaven) was built up here; an image radiating power by which the earthbound spirits could gain release.

Lastly came the banishing of undesirable presences at the 'wailing wall' where victims of many nations died. In front of it is a high monolith, put up by the Germans. The ritual began with the summoning of the Group Spirit of Germany. The banishing was performed at each of the four quarters; at the end of it a great figure of Peace built up over the central monument.

Then the Hierophant (who had performed the cleansing ceremonies) spoke the name of other centres of suffering and despair; among them Dachau, Ravensbruck, Oranienburg, Auschwitz, Kragujevac: so that through resonance, the purification ritual might cleanse them also.

This procedure was objective in that the resulting experience was shared by several people, and the figures which built up (which they felt differed from those which would have been their personal choice)—were seen by all.

The power inherent in strongly-concentrated thought, the essence of ritual, was used here. Also it is possible that force of some sort emanated from the figures which built up, it being a widely-held theory that projected thought-forms have energies of their own; energies which reproduce those of the idea held in the mind from which they were projected, or of the aspect of nature of which they are the personalisation.

We cannot today dismiss thought forms and the possibility of their interaction in our life in some way as fantasy. Scientific research has shown that thought-forms have objective existence; they can be photographed. In my book, *Why Grow Old?* I mentioned the Baraduct, experiments in Paris; they were conducted with subjects who represented a cross-section of mental levels, ranging from scientists to 'teenagers. Each subject concentrated upon a mental image as strongly as possible for a given period of time; at the end of which a photograph was taken. Clearest results were produced from the scientists, the photograph of an ornithologist's mental picture of a golden eagle could have been taken from the living bird. Next most satisfactory were reproductions of girls' visualisations of their boy-friends.

Professor Fukurai has made similar experiments in Japan, during which excellent 'thought' photographs were produced. The Delawarr Laboratories, Oxford, among others working along these lines, also had a high percentage of successful results.

What is known as the 'London-Leeds Experiment in Thought

Photography' comes into a different category. In the investigations just mentioned, a camera was used; in the London-Leeds test the only physical equipment was photographic paper, apart, of course, from the paraphernalia for developing the photographs. What could be called straightforward photography of a mental image was the object of the researches first described; the second involved an attempt to impress thought forms direct upon photographic paper; not only in the room in which the experimenters were, but also in another town. The 'transmitter' of the images, in this case, was, instead of a camera, a well-known psychic or sensitive, Mr John Myers.

Arrangements were made for seven people to meet in London, and seven in Leeds, at 8.30 p.m. on 9th January, 1930. In London, at 5 Smith Square, W.1. (the W. T. Stead Library and Bureau) were John Myers, the daughter of W. T. Stead, (the journalist and psychic researcher who was drowned in the *Titanic* disaster of 1912) and four other people, including the news editor of a national newspaper. In Headingley, Leeds, the group consisted of a Mr and Mrs W. T. James (whose idea the project had been in the first place), a Post Office clerk, a railway claims clerk, a secretary, an insurance inspector, and a religious administrator. In both Leeds and London were photographic papers, which had been bought beforehand and kept in a locked cabinet, opened on the night of the experiment before members of each group, and signed by two of them on the reverse side. There were also in readiness hypo, dveloper and a red lamp.

In London as Miss Stead picked up the papers from the table, each member of the group in turn described the image he or she wished to have reproduced on the paper. A cross, the letter T (for *Titanic*) flowers, were among the requested pictures; Miss Stead asked for a copy of her father's portrait, hanging then in the house.

After a few minutes, the photographic papers were put into the developer. At 10.30 p.m. they were examined. In each case there was a good, clear reproduction of the picture asked for.

In Leeds, at 9.10 p.m., after routine examination of the photographic papers, they were placed in a quarter-plate negative box, which was carefully inspected by everyone present both before and after transferring the paper to it. At 9.30, Mrs James picked up the box; at 9.37 it was moved about so violently that she dropped it.

When she held it in her left hand again, her right hand began to trace signs in the air, which were recorded and later were found to be recognisably the same shapes as those on the photographic papers. By 10.30 the papers had been placed in the developer. At 11 p.m., after the results had been examined and listed, one of the group rang through to London, describing the pictures recorded on the Leeds papers. They were found to be almost exact reproductions of those produced in the Stead Bureau. Among minor differences were that the Leeds pictures were smaller than those received in London; there was greater detail in the London flower picture; the cross was larger; the downward stroke of the T (for *Titanic*) joined the cross stroke whereas in the Leeds photograph there was a small gap between them.

The whole experiment was made under strict test conditions, for instance everything possible was done to make sure that the photographic papers were not interfered with in any way. In both cities it took place in bright light; an unusual feature. In most such cases of sixth sense manifestations, light has been found as a rule to inhibit the raising of whatever form of power produces the effects. Photographically-speaking the results of the experiment should not have happened. Penetration is known to take place in photographic plates which are stacked together, but in this case each image (except the topmost) had to pass through one or more layers of paper without affecting the picture on each layer and without leaving any trace of its passage. According to physical laws the whole thing is impossible, but apparently in such instances they are not the whole story. As Dr Rhine said of E.S.P. experiments: 'Physical laws do not hold'.

According to findings in a number of cases, it appears that a thought form can have a dynamic aspect through which it can react on matter. This is an explanation advanced by Mr G. Delawarr of some of the results obtained in experiments made to show the effect of 'blessing' on plants. He says: 'It is our contention that when a person *thinks,* he produces a thought form which can be used to effect living matter. We also postulate that the energy pattern thus produced will vary with that person's inherent ability to perform the rite and the character of the particular thought that he is using.'

The 'blessed' plants, whether they received energy through the agency of a thought-form or by some other channel, in most cases grew into specimens better in every way than the 'unblessed' controls. Mr J. Rawson of Easingwold, York, found an increase of fifty-three per cent in weight in 'blessed' plants over the weight of those 'unblessed' at the end of the experiment. Some of the participants found that not only the plants but also weeds in the treated pots, flourished luxuriantly. The gardener of a participant in the experiment was disappointed to find that when the two groups of plants began to grow, the 'unblessed' grew faster and taller than the others. But as they matured, he found that although the 'blessed' plants were shorter, they were thicker, stronger, more vigorous, bearing a much heavier crop of flowers than those 'unblessed'.

Professor Otton Rahn of Cornell University U.S.A., showed by a series of experiments that plant-growth and yeast cells could be affected by emanations from human beings. He told a meeting of the American Association for the Advancement of Science in Syracuse, New York, that some years ago scientists had discovered the human body in common with all living things, produces ultra-violet rays. These rays, it seems, can either damage or benefit, according to volume. Yeast cells, he said, can be killed by a subject looking intently at a glass slide on which the cells are placed for several minutes when held close to the eyes. The tip of the nose was discovered to be a fine ultra violet tube. These rays are not always harmful—tests on plants showed that they can be beneficial. There seems to be no difference in kind but the volume differs; when large, it is lethal to yeast. The same person emits rays at different rates. He may be 'killing' at one time the 'benign' at another. The right hand appears to radiate more power than the left, even in left-handers.

'These body rays seem to be given off most strongly by the parts of the body which are replaced most rapidly, such as the palms of the hands and the soles of the feet. . . . The tips of the fingers are very strong emitters of this energy. . . . The sex organs of both sexes and breasts in women emit these rays quite strongly.

'The first scientific proof that there is a personal electric field, a sort of electric aura, within and in the air around a living body, was announced in the Third International Cancer Congress. The report was made by Dr Harold S. Burr, of Yale University. . . . Human eyes are powerful electric batteries. This discovery, showing that each eyeball is an independent battery was announced to the National Academy of Sciences in 1938 by Dr Walter H. Miles,

Yale University pathologist. . . . The fact that eyes produce electricity has been known to science since 1860, when it was discovered in frogs, but the source of this electric power, its variations and especially its high power in human beings is little known'.

Not much more than two centuries ago the experiments of Professors Rhine and Rahn, the Meyers-James groups, Mr Delawarr and those of other pioneers in these lines of research would have ended at the gallows or the stake. The discoveries of modern science and the old witch beliefs are so similar that no inquisitor would notice the difference. Precognition, telepathy, the whole range of E.S.P., projecting and activating thought-forms, blessing (and cursing) plants or crops, are all part of ancient witchcraft teachings. Witches have always believed that the human body is a storehouse of energy, which can be put to many uses; that this energy can be transmitted by the finger-tips and the hands, that the human eyes have dynamic power.

Once it would have seemed impossible that witchcraft and science could ever have anything in common; they have come together because of the growing realisation that there is more to life than the five senses tell us of, as I said at the beginning of this chapter.

This belief in the paraphysical world has always existed in a deep layer of the human mind, from which waves of rationalism and materialism have never dislodged it, although for a time they might submerge it, as happened in the nineteenth century. This was the beginning of the 'modern' scientific age; which taught that all the phenomena of life must be the result of the action of a physical law; that anything which could not be explained in these terms did not exist. Only the unintelligent could believe in the reality of an experience outside this framework.

The more reasonable approach developing today looks on a phenomenon which cannot be explained by known laws not as necessarily superstitious nonsense, but as a challenge to discover its cause. Or perhaps rediscover would be the better world; most of today's world-shaking scientific 'finds' seem to have been known centuries ago.

Democritus, Leucippus and Epicurus evolved atomic theories; according to Sextus Empiricus these were not original but derived from Moschus the Phoenician, who taught that the atom was divisible. Long before the telescope was thought of, Anaximenes and Thales declared that the Milky Way was a galaxy of solar systems, suns and planets. Lucretius' theory was that there were an infinite number of worlds in infinite space. Vaccination was described in one of the Vedas: 'Collect the fluid from the pustules on the point of a lancet and insert it into the arm, so that the fluid mixes with the blood. This will produce fever but the disease will then be very mild and there will be no cause for alarm.'

Daguerre is usually credited with having discovered the principle of photography, in 1839. In 1566, Fabricius in his treatise, *De Rebus Metallicus*, described the properties of certain metallic bodies, which he said, could be used to retain a pictorial image. And in 1729, Tiphaigne de la Roche, brought out a book *Giphantie*, in which he gave an account of an photographic process. 'The image is imprinted instantaneously on the exposed sheet (toile) which is then at once removed and placed in a dark room. An hour later the prepared surface has dried, and you have a picture all the more precious in that no work of art can imitate its truthfulness.'

And penicillin, hailed not so long ago as a great 'discovery', was the subject of a thesis written in 1897 by Ernest Duchesne, a student at Lyons. His theme was the antagonism between moulds and micro-organisms; in particular he mentions the action of *penicillium glaucum* on bacteria. The effects of oxygen were noted and studied in the fifteenth century by an alchemist, Eck de Sulsbach. Early in the sixteenth century, Paracelsus was saying that a flame is sustained by an ethereal agent. In 1636, the principles of the electric telegraph were investigated by Schwenter. On 26th November 1695, Fenelon described, in a letter to the King of Poland's secretary, Jean Sobieski, experiments in telephony, in which a loud speaker was used.

Aristotle refers to the earth's globular shape in his treatise, *De Coelo*. Anaesthetics, glass-making, industrial gas, metallurgy (including the making of alloys, such as electrum) are a few of innumerable examples of subjects of which present-day science is thought to have unravelled the secrets, but which history shows to be old knowledge exhumed. As Marie Antoinette's milliner, Mlle. Bertin said when rehabilitating an old hat: 'There is nothing new but what has been forgotten'.

So it seems that the story of rediscovering physical laws and processes is being repeated on the non-physical level, and presented in fresh forms, since, as was said long ago, 'truth needs to be restated'.

The teachings of philosophers, metaphysicians, mystics in past generations are echoed in scientific pronouncements of today.

Non-reality of the material world has been a basic theme of the world's great teachers and avatars. Modern scientists have the same idea. Sir James says '. . . modern psychics is pushing the whole universe into one or more ethers'. And—'The material universe is derivative from consciousness, not consciousness from the material universe.' He said there was general agreement that modern psychics is heading towards the conception of the universe as a non-mechanical reality. Professor Max Planck states: 'I regard consciousness as fundamental. I regard matter as derivative from consciousness. We cannot get behind consciousness.' Prince de Broglie regards 'consciousness and matter as aspects of the same thing'. Professor C. E. M. Joad in his *Guide to Modern Thought*, says that Einstein and Schrodinger agree with Planck's views.

In the seventh of a series of broadcasts dealing with the mind, Sir Cyril Burt told us that '. . . the physicist has arrived at the stage when he is ready to assure us that he has a conscious mind but doubts whether he possesses a material brain'.

So, with every year, the wheel turns a little further from materialistic concepts back towards the non-physical or mystical interpretations of life and man's place in it. But the turning back is not retrogression in the sense of retracing tracks; it is rather the motion of the spiral, the curves of which repeatedly pass over the same place, but each time on a higher level. The discoveries of modern science relating to the invisible world and its forces can be a means of presenting great spiritual truths in a form in which they can be recognised and used by the majority, instead of the enlightened few, in the overcoming of human problems and in the achieving of a fuller, more satisfactory way of life.

Science is opening the door, which it once slammed shut, to a world in which anything can happen, because it is a world in which mind affects matters, and mind has no discoverable limitations. Jeans believed, as we have seen that differentiated human beings could be likened to cells in a Universal Mind; Professor Wood-Jones put forward much the same idea in his *Design and Purpose;* as does Professor I. M. Lowson in *Science and Reality*, while Professor V. H. Mottram, in the *Physical Basis of Personality*, says:

'. . . I throw out the suggestion that the real "I", the core of our being is a spark, an atom of the fundamental reality of the universe'.

We know that 'a part is the same in kind and quality as the whole; the only difference being one of degree'. Therefore if indeed we are a part of a Universal Mind, which is the sum of and the only power in the cosmos, we must possess limitless potentialities which will unfold as we recognise and develop them.

CHAPTER XIII

The Role of the Clairvoyant

CLAIRVOYANCE ranks as at least one of the oldest professions in the world, or perhaps it would be more accurate to say the use of the psychic senses, of which clairvoyance is one. I am using the terms clairvoyance and clairvoyant, as meaning all the psychic faculties and one who possesses them; not relating the word only to the specialised channel of seeing. I think this is not stretching too far the technical description; although psychics may class themselves as clairaudient, psychometrist, clairvoyant, most of them find themselves operating, at least occasionally, through all the psychic senses. 'Seer' which is defined in the dictionary as a 'person of preternatural insight' would probably be the best word for the psychic. But seer has an archaic sound; let us settle for 'clairvoyant'; one who has the sixth, or psychic sense.

Most people, from the Stone Age to the twentieth century, have wanted to discover what is waiting round the corner of toworrow or next year. Through the centuries the popular attitude to men and women, who could satisfy this urge through foresight or fore-knowledge, has varied from respect and reverence to contempt and persecution.

Very probably the Wicce (the Wise Ones) were the first clair-voyants. In the days when their role was a combination of priestess (or priest), healer, and citizen's advice bureau, their psychic faculties would have been put to multifarious uses in everyday life. The idea that these faculties were in any way evil had not yet been born; they were thought of as natural; to be treated with respect, but not feared.

The great foci of psychic force in the ancient world, the Oracles, were looked upon much in the same way. They were prophetic revelations which could be spontaneous, or received by consultation made after performance of rituals at certain places. The sanctuary in which the revelation manifested was itself called Oracle, the meaning of which is place of invocation, place of sacred Word.

The most famous of these is probably the Greek temple at Delphi in Phocis; among other almost equaly well-known were the Oracles of Dodona in Epirus, of Lebades in Boeotia, and of Taenarus in Laconia. To these places came most of the great men of history, at least once in their lives, hoping for a clue to the riddle of their fate; just as today clairvoyants are consulted.

Delphi stood at the foot of two spurs at the southern end of Mount Parnassus; it was surrounded on three sides by precipices. Situated in a vast enclosure, a magnificent temple to Apollo, the god of eloquence, dominated the highest part of the town. An inscription on the temple pediment read: 'Let no man enter this place except his hands be pure'. An equally vital but unwritten injunction was apparently: 'Let no man enter this place except his hands be full'. Every visitor was expected to bring an offering; the temple was heaped with treasures, gifts of the Greeks and of visitors from other countries.

At one end of the temple was a great golden statue of Apollo; behind it was the entrance to the cave of the oracle itself. Plutarch says that the cave was discovered through the behaviour of some goats, who suddenly developed convulsions when grazing near a cavity in the rocks. The shepherd and others who investigated, also also acted in a strange way; they seemed to be in a trance, and while in that condition, they muttered words of which no one knew the meaning.

The priests, decided that these were signs, not only of mephitic gases escaping from the caves, but that Apollo wished to communicate his wisdom to humanity through the medium of human speech. They arranged that once a month a virgin, the Pythia, should go down into the crypt and there, the reasoning mind having been subdued by the vapours, utter the wisdom given to her in this condition by the god.

The Pythia was seated upon a tripod, crowned with laurel, her forehead bound by a white wool fillet. In the cave were also the pythons sacred to Apollo, who had conquered this colubrine species; sometimes the Pythia, in trance, wrestled with them. At

first the Pythia were chosen for their beauty from the most important families of Delphi, but after a scandal caused by the elopement
of one of them with a handsome Thessalian, the minimum age for
the Pythia was set at fifty.

A detailed account of a visit to the oracle is given by Apollonius
of Tyana, the great philosopher, who consulted the Pythia with his
disciple Damis.

First came the ceremony of purification in holy water. After the
sacrifice to the god of a bull and a goat, says Apollonius, 'we
entered the temple, our heads crowned with laurels, holding in our
hands a laurel bough decorated with a band of white wool. These
are the symbols with which consultants must approach. We were
shown into a cell, where, say the priests, at a moment neither pre-
arranged nor foreseen by themselves, one suddenly smells a
wonderfully sweet perfume. A litle while after one of them came to
find and take us into the hidden sanctuary whose walls are
decorated with the rich offerings that attest the truth of the oracles
and the gratitude of those consultants who have been favoured by
fate. . . . Behind the statue of the god is the crypt, into which one
descends by a gradual slope, but the servants of the temple keep
the consultants far enough away from the Pythia to make their
presence unnoticeable.

'The Pythia, much fatigued, refused to answer our questions. The
priests around her overwhelmed her now with prayers, now with
threats. Finally, giving way, she place herself on the tripod, after
having drunk the water that runs through the sanctuary, said to
have magic properties. Hardly had the woman sat down when we
saw her chest swell, her face flush and pale; all her limbs were
seized with nervous trembling, but she uttered nothing but broken
cries and long-drawn moans. Gradually her convulsions became
more and more violent, her eyes sparkled with fire, she foamed at
the mouth and her hair stood on end. Unable either to resist the
overpowering fumes or to leave the tripod on which the priests held
her firmly seated, she tore off her fillet and between the most
terrifying howls pronounced a few words, which the priests hastened
to note down. They . . . handed us the message in writing. I had
asked whether my name would be handed down to posterity; my
disciple, without having consulted me on the subject, had asked the
very same question. The reply was that my memory would
pass into future ages, but would owe its perpetuation to the

calumnies that would be attached to my name. I tore up the paper as I was leaving the temple; that is what all consultants do whose pride has not been satisfied.'

The Oracle's forecast may not have suited Apollonius, but it proved accurate. During his lifetime, he had a great reputation and following. After his death, the leaders of the Christian church had nothing good to say of him; he is remembered chiefly by their denigrations.

The work of the priestess of the oracle at Dordona must have been much more pleasant than Pythia's. Instead of a dank unpleasant-smelling cave, her sanctuary was a clearing in a forest of oaks, at the foot of Mount Tomaros in Epirus. The town of Dordona was sacred to Zeus; its temple was endowed as richly as that at Delphi with thank-offerings from satisfied visitors to the oracle.

The site of the oracle was a sacred oak-tree. At its foot ran a stream which dried up daily as the sun reached its zenith, beginning to flow again about midnight. Traditionally the oracle had come into being when two black doves, sacred to Isis, flew out of Thebes. One made its way to Libya, the other reached Dordona, where it perched in an oak-tree. People from the town, resting under the tree, saw the dove and heard a voice saying: 'This is a place beloved by the gods; here they will reveal the future to worthy men.' The legend is thought to be a dramatised version of the Egyptian records concerning two Theban priestesses, who were inspired by God to travel as far as their strength would take them, making known his teachings as they went. One got as far as Libya; the other came to Epirus; both were successful in their mission. The ancient word in Epirus for 'dove' was the same as that for 'old woman' which may give a clue to the legend's origin.

When the oracle was consulted, the priestess went in procession with the temple scribes to the foot of the sacred oak. Here she listened to the soughing of the wind in its branches and the voice of the stream at its foot, translating these sounds according to an ancient ritual which gave the answer to the seeker's question. Like Aradia's disciples, she could 'understand the voice of the wind'. Seven copper vessels, suspended so closely in the inner walls of the sanctuary that if one were struck the others vibrated, were set echoing; the same ritual interpreted their resonance, as guidance or warning.

The third oracle, Triphonius, in Boeotia, has been described as an imitation of the oracle or Delphi. It seems to have been almost as popular, incredible though this may appear from descriptions of its functioning. To begin with the cave of the oracle had been chosen by its priests for its terrifying properties. The approach to the sanctuary was first by a ladder; then the inquirer had to crawl down a long, narrow tunnel, feet foremost. At the end of this, he or she was hurtled forward with an impetus so great that it could not be resisted. Apparently a mechanism controlled the violent propulsion; it could not be stopped or modified by the pilgrim, who, on pain of death, had to hold a honey-cake in each hand.

The visit to the oracle could only be taken at night, after a period of preparation which was in itself an ordeal, so Pausanias records. He says that a would-be consultant of the Oracle, a Theban named Tersidas, was locked for three days and nights into a chapel sacred to Fortuna, with little or no food. When released he was given water to drink from the spring of Lethe and of Mnemosyne. One draught (forgetfulness) obliterated all thought of the past; the other (memory) enabled the mind to remember everything seen or heard in the sanctuary. Then Tersidas was dressed in a linen alb, and led by torchlight down a ladder to the oracle, where he was left until morning.

According to Pausanias, he had to be helped out by the priests. His eyes were glazed, he recognised no one. He muttered a few words, which the priests recorded as being the oracle's reply, on his way back to Fortuna's temple where he stayed until he had recovered his senses, more or less. Apparently he never entirely got over the effects of his visit to Triphonius, nor did most of those who penetrated to the shrine.

Plutarch relates the experience there of an acquaintance of his, Timarchus, as told to him by this man. Timarchus went to Triphonius to ask the oracle 'what one should think of the dai-monion or familiar spirit by which Socrates believed himself to be inspired.' After lying on the ground in the darkness, scarcely conscious, he heard music from far off, he saw a wavering light, different-coloured islands in a lake of fire, a pit like that of a volcano, on the edge of which were radiant sparks of differing luminosity. A voice told him that the islands were sacred regions inhabited by pure souls, 'man cannot enter there until he has cast off the bonds of the flesh'. The sparks were souls just departed from earthly life. The soul of Socrates, said the voice, 'had become worthy of entering into communion with invisible worlds and his familiar spirit, a deputy sent from them, taught him a wisdom that men did not appreciate and therefore killed. You cannot yet understand this mystery; in three months it will be revealed to you.'

Three months after this experience, Timarchus died, 'babbling', says Plutarch, 'of luminous islands and lakes of fire and holding out his hands towards the image of Socrates which he said was coming towards him'.

Less difficult to consult, but to judge from the existing records of their prophecies, rarely more encouraging, were the Sibyls, women who claimed to be possessed by a spirit, whose mouthpiece they became.

Traditionally, there were ten Sibyls: Sambeth (supposed to be the daughter of Noah, who made Nostradamus-like prophecies concerning the succession and fate of the world's empires from the deluge to the coming of Christ), Elissa, known as the Lesbian Sibyl, daughter of Zeus and Lamia; Artemis, daughter of Apollo; Manto, daughter of the famous soothsayer of Thebes, Tiresias. Manto was called 'the Thessalian'; as Thessaly was traditionally a witch-stronghold, and the gift of divination was one of the powers of the witch, the Sibyl and the Craft may be connected in some way. The fifth Sibyl was Sarbis, from Phrygia; Cassandra, Lampusa, Phyto, Amalthea and Hierophila completed the list. Their prophecies seem to have been mainly concerning political or world events; Cassandra foretold to Octavius (who took the name of Augustus) the birth of Christ, when he asked her whether there would ever be a greater prince than he. At that time the 2160 year period rule by Aries was ending; with the beginning of the Piscean aeon the coming of a saviour was expected by the ancient peoples who understood the principle of the Precession of the Equinoxes . . . which may have influenced the Sibyl's prophecy.

In Rome, clairvoyance (or divination) was a flourishing business. To maintain a private astrologer was almost a status symbol; every noble family had one, from the Emperor downwards. The occupational risks of such a position were high; if the astrologer took his profession seriously and predicted an unpleasant event, especially to Caesar, he disappeared. If a catastrophe happened which had not been predicted, he was blamed for not having forewarned the employer, and the end was the same. After a time, the practice of divination of all types was banned by successive Emperors; not because it was considered fraudulent, but because it might be used as an instrument for imperial overthrow. Augustus ordered the burning of one thousand books on magic, although he himself continued to use it privately. Tiberius banished everyone known to practice the art. Vitellius also made a decree of banishment of magicians and psychics from Rome. It did not work out perhaps quite according to plan; the departing magicians placarded every cross-road with a notice foretelling Vitellius' imminent death, which in fact took place before the end of the year.

Successive emperors made their attempts to suppress the practice of divination and of magic and witchcraft. They failed, as all such attempts have failed and would fail, in the unlikely event of their being made today, when the discoveries of science relating to the psychic world make possible a more rational attitude towards its phenomena. History shows clearly the futility of trying to prevent by law the expression of basic urges in human nature—of which the need to make contact with the invisible forces is one, whether by direct means or indirect, such as clairvoyance or any form of divination. And history itself has been shaped to some extent by the predictions of clairvoyants, as we have seen, not in ancient Rome and Greece only, but in modern Germany and other periods.

Four hundred years ago, Dr John Dee was the power behind the throne of England, upon which Elizabeth I then sat. He was born in London in 1527. His parents were wealthy; he was sent to France to study mathematics and geometry; he made a great reputation as a scholar before he was twenty-five. The rectorship of Upton-on-Severn was offered to him as a tribute to his academic attainments: his reputation as an occultist was growing, also, with not such immediately happy results. He was imprisoned on a charge of trying to assassinate Queen Mary by magic, but released without suffering more than, as he complained in his preface to his English translation of Euclid, 'being regarded as a companion of hell-hounds, a caller, and a conjurer of wicked and damned spirits'.

At one time Elizabeth relied to a great extent upon Dr Dee's predictions and advice, which were based on astrology and scrying (crystal-gazing). He is supposed to have foretold some years before her sister died, that she would be Queen; at any rate he must have satisfied Elizabeth who was a clear-thinking, hard-headed woman, as to his clairvoyant powers. She rewarded him with the Chancellorship of St Paul's Cathedral, and the Wardenship of Manchester College; posts for which he must have had the intellectual qualifications. When the Gregorian Calendar was introduced into this country, it was based upon Dee's methematical and astronomical calculations. Later Dee seems to have gone downhill. He became poor, he presented a petition to James I on 5th June, 1604, asking for protection against slanders and libels; soon afterwards he died.

Albertus Magnus, Bshop of Ratisbon, had many Royal consultants including Prince William of Holland. He was called the greatest magician living; one of his more famous experiments was the construction of what was no doubt the first robot, a mechanical brass man, which worked for him in his house. It may also have been the computor's ancestor; it used to give Magnus the answers to difficult questions of astrology and theology . . . or so it is said. Finally, the brass man talked so much that St Thomas Aquinas, then a student of Magnus', smashed the robot with a hammer. Even then, he could not work in peace; a continuous procession of horses and carriages clattered past his window. St Thomas settled this nuisance by making a waxen image of a horse, which he buried in the road outside Magnus' house . . . after that no horse would pass it.

During the first half of the sixteenth century, the policy of King Charles IX and Henry II of France was more or less dominated by Nostradamus, the great occultist—one of the few to die peacefully and in comfort, perhaps because he was wise enough to make his predictions so vague that they could be interpreted in several ways.

The eighteenth century produced Count Cagliostro and Franz Mesmer, with whom Cagliostro is supposed to have studied at one time. As Cagliostro understood hypnotism and Mesmer was then the great exponent of its use, under the name of 'animal magnetism', this may have been so.

Among Cagliostro's predictions were the fall of the Bastille, the monarchy and the Revolution. He died in 1795, in a dungeon of the Castle of San Leo, Montefeltro, a victim of the Inquisition.

In our own century, Rasputin, monk of the Khlysty sect, occultist, magician, and probably many other things, dominated the Court of Russia, the Tzar and Tzarina. During the disastrous years of his influence, officials were appointed or dismissed and the entire administration of the Russian Empire was conducted by his whim. Like Dee and many other Court 'magicians' Rasputin used a crystal for making his predictions; perhaps the most memorable of which was: 'The monarchy will die with me'.

He died on 16th December, 1916, ten weeks after this the February Revolution exploded . . . the Russian monarchy was wiped out by the shooting of the Tzar, Tzarina and their children in the cellar at Tsarskoyeselo. Rasputin's death was as strange as any episode in his life. At the end of 1916 some of the most powerful men in the Russian Court decided that for the safety of the country, he must be removed. A dinner-party was planned at the house of Prince Youssopov, who was a great friend of the Tsar Nicholas, with Rasputin as guest of honour. During its course he was to be poisoned.

The setting must have been superb; the long dining-table has been described as covered with thick white silk set with a fabulous gold and silver service. Wine and vodka were served in Venetian crystal glasses. The chairs were red velvet; their occupants were holders of the greatest names in Russia, Princes, Grand Dukes, Counts . . . and the Titanic figure of the black-bearded monk, who stood six foot five in his sandals. At midnight a toast was proposed. Rasputin drained his wine in one gulp, then instead of collapsing from the effects of the quick-acting poison with which it was laced, drank a second, then a third glassful. Prince Youssopov snatching up a long, thin dagger, burried it to its hilt in Rasputin's chest, the monk wrenched it out. Three times then the Prince shot Rasputin in the body. Bleeding, he got up from his chair and advanced on Youssopov, who emptied the magazine of the pistol into him. Rasputin fell down; Youssopov and the other men dragged him out, bundled him into a car and drove off to the Neva, which was frozen over. They threw him onto the ice, believing him to be dead, but he began to crawl towards the bank. Rasputin finally died in the river, into which his body was thrust through a hole cut in the ice. A few years ago I met in London Prince Serge Obolenski, who was one of the guests at this dinner-party. His most vivid memory of it, he said, was a moment of almost superstitious fear which he thought they all felt, when Rasputin apparently was unaffected by poison, steel or bullets. Roehm, Hitler's favourite who was shot during the purge of the Night of the Long Knives, apparently also had powers of unusual resistance. Enough bullets to kill six ordinary men were fired into him before he died, so an ex-storm-trooper who was present at the execution, told me.

In this half of the twentieth century we have no Rasputin or Magnus or Dee or oracles such as those of ancient history, probably because in the world as it is today the spheres of influence in which they could function no longer exist. Still, though psychics at this time may not be as spectacular as in the past one must conclude that their role in our society is in some ways more important than at any other period of time. Per capita, they are more numerous now so far as can be judged, than they were even in Roman times, which indicates a wider need for them.

No one knows exactly how many practicing clairvoyants (the word is used in the meaning established at the beginning of this chapter) there are in this country. Fifty thousand has been suggested as a possible basic figure; probably eighty thousand would be nearer the mark. In Brighton, with a population of 162,910, there are between seventy and eighty psychics; larger towns possibly support twice or three times as many. It is estimated that at least seventy-five per cent of our population of 46,071,604 consults a clairvoyant at least once a year; many go as often as once a month. According to an opinion poll published in the London *Daily Sketch* on 14th September, 1964, at least fifty per cent believe the predictions made to them.

Approximate as the estimate of clairvoyant's clients is, it gives an idea of the money spent each year on psychics' consultations. £350,000 was given to me as a conservative figure, taking into consideration that fees may vary between five shillings and fifteen guineas. In France about the same sum is spent on clairvoyants each year; in America at least one million dollars is the estimate.

As well as this the money paid for psychic journals each year must run into thousands of pounds. One of them, *Prediction*, has a circulation of 50,000 monthly in this country alone (where a copy cost 1s. 6d); it sells also in America, Canada, Australia, New Zealand, Africa, France, Germany, Scandinavia, China and India.

Three internationally-known societies, the College of Psychic Science, the Psychical Research Society and the Spiritualist

Association of Great Britain, with full time schedules, and impressive membership lists, are additional signs of the growing significance of the psychic in present-day life.

The oldest of these societies, I understand, is what is now the College of Psychic Science. It was founded in 1884, as the London Spiritualist Alliance, by the Rev. Stainton Moses, and Edmund Dawson Rogers, a journalist. Incorporated in 1896, among the signatories of its Memorandum of Association were Lord Radnor, the Hon. Percy Wyndham, Alfred Russel Wallace, o.m., and Major-General Drayson. The objectives of the College are given as 'the investigation, study and classification of psychic phenomena; their co-ordination with the existing body of philosophical and scientific knowledge, and their application to the subject of survival and communication with the discarnate.'

Many famous mediums and psychics have been associated with the College. The first president and founder of the L.S.A., Stainton Moses, was I am told, one of the greatest of these; among others are D. D. Home, Florence Cook, Hearne and Williams, Cecil Husk, R. J. Lees, George Spriggs, Percy Street, Mrs Everitt, and Mrs Etta Wreidt. W. B. Yeats, the poet, was a member—he met his wife, Georgina Hyde Lees, through the Alliance. Mrs Despard, the great suffragette, joined the L.S.A., and Mrs Bernard Shaw, the mother of G.B.S. She was an automatic writer herself; G.B.S. she used to say, never commented on or criticised her performances.

The policy of the College is to further the increase of knowledge of psychic matters. It is a clearing-house for information on these lines; one of its most important functions is the investigation of the claims of mediums and clairvoyants. Only psychics who can satisfy the high standards of the College as to ability and integrity appear on its 'approved' lists; a recommendation from the College ranks as a guarantee of a certain standard of psychic ability, as four stars in an A.A. guide-book indicate a first-quality hotel.

The C.P.S. looks on this scrutiny of psychics as a service to the public; it also provides a service to psychics by protecting them from the public. Would-be consultants who book appointments through the College are 'vetted' discreetly, to make sure they genuinely need clairvoyant help.

The College also gives guidance and instructions in various forms to people who wish to develop their psychic gifts.

The flourishing of these societies, the thousands of pounds paid every year to clairvoyants, show that the psychic is filling a public need; probably a need more complicated that it used to be, although of course the basic urge to know what lies ahead still operates. People today tend to treat psychics as they used to treat their priests. Often they go to them for counsel on matters which they would not mention to husband, wife, parent or intimate friend. Today the psychic's consulting-room is a repository of secret hopes and fears.

Because of this the men and women who practise as clairvoyants probably know more about their fellow beings than even priests or doctors or psychiatrists know. The psychic is in a position of great responsibility to the client, whose whole life may be influenced by a prediction, or by the advice given. The majority of people are in a suggestible condition, for one reason or another, when they consult a clairvoyant; what is said is likely to sink into the subconscious and may produce far-reaching results.

Not all clairvoyants realise fully the onerous nature of this responsibility but a great many of them do, and are prepared to meet it. Such a psychic can be of very real service to the sitter. Using a range of perception which is beyond and more subtle than is possible to the average person, he or she may be able to see the roots of a given problem within the client's own subconsciousness, and to suggest ways of dissolving it. There is too, the therapeutic effect which a prediction of happiness ahead can have upon someone in a depressed state of mind.

The reassurance and comfort given by a psychic of integrity can even be the impetus enabling the client to struggle through one of the dark patches which most of us encounter now and again. Some people of course may become clairvoyance-addicts; feeling that they cannot get along without the constant stimulus of the psychic's help, but this is a pattern which is met with on every level—the urge to repeat any experience which gives pleasure or an illusion of escape. Most psychics deal with this kind of situation by arranging appointments for such a sitter only at reasonable intervals.

A clairvoyant is helping his client by refusing too-frequent sittings, and in doing so he is not turning away his own bread-and-butter. A good clairvoyant is usually fully booked for weeks or even months in advance. Today the psychic has more status than he has had for many centuries; clairvoyance has attained the dignity of a profession. Members of every income group and social stratum consult him, from Royalty downwards. Bankers and stockbrokers are frequent visitors. Through his gifts the clairvoyant opens the door, even if only a little, between the known world and the unknown, which for most of us is tightly closed. And for the privilege of a glimpse of that world men, because they need what he has to offer, will as Emerson said, 'beat a path to his door'.

CHAPTER XIV

The Sixth Sense at Work (1)

THE senses from one to five broadly can be described as mechanisms by which we perceive whatever enters our normal field of experience. The sixth sense seems to work in much the same way, as one would expect; registering impressions received on the level at which it functions.

There are numbers of theories or explanations as to the ways in which the sixth sense works; the opening of the 'third eye'; through activity of chakras (psychic centres of awareness), and so on. What does seem essential—at any rate, where the deeper levels of clairvoyance are concerned—is the ability to 'tune in' to a different plane of consciousness from that of ordinary physical awareness.

Probably few psychics know how or why their sixth sense works, but all seem agreed that it cannot be turned on at will. It is like the wind 'which bloweth where it listeth'. It is subject to no hard-and-fast rules; there are no conditions which guarantee its functioning or non-functioning. Some clairvoyants cannot work unless they are in good physical form; others are at their best if a little under par. Some 'see' better after fasting, others need food for optimum functioning. Alcohol, meat, sleep—all seem to be necessary—or not—in varying degres to the individual clairvoyant.

However it works and whatever its real nature, the sixth sense demonstrably provides a bridgehead between us and the invisible world. And since as we grow, the need for contact with this world grows also, even the glimpse of its existence, which the clairvoyant's power gives us, can be valuable.

How do psychics themselves feel about their gifts and the responsibility it brings with it? What do they think of the sixth sense and its manifestations in their particular case? How do they make their predictions? In order to answer these questions and to get a picture of the functioning of the invisible forces through these channels, I have asked a cross section of clairvoyants for their impressions, ideas and experiences on the subject, and for documented records of results of their predictions. All the cases I have quoted can be verified, which I submit makes them admissible (at least by the open-minded) as evidence of the action of the faculty of extra-sensory perception.

The man who has been called the doyen of modern psychics, William S. King, has beliefs as strong as his personality and charm. 'Clairvoyance', he says, 'is a real truth. And a real responsibility'.

From his earliest childhood, his sixth sense has always been active; the story of how it operated in him then and in his later life has been told by Charles Drage in *William King's Profession* (published in paper back form under the title *The Strange Profession of William King*).

I mention here one episode of those early days which was not included in this book, which shows how strongly clairvoyance was developed in him, even when he was very young.

Born in Ireland, he lived there for the first two decades or so of his life. When he was ten years old, he visited with his parents a widowed sister of his father's who had a farm in County Armagh, which she managed with the help of one of her sons, John Gordon. A big handsome man in his twenties, his little cousin hero-worshipped him. As a rule William hardly dared to speak to him, but one day he told him: 'John you're going to join up'. His father told him to be quiet. There was no war on—what force could John join? Mr King says: 'Although usually I was an obedient child, I could not stop myself from telling John: "You're going to wear uniform—soon—and you're going to die on a wide road before you're thirty".'

When William King went with his parents to Armagh the following year, John was in the police force. Next year, while patrolling a main road, he was shot dead.

His sixth sense, William King says, has guided him all through his life. He has always obeyed its promptings and it has never been wrong. During the last war, he would almost certainly have been killed if he had not listened to the inner voice which warned him to sell a house which afterwards received a direct hit in a bombing raid, and to leave for the evening a house which was destroyed by a land-mine while he was out. He was shown the house in which he now lives in a dream before it was even on the market and advised psychically to move into it.

Clairvoyance not only cannot be turned on and off; sometimes it suddenly takes over, apparently spontaneously. In September 1962, I was one of a small party in Mr King's house; in the middle of a completely ordinary conversation, he said: 'Mr Gaitskill is going to die early next year'. Mr Gaitskill was not even ill at the time. Later in the year when the Labour Party leader's health was deteriorating, I said to Mr King: 'I hope you're not going to be right'. He answered: I am, you know'.

Another friend of Mr King's and I were with him when the B.B.C. telephoned to make arrangements about a television programme in which he was to appear. We heard Mr King say: 'I don't want to know his name or anything about him. I work much better if I have no information at all about a sitter'.

When he put down the receiver, he told us: 'The B.B.C. wants me to read for someone on their staff.' He then said casually, as if speaking of someone he knew well, that this man was married; he had children, one of whom had been seriously ill (describing the type of illness). The man, he said, wrote privately as well as for the B.B.C.; he had recently been offered new work on these lines, and other points about his life and career, all of which proved to be accurate. 'And,' he added, 'his grandfather died violently in a rather dreadful way—I think he must have been murdered'.

The man whom the B.B.C. had chosen as Mr King's sitter turned out to be Erskine Childers, grandson of Robert Erskine Childers, who was shot in November 1922 at Black Bush Barracks, Dublin, by the Free State Army because he had espoused the cause of the I.R.A. One of his books, *The Riddle of the Sands,* a spy thriller which still sells and ranks as a classic of its kind, is considered by some to be more fact than fiction.

Another instance of Mr King's 'extra-sensory knowing' which I personally experienced, occurred when I recommended to him a doctor, who so far as I knew, was a general practitioner, also specialising in biochemic therapy.

'What do I want with a gynaecologist?' Mr King objected.

In the course of a subsequent conversation which I had with this doctor, he said: 'Of course you know that I also specialise in gynaecology'. Mr King could not have got this fact from my mind, because I did not know it when I spoke to him about the specialist.

Whatever the form of sixth sense involved—telepathy, precognition and so on—it manifests in Mr King's consciousness generally in the form of pictures, which, he says, build up not in his mind, but apparently outside and beside him. Sometimes these manifest as symbols, which he is able to interpret intuitively; occasionally they may be accompanied, as it were, by the sound of a piano, violin or orchestra. This only happens, as a rule, when the sitter is concerned with music in some way. And the music seems to be beside his ear, not inside it.

He told a client when he heard music very distinctly and persistently during a sitting: 'Your ambition is to be a singer. You have all the necessary qualities and ability but so far you have got nowhere. If you will do what I tell you you will be successful.'

He said that as well as the usual routine of training and practise she was to visualise every night the stage on which she wished to sing. If possible, she should go and see it. The visualisation must be of the stage only, not the audience. She must sit quietly for about ten minutes, meditating on success, believing it was already hers. Then she was to look in a mirror, hear herself singing with her psychic ear. 'Sing from your subconscious', said Mr King.

This technique is familiar to most students of mind training and psychology, but Mr King says the advice he gave to this woman came to him through psychic channels. He did not know of it consciously.

At any rate, it achieved its object. Soon the sitter began her climb to the success which she achieved when, within a year of consulting Mr King, she sang at the Albert Hall.

He often advises clients to believe in and meditate upon their ambitions. 'You must create the pattern you want and then give it to God to fulfil,' is how he puts it. He believes that the pattern of human life can be changed by constructive thinking, but this must be used as a purposeful and regular routine. Anyone can achieve what they desire—provided they have the will to succeed and are prepared to work for it through meditation and by doing whatever is necessary on the physical level.

He is a great believer in the power resulting from meditation, which he considers is as necessary to everyone's well-being as is food. 'There is no question that clairvoyant faculties are increased by meditation,' he says. Clairvoyance he describes as the opening of a door; the more this power is used, the wider the opening becomes and the vision of what lies beyond. It cannot be forced open; any effort to do so may result in its complete closing; it opens when least expected.

Everyone can open this door, Mr King thinks, but most of us do not realise it, or perhaps are unable to make the attempt without training. Or are afraid. . . .

Physical reactions can interfere with or stop the functioning of the sixth sense. Mr King finds that a heavy meal dulls his psychic perceptions; so does anxiety or annoyance. On the other hand, he says he has given some of the best readings of his career when feeling really ill.

During his life, William King has run the whole gamut of psychical experience. He has produced phenomena at seances (including a canary which flew about the room, surprising him as much as anyone, before it dissolved into the air), he has been a direct voice medium, has healed many illnesses, including polio, has material-ised entities, produced automatic writing in many languages, among them Urdu, Greek and Hebrew, of which he has not the slightest conscious knowledge.

The precognitive faculty functions in every true clairvoyant; sometimes it manifests spontaneously, as in the example I quoted of the foretelling of Mr Gaitskill's death; sometimes when sitting with a client, the psychic enters into a state of mind—not neces-sarily a trance condition—in which he will be receptive to impressions of the sixth sense. Evidence of the range and accuracy of the functioning of Mr King's precognitive faculty would fill a library, since he has had a full appointment book for perhaps thirty years. Although he never takes the names of a sitter, people telephone to tell him his predictions have come true, as in the case of a business man who made a fortune in tin through Mr King's advice. Or they tell the Press, as did Lady Dufferin and Ava, who gave an interview to the magazine *Nova* in March 1965, describing how exact Mr King's forecast for her had been.

Newspaper headlines confirmed the truth of his prediction con-cerning two women who consulted him. Not long ago Mr King was happily telling a young, attractive woman, whose life seemed full and pleasant enough, of its possibilities, when these impressions jolted to a sudden stop. He said: 'You have made plans to take a journey abroad by aeroplane very soon. Do not go. Cancel the flight at once.' She said it was not possible. 'But I tell you,' said Mr King, 'that you must'.

The following week, he gave a sitting which followed much the same pattern. To this client he said: 'I must have an aeroplane fixation. Last week, I told one of my consultants to cancel an aeroplane flight, now I must say the same thing to you. Do not go.' 'Mr King,' the client answered, 'the woman whom you advised last week to cancel her flight was my daughter, Mrs X. My name is Mrs Y. She and I are travelling by aeroplane together next week. We cannot possibly put off the journey.'

'I implore you both not to go,' Mr King repeated.

The following week he saw the names of mother and daughter in the list of passengers killed in an aeroplane crash.

He believes in survival. Death he describes 'as simply passing from one room to another.' He constantly sees people in the 'other room', he thinks as little of it as you and I think of encountering men or women in the street. He shared the three hundred year old cottage he once owned in a Sussex village with a former tenant whom he came to believe had been a smuggler. The first indication Mr King had of his presence was footsteps which patrolled the place from about midnight onwards. The cottage, which is in fact three cottages knocked into one, has in its main room an inglenook made out of ships' timbers. And one night the new owner saw sitting there a man in a navy blue fisherman's jersey, a rough frieze coat beside him. He used to appear frequently in his corner watching Mr King for hours on end. Sometimes he would sketch recognisable initials—always the same ones—in the air with his forefinger. One day Mr King went over the inglenook with the beam of a strong torch. Carved into one of its corners he found the initials which his visitor drew with such care. He discovered they were the initials of a man who had once lived in the cottage, which had been used as a smugglers' hideout. But what the man wanted with him, he never knew.

It is easier, Mr King says, to tune in to lower than higher forces; therefore he believes it important for a clairvoyant to keep his mind as much as possible on a positive and constructive level. He thinks that perhaps his attitude to life is summed up by his family motto; 'Return good for evil', which is inscribed in Latin on the ring he always wears, made from his grandfather's and grandmother's wedding rings, joined together.

The faculties of extra-sensory perception, we know, must be basically similar in all clairvoyants, but the way in which they manifest in each person is subtly different. Different, too, is every clairvoyant's approach to the use of these faculties.

Mrs Ena Twigg, for example, is interested in scientific experiments in connexion with the functioning of the sixth sense. Her powerful psychic abilities are at the service of parapsychologists and doctors whenever she has time to spare from her clients.

She comes from a psychic family. When she was very young, she was conscious of what she calls 'the misty people', who seemed very real to her, though their bodies were not solid as were those of the physical world. When she was fourteen years old, the 'misty people' told her 'You're not going to have your father for long. In a week he'll be with us.' So far as was known her father was perfectly healthy at the time but on the following Monday, he suddenly died.

Mrs Twigg had a very serious illness when she was a girl. None of the specialists called in could discover what was wrong with her. One night when the doctors thought she was dying, the 'misty people' said to her: 'We have arranged to heal you'. By next morning her condition had improved, although the cure took six months to complete.

In the last war Mrs Twigg often was helped in periods in anxiety by the working of her sixth sense. She always knew the whereabouts of her husband, who was in the Navy, even though they were 'top secret'. She knew from which ports he would sail. On one occasion she says that she had a vision of D day (which she recorded) some months before the happening. The date of the war's end was also told to her psychically—again she made a record of the details.

Mrs Twigg works often, though by no means always, through trance conditions. Phenomena and materialisations of all kinds come through then, although they sometimes occur even when she is giving a 'conscious' state reading. The phenomena usually manifest in the first floor room she calls the 'sanctuary', but she remembers that during a sitting in a downstairs room, a large vase full of flowers took off from a table, circled, and wove to and fro, about six feet in the air. 'I never know when something like that may happen', she says.

Mrs Twigg believes, as Mr King does, that the individual survives death. She quoted three of many instances in her experiences which seem to indicate survival. Their significance lies in the fact that information was given by the communicator which was not known to the sitter at the time. While I am not arguing against survival, I think we have to admit that from a scientific point of view although these instances are additional evidence of Mrs Twigg's exceptional psychic powers, neither they nor the great majority of such cases constitute proof that the information came from a discarnate entity.

Usually the details given could have come from the sixth sense, of the medium or clairvoyant, functioning as telepathy or other such faculty aided by the subconsciousness' talent for dramatisation. Probably we do not yet know enough to be sure just what survival means. . . .

However we interpret them, the cases quoted to me by Mrs Twigg from her store of such records, are interesting as manifestations of the sixth sense. To a woman client who had just arrived from America, as Mrs Twigg knew psychically, she said 'Do you know your mother is dying?' 'My mother is quite well', the sitter answered. The next day she telephoned to Mrs Twigg saying that a cable had arrived telling her her mother had died the day before. The next time she came to see Mrs Twigg the mother came through. To give her daughter proof of her identity, she said: 'My wedding-ring slipped off my finger after I was dead, and someone threaded a rosebud through my fingers.' These two points were confirmed later by a relative who was with the mother when she died. The client did not know these details when she sat with Mrs Twigg.

The second case concerns a wife who was likely to lose her property because an important document concerning it could not be found. Her husband, through Mrs Twigg, told his wife that the paper was hidden in a place where she later found it.

A woman whose husband died suddenly was left with a factory containing a specialised type of plant of which she knew nothing, as her only source of income. Through Mrs Twigg, the husband told the wife that he would enable her to run it. He gave detailed instructions which his widow relayed to the staff; for some years the factory was run successfully apparently from the spirit world.

The last case of this type concerns a man whose little daughter had just died. He used to sit with Mrs Twigg regularly; one day the child appeared, and told her father: 'I am being born again'. Soon after this his wife became pregnant; when the baby arrived she was, the father said, a replica of the child they had lost, and as she grew older, not only in appearance, but in character and mannerisms as well.

One of the most surprising experiences of Mrs Twigg's career was with a man who telephoned asking so urgently for an appointment that she agreed to see him 'after hours'. As she had had no sort of introduction with this client, a point on which she usually insists, she asked her husband if he would be in; he said he had a meeting which he could not very well cancel.

The client was a large man; she particularly noticed that his hands were huge and of peculiar shape. However, his manner was pleasant and inoffensive and rather to her surprise, Mrs Twigg was able to get excellent results for him. When the sitting was over, he said: 'This has been wonderful. You have convinced me of survival—now I'm going home to kill my wife'.

And he was serious about it. He said that the woman to whom he was married had nagged and made him miserable for twenty-five years. The reason he hadn't killed her, though often he had wanted to, was that he believed that to take her life would mean the end of everything for her. Now that he felt certain she would survive death, there was nothing to hold him back. . . .

For two hours Mrs Twigg tried to talk him out of his decision, wondering now and again whether he might feel inclined to experiment with her. After his visit she watched the papers for some days but as no murders which fitted the conditions were reported, she hoped that he had thought better of the idea.

Trance mediumship could be called the forte of Mrs Marjorie Staves—though she prefers to give clients a 'conscious' reading at their first visit. While 'controlled' she has spoken in five languages, of which her waking self has no knowledge. She has worked in Washington, New York, Philadelphia, Canada, and Germany; tests of her powers were carried out by twenty-one scientists for twelve months.

During one of these tests, she was given a sealed envelope, in which was a personal object which she was told belonged to a celebrity of the entertainment world. The envelope, Mrs Staves knew as soon as she touched it, had nothing to do with a stage or screen star; it came from a fellow-psychic, and she gave an accurate reading to its owner.

Sixteen people materialised at one seance, at which a Press photographer was able to take a picture of her guide, White Hawk, who had been her 'control' for about twenty years. He spoke to me through Mrs Staves, in a deep, rather gutteral voice, manifesting suddenly while she sat holding my watch. The only sign of his coming was that Mrs Staves' eyes closed, and shivers which amounted almost to convulsions shook her three times. When he left the spasms recurred; passing, as her eyes opened and her normal personality took over.

White Hawk seemed to know all about my past and present conditions. He foretold future happenings in some detail, which I hope will prove equally correct, giving several dates. This is unusual; since the psychic sense functions on a level at which time and space as we know them are non-existent. A clairvoyant seldom gets an impression of when an event foreseen is likely to occur.

All her life, Mrs Staves' sixth sense has been so active that when she was a child of only twelve or fourteen, her mother used to ask her psychic advice. She believes that the gift should and can be used to enable men and women to make contact, even if briefly, with the invisible world; a contact which she thinks necessary because it helps them to realise the reality and possibilities of this other world. An experience she had when she was confirmed, to her is corroboration of her belief in the purposiveness of clairvoyance. When she and her twin sister were kneeling before the Archbishop of Canterbury, seemingly by chance, he put his hands twice on Mrs Staves' head, 'My child, you are doubly blessed', he said.

Among many remarkable incidents in her career, she remembers particularly a woman who came to her in deep distress. 'You have just come from a mortuary,' said Mrs Staves, 'where you identified your son who was killed a few hours ago in a car accident. Try not to grieve; he is here now with you. Don't think of him as dead.' And the mother went away comforted.

She told a woman whom she 'saw' had just received a cheque from an insurance company in compensation for a lost diamond watch and ring, 'Send back the cheque. You will find your jewellery in a wardrobe which you have not used for a long time.' The woman did not believe this possible, but having searched as Mrs

Staves told her, she telephoned to say she had found the watch and ring.

On 12th February, 1964, the London *Daily Express* asked Mrs Staves to forecast the results of the Liston-Cassius Clay fight. She said: 'Cassius Clay will take his man in the second round', and as it turned out, he did.

The night before the air crash in which Nancy Spain, the columnist, Jean Werner Laurie (Editor of *She*) and several others were killed, Mrs Staves was a fellow-guest with them at a dinner given by Mrs Dolly Goodman and her husband. Most of the party were to travel in the same aeroplane to the Grand National next day. Mrs. Staves begged them not to go. They made the irreparable mistake of not taking her warning seriously.

A number of well-known people are among Mrs Staves' clients; on the list are Harry Secombe, Peter Finch, Vera Lynn, Bob Monkhouse and Donald Campbell.

CHAPTER XV

The Sixth Sense at Work (II)

IN one of the monastically peaceful rooms set aside at the College of Psychic Science for consultations, Suffolk-born Mrs Allingham told me that the activities of the sixth sense were among her earliest memories. When she was four years old she was taken by her father on board a Dutch schooner, where she created something of a stir by insisting that there was in the saloon a woman (whom no one else could see) playing a harp.

This is her first recollection of contact with a non-physical entity. After it, appearances from the 'other side' were so frequent that her nightly prayer was: 'Don't let me see anything please, dear God. Amen.'

When she was taken to the Tower of London, among the crowds of ordinarily-dressed people, she saw men and women in satins and brocades, sparkling with jewels. Some of them were crowned. At first she thought they were in fancy dress; then when she saw it was obvious that no one else was taking any notice of them, she realised what they were. None of the scenes of violent death and suffering which are so large a part of the Tower's history came through to her; she believes this did not happen because children are protected psychically from sights or sounds in the other world which might harm them.

Before she was twelve, the faculty of precognition began to show itself in her. She found that tea-leaves left in the cup formed pictures for her of what would happen to the person whose cup it was. She knew in advance what people would come to the house the next day or the next week; when people would put off appointments . . . and although her mother said 'Nonsense' when her daughter made these predictions, she had to admit they were always right.

When she fell in love, and married, she knew that she would be widowed soon afterwards. Her husband died as foreseen, but, she says, almost immediately after his death she was given signs that he was still with her.

When she went to the cemetery, where he was buried, for the first time after the funeral, she could not find the grave. As she wandered about, unable to find an attendant, she felt as if she were being pushed towards a certain grave. She was so certain it was his that she left there the flowers she had brought; a later check showed that it was indeed the grave for which she had been looking.

One day a bunch of red roses, flowers which her husband had always given her, materialised in an empty fireplace; another time she saw one of her husband's feet, then one of his hands. She knew then, she says, that her husband had survived as a conscious individual. If he were able to make contact, he had said, he would materialise partially; this was to be her assurance of his continued existence. She believes that ever since then he has acted as her guide; she says sometimes he communicates with her in a pre-arranged code during a sitting giving information which she needs to have at that moment.

Sometimes Mrs. Allingham is asked by men or women for her help, from the 'other side'. A man whose looks and aura repelled Mrs Allingham seemed in such great distress that in spite of the distaste she felt, she knew she must do what she could for him. He said he was a gangster named Podola, who had shot two policemen, would she please pray for him. Evidently her prayers were successful. After a time she never saw him again.

There were difficult times in Mrs Allingham's life but always the helped she needed, financial or otherwise, appeared in time to save the situation. When she was forced to sell her house, up till almost the date set for handing it over to the new owner she still had not been able to find anywhere to live. She was in a state of near-despair when she semed to hear a voice saying: "You'll hear of a flat tonight'.

That evening Mrs Allingham had a sitting with a client for whom she had felt rather sorry; she had the idea the woman was hard up. Somehow after the sitting Mrs Allingham's problem was mentioned. The client turned out to be the wealthy owner of a large house in Kent, where there was an empty flat; this she offered to

Mrs Allingham on the spot, saying: 'My husband will call for you in the car and drive you down.'

When she was visiting an old house near Felixstowe, Mrs Allingham was given a bedroom known as the Drawbridge Room. She knew at once that it had an atmosphere which she described as 'eerie'. She heard nothing but saw a man in a brown suit walking to and fro in a distracted way. Presently he came near to the bed. 'Pray for me. Pray for me.' he kept saying. And then he disappeared. The man had never appeared in the house before, apparently her hostess knew nothing of him or his story. But later Mrs Allingham met a woman who knew the house well, and who was not surprised to hear of the man's visit. He had committed suicide in the Drawbridge Room.

The three materialisations just mentioned—of Mrs Allingham's husband, the gangster and the brown-suited man—seem to be manifestations of conscious entities, as distinct from the 'gramophone ghost' which it is thought may operate on the lines of a disc or film. The idea that there is a medium which holds visual or auditory impressions in much the same way as they are retained on photographic plate or wax disc, is so far only theory; but it seems likely that it is a theory not far wide of the truth: it fits in with the usual pattern of a certain type of manifestations. The 'ghost' in such cases plays the same scene over and over again when the film or record is set going, apparently by the power given off by a psychic.

The type of manifestation when what appears to be a conscious entity is concerned does not follow a pattern of this kind. These entities are thought to be projections of ectoplasm borrowed, it is supposed, from the physical body of a medium by the spirit as a temporary vehicle for manifestation. Ectoplasm is usually supposed to be a substance which is part of or can be generated in the human body, since photographs of ectoplasm flowing out of or returning to it have been taken under test conditions. It may be the basis for and explanation of a great deal of supra-physical phenomena, such as some types of thought-forms, apportages and so on.

The non-gramophone type of manifestation apparently is directed by individualised intelligence, which may or may not be discarnate. . . . The more we study the fascinating subject of what 'lies round the corner' the more we realise the existence of infinite possibilities, concerning which much research is needed before we can come to definite conclusions concerning them. And while steering clear of too abstract metaphysical speculation, I think we have to keep in mind the realisation that the explanation of non-physical phenomena may not be what it seems to be or even what we would like it to be. A scientist described to me a recent experience of his own in terms which show the necessity for suspending judgment. He said that he had seen what appeared to be the Ba (one of the series of psychic bodies belief in which was part of Egyptian theological doctrine) of a woman whose headdress indicated that she had been an Egyptian princess. 'I could have imagined her, which explains nothing because we don't know what constitutes imagination. Or I could have strayed into another time dimension and experienced something from the so-called past. Or the girl could have projected herself in a dream (or by some other means) into the so-called future and had a glimpse of the modern world of which I happened to be part . . . which I should think must have given her a shock. . . . Or she might have been a materialised spirit. And there may be other "ors" of which we do not at the moment know.'

If ectoplasm is a constituent of the life-force which animates the body, this may account for the tiring effect its withdrawal in materialisation phenomena has on most mediums. Among psychics who have told me that they prefer to avoid producing materialisations if possible because it leaves them so exhausted, is Mrs Leith-Walker, a clairvoyant some of whose work is done under the aegis of the College of Phychic Science.

But as in all forms of the sixth sense, materialisation is not always under conscious control. It can happen without the consent or intention of the medium. When Mrs Leith-Walker saw her husband, who had died not long before, walking in front of her down the street she had made no conscious attempt to contact him. She followed him into a nearby post-office. After a minute or so he came out into the street again, took a few steps—and then was not there any more.

For a time after his death, she used to hear his footsteps in the flat every evening; sometimes would see him. His visits became less and less frequent until they ceased altogether.

Psychic awareness began for Mrs Leith-Walker in childhood. With her it first developed as intense sensitiveness to the feelings and reactions behind the facade with which most people disguise their inner selves. She remembers praying, at the age of ten, 'Let me see beyond the masks of people'.

In her late 'teens she worked with a Swiss doctor as secretary-receptionist in a house in Norland Square. He also had a School of Wisdom (soi disant) in Gower Street. Whether he or she were the activator, phenomena of every kind manifested in the house, from footsteps and knocks on doors, to discarnate figures. The doctor had an altar in one of of the rooms; Mrs Leith-Walker never discovered its purpose. The atmosphere of the house she found disturbing; she did not stay long with the doctor.

It seems that most clairvoyants do not choose their profession; it chooses them. Mrs Leith-Walker describes herself as a 'reluctant clairvoyant'; quite content with her work as an artist. But she was so much beset with psychic experiences, circumstances so often arose in which her faculties were the means of helping somebody, that eventually she found herself practising as a psychic.

Her chief interest is still—as when a child—to sense the inner feelings of people. To do this enables her, she says, to establish contact with clients and to help them with their problems. In the case of women, she finds these are mostly emotional. Men chiefly want advice on business matters.

Among the psychic experiences she remembers most vividly is the appearance of a tall man with brown hair. He gave her facts about himself which Mrs Leith-Walker was able to check; his name, that he had committed suicide, that he was a schoolmaster and a clergyman. Because he had taken his own life, he had been buried in unconsecrated ground; this seemed so dreadful to him that he begged her to try to arrange for his body's re-interment in a cemetery.

Another experience which stands out in Mrs Leith-Walker's memory is precognitive. She dreamed of a house, which she saw very distinctly, in a country she realised she did not know. She saw this house so distinctly that she made a drawing of it when she woke. Some time afterwards, visiting Morocco for the first time, she was taken to the house of her dream; her drawing could have been made from the building itself. She lived in this house for some time, partly because the country fascinated her, and partly to study the pronounced psychic development of the Arabs, among whom the sixth sense is said to function as normally as the other five.

One of the rituals at which she was allowed to be present, the purpose of which was to obtain some wished-for end, had a corpse as its main feature. Having rifled a grave, the celebrants fed the body with cous-cous, then danced around it, chanting and concentrating upon the result they hoped to bring about.

In the Romanies (the gypsy people) the psychic faculties are supposed to be as general as they are in most Arab races. Apparently although some male Romanies are psychic—the celebrated Gypsy Petulengro, who died a few years ago, was an example—the gift descends chiefly in the female line. Very little is known factually about the origin of the Romanies. For centuries the world has been their country; they travelled America, Russia, Europe and the East in their 'vardos' (wooden, horse-drawn caravans), following for about two thousand years the ancient pattern of nomadic life. The Romany language indicates that they are a nomadic tribe which migrated from Central Asia several centuries B.C.; this is born out by the fact that their clairvoyant techniques are of Eastern tradition.

The Petulengro family seems to have a lion share of the Romany psychic gifts. The sixth sense of Eva Petulengro, great-niece of 'Gipsy' Petulengro, is making a reputation for her as a clairvoyant remarkable as her great-uncle.

Eva Petulengro was born twenty-five years ago in a vardo parked in a football-field behind the Black Swan at Spalding, Lincolnshire. The first light she saw came from a hurricane-lamp swinging from the roof of the 100 year old caravan, which had been built for her great-grandfather in Norfolk. In it she travelled up and down the country with her family, who 'worked' fairs, amusement parks and entertainment centres in seaside and holiday towns, until she was about twenty.

The Petulengros first came to England with the Romany 'invasion' five hundred years ago. After their long wanderings the family settled in Brighton, if not permanently, at least for longer than they had stayed in one place before—'two winters and three summers'. Neither they nor their ancestors had ever lived in a house before; Eva has one of her own now, into which she moved in 1964 when she married a 'gorgio'—a non-Romany.

She says she cannot remember when her sixth sense was not active. Its working is so much a matter of course among Romanies that its absence, not its presence would be remarkable. At fourteen she took up clairvoyance seriously; she began to read hands at fairs, not by ordinary methods of palmistry—'Romanies have their own system, which my mother taught me as soon as I was able to understand anything. Her mother taught her, and so it has always been.'

Without knowing anything about me, or my books on health and longevity (*Eat and Stay Young, Nature's Way to Health, Why Grow Old?, The Earth Heals Everything*, and so on) which I have studied for many years, Eva Petulengro, looking at my hand, said: 'I have never seen such a long life line, and I have seen a few. And even that is not so remarkable; usually in a long life line I see signs of the deterioration which will finally cause death. But here I can't find any; you seem to get stronger and healthier.'

Among records of her verified predictions are the foretelling of the sex of the Royal babies, an air disaster which occurred in February 1964; to Michael Cranford, of the long run which *Come Blow Your Horn* would have; to Jerry of the *Pacemakers* that he would become engaged shortly; to her husband that a yacht in which he was scheduled to race would have an accident resulting in loss of life. The yacht—in which he decided not to sail—was wrecked and sank; at least one member of the crew was drowned.

Eva has told Harry Corbett of *Steptoe And Son* that a political career is likely for him. Godfrey Winn, Brian Rix, Frankie Vaughan, Alan Melville, Cilla Black, George 'Beatle', and among other celebrities who consult her.

Materialisations, impressions received clairvoyantly, or as symbols and pictures, are the chief ways in which Anthony Trevor's six sense manifests.

The first psychic experience he remembers came to him when he was seven years old. He and his brother were sent for a holiday with their grandparents at Gorleston-on-Sea. When they came back they were told that their mother was away. At bedtime no one came to tuck them in, as their mother always came. The little boys were crying bitterly, when they both saw their mother come into the room. She kissed them, she dried their tears and tucked them up snugly. Anthony and his brother both remember that the bed-clothes in the morning were just as she had left them, the night before.

At breakfast, their father told them that their mother had gone on a long journey. When both the boys insisted that she had come to their room the night before, their father first thought they were lying and then that they were dreaming. 'If it were a dream,' Anthony Trevor said; 'it seems odd that my brother and I should have dreamt exactly the same dream and that our mother's handkerchief with which she had dried our cheeks, was on my pillow when we woke.'

Mr Trevor went to sea for some years before taking up psychic practice professionally. He found that he could produce manifestations of phenomena in circles in which he was sitting without effort. At one sitting a newspaper reporter was one of five people who with hands linked formed a circle. The room was not entirely dark; soon they could see trumpets moving about in the air above their heads, advancing and retreating, as if dancing a minuet. Suddenly one of the trumpets dived and tapped a sitter smartly on the nose; he said afterwards that he had issued a mental challenge to whatever power was controlling the trumpets to do this. Presently chairs and a table, which two men, using physical strength, could lift only a foot and that with difficulty, took off from the floor and cavorted four or five feet above the floor. When the sitting was over, the newspaperman took the room apart to discover if there were any possibility of what Mr Trevor calls 'spoof'. He found absolutely nothing of the kind.

The sixth sense sometimes operates powerfully in a psychic at public meetings; perhaps because a force is generated by the gathering upon which the clairvoyant is able to draw; actors, singers, speakers also experience a current flowing to them from the audience. This surcharge can give, Mr Trevor says, the extra confidence needed to carry the psychic over doubtful moments which often arise at open meetings.

One of these came to Mr Trevor early in his psychic career. He had the impression that a wife was anxious to get through to her husband whom Mr Trevor was able to pick out. But for this flow of confidence he says, he would never have had the courage to give the man before several hundred people his wife's message, which was that she was there with a pair of kippers. . . .

The husband was so overcome he could hardly tell Mr Trevor that those kippers meant proof of survival to him. He said: 'My wife used often to cook kippers for me because I like them so much. She always said if she could come back, she would bring a pair with her, to prove that she really was there.'

William Redmond, whom I met at the headquarters of the Spiritualist Association of Great Britain in Belgrave Square, gives the impression of being an unusually collected kind of man. Like so many psychics, the sixth sense began to function actively in his childhood. At fourteen he had a sense of contact with the forces of the invisible world. At seventeen he was asked to take his first public psychic meeting, at Forest Row; the scheduled speaker had been prevented from coming at the last moment.

Mr Redmond keeps detailed records of his sittings and experiences. Among them, he said, he found three which he considered useful illustrations of the workings of the sixth sense.

Five years ago, said Mr Redmond, he took a seance at which six people were present, at Birkenhead. Mr Redmond told one of the women that her husband had come through. 'That's impossible,' she said. 'He is still alive.' The time was three o'clock in the afternoon. She explained that her marriage having broken up, she and her husband lived apart, but in houses in the same street; she had seen him going to work that morning.

Later she telephoned to Mr Redmond. At three o'clock that afternoon, her husband had been killed by a lorry.

Mr Redmond's second case concerned the granting of a Queen's Pardon, which is given perhaps six or seven times in a hundred years. The client to whom he foretold it was a woman who had consulted him previously. On one occasion he had warned her not to go away for Christmas. She stayed at home, as he advised—and on Christmas Day her husband died.

Some time afterwards she came to Mr Redmond in great grief. Her son, who was in the Army, had been accused of falsifying accounts, cashiered and sent to prison for ten years. His mother insisted that he was innocent—how, she asked Mr Redmond, could she get his name cleared? Mr Redmond told her that there was no need for her to do anything. Fresh evidence would come to light unexpectedly; there would be a retrial and a Queen's Pardon. The mother said the case could not be re-opened, only a miracle could help her son. 'The miracle will happen,' was Mr Redmond's answer.

Six months afterwards new evidence was discovered which established that his client's son had been convicted through mistaken identity. A retrial was ordered; the result was a Queen's Pardon, as he had foretold.

The third case on Mr Redmond's list concerns a sitting he gave to a Mr Donald Lloyd of Richmond four or five years ago. Mr Redmond told Mr Lloyd he would leave the company for which he was working for six months, and then go back. Mr Lloyd was certain this could not happen, because, 'If once I decide to finish with anything, it is final. I would never go back to any situation or thing'. This was in the November. Nothing happened until the following June, when the directors who employed Mr Lloyd told him that a company had been formed with which they had some association. This company proposed to open a section dealing in the type of work in which Mr Lloyd specialised; a request had been made that he should join them for six months. If he would consider the idea, the directors said, his present job would be kept open for him. So as Mr Redmond had foretold, Mr Lloyd left his firm for six months and then went back to it. At the time of the prediction, the new company had not made the decision which led to Mr Lloyd's visit to them; his own company knew nothing of it, and neither, of course, did he.

Telepathy seems to be ruled out as an explanation in this case; the event when Mr Redmond described it, had not even taken shape in thought. This is an experience which all clairvoyants have, it seems; so far, although numerous theories have been put forward, no one knows just how or why precognition works on this level, or what factors are involved. The most popular rationale probably is that there being no time in a real sense, and therefore no past and no future, it is as easy to glimpse happenings of, say next year, as to look back on those of twelve months ago; that is if one has the working equipment, the sixth sense. But this may be an over-simplification; questions of time and consciousness dimensions have to be considered, and the claims of free will—which many scientists and philosophers admit. And these, if viable, must be incorporated into an acceptable framework.

This is still only speculation and theorising—which is necessary so that more may be discovered about the sixth sense—but what interests most people in the meantime is evidence of its existence. So let us watch it at work again, this time in the top flat of an old house in Covent Garden where Mrs Penrose lives, the widow of Charles Penrose, the 'Laughing Policeman' of music-hall, stage, television and gramophone record fame, who died about eight years ago. She herself was well-known for her children's stories of which she made recordings, such as the *Inkwell Fairy* and *Dismal Desmond*, under the nom-de-plume Billie Grey.

Mrs Penrose came to Covent Garden as a bride of eighteen to the house next door to her present flat. Her first home was supposed to be haunted though the only evidence of it she herself saw was a woman in a crinoline who passed her on the stairs. From time to time, visiting friends would see or hear psychic manifestations. Stanley Lupino, who was a sensitive, several times saw a man in knee breeches, smoking a churchwarden pipe—but his connexion with the place was never discovered.

She realised that she had clairvoyant powers when at the age of fifteen she foretold to a school-friend her mother's illness. Mrs Penrose said she never tried to use these powers; she 'was scared' of seeing the pictures in her mind which later took shape as events in her own or other people's life.

After her marriage to Charles Penrose; except for the occasional prediction as to the success or otherwise of one of his shows, she more or less ignored the psychic side of her life. But it would not be suppressed. When she was in Egypt with her husband a 'wise man' in one of the 'souks' (bazaars) told her that she had marked psychic gifts, which she would have to use one day, at first to help friends and family, later professionally. A few years afterwards, she and Charles Penrose, who was making 'laughing records' in Bavaria, went searching for cuckoo-clocks (a hobby of his), to a small village, in which lived an old woman who had learnt palmistry and cartomancy from the gypsies. They had accepted her as a friend, although she was a gorgio, and as a token of their friendship had given her one of their greatest treasures, a pack of cards.

The card were so old that the gypsies did not know their age. There are thirty-eight of them, all numbered on the face, which instead of the usual suit, knight, queen or king symbol, carries a picture; a house, clover, a book, a key, a cross, of the same type, but different from Tarot representations. They are smaller than ordinary playing-cards.

The 'wise woman' told Mrs Penrose that one day she would practise as a clairvoyant. When they parted, she gave her the gypsy cards, telling her: 'You will be able to use these—I do not need them; the time I have left is very short'.

Mrs Penrose heard that a few weeks' after she and her husband left Bavaria, the old woman died. As foretold she did use the gypsy cards; and in spite of being offered substantial sums for them by collectors and experts, who say they are extremely rare, is still using them. Until she, too, has no further need of the gypsies' gift she will not part with it.

Mrs Penrose does not always use cards; sometimes impressions about a sitter's health or circumstances form as pictures either in her mind or round the client. Stage and screen people are among her consultants; executives of the entertainment world, of whom the producer Stanley Willis Croft (*Gentlemen Prefer Blondes, etc.*) is one, will not sign a contract without asking her psychic advice. An accident to Mr Willis Croft's uncle was foretold by Mrs Penrose; two deaths which she said were imminent in his circle, occurred the next day. Her son, Peter Penrose, production chief of Moss Empire, always consults her before making decisions. He was once offered two contracts, one of which carried a larger salary and apparently better prospects than the other. His mother advised him to accept the less obviously attractive proposal, which he did. It turned out to be better in every way than what had seemed the more tempting opening.

To avoid the pitfalls which are hidden from the reasoning mind, Mrs Penrose sees as the most important function of her psychic power. 'So often', she says, 'it helps people to avoid making mistakes, and puts them on the right path'.

CHAPTER XVI

On The Threshold

WE are said to be on the threshold of a new cosmic phase, the Aquarian Age, the era of light, victorious over the Kali Yuga, or Dark Age. For nearly two thousand years, under the dominating influence of Pisces, man has been hypnotised into the belief that he was born in sin, born to suffer; his only hope of salvation the denial of everything that gave him joy—in the words of Ogden Nash: 'Vanity, vanity, all is vanity, That's any fun at all for humanity'. One of the signs of the approach of the new age is the growing refusal to accept any longer this negative doctrine.

The concept of Cosmic Ages is very ancient; a belief that Time moved in a Great Cycle, which spanned approximately 28,000 years, measured by the periodical backward movement of the equinoctial axis in zodiacal latitude. The Great Cycle was separated into twelve Ages, the length of each of which was estimated to be about 2160 years; an estimate arrived at by dividing 25,868 (the number of years, more or less, through which the cycle of the precession of the equinoxes runs) by 360, the degrees of the zodiac, which gives seventy-two years per degree of precession. Seventy-two multiplied by thirty, which is thought to be the number based on primitive observation of planetary movements, produces 2160, generally accepted as the period of an age.

As the precession of the equinoxes is retrograde, the cosmic cycle moves backwards also. It begins with Pisces, passes into Aquarius, thence into Capricorn, and so on. The Piscean Age is thought to have begun in about 100 B.C.; according to this reckoning it is in its last phase.

The last phase of an old and the beginning of a new era are considered to be of great importance. They are transition periods, in which trends and impulses which affect people and affairs, begin to show themselves. Upheavals seem to be inevitable as the old order passes; the breaking-down before the building-up, katabolism before anabolism. But one of the characteristics of the Aquarian Age is order, before the end of this century, we can hope to see signs at least, of its manifestation.

Realisation that the birthright of humanity is not suffering, disease, lack and sorrow, but happiness, dominion, fulfilment, as I mentioned at the beginning of this chapter, is a herald of the Aquarian phase. We are beginning to accept that manifestations of the life-force are not necessarily libidinous; that they can be equated with zest, joy, the ecstasy of living all of us ought to, and few do experience; which is allegorised in the Invocation to the Cyprian, in Professor Gilbert Murray's translation of Euripes' *Hippolytus*:

> For mad is the heart of Love
>   And gold the gleam of his wing
> And all to the spell thereof
>   Bend, when he makes his spring.
> All life that is wild and young
>   In mountain and wave and stream
> All that of earth is sprung
>   Or breathes in the red sunbeam.
> Yea, and mankind.
>   O'er all, a royal throne,
> Cyprian, Cyprian, is thine alone.

And again the growing awareness of and interest in the non-material is the very autograph of the Aquarian phase. Professor Julian Huxley talks of this change which is taking place in consciousness in *New Bottles For New Wine*. Although no doubt he sees it from a different point of view and expresses it in different terms, expansion into fresh dimensions of mind is basically the idea which we are considering here. He says: 'As a result of a thousand million years of evolution, the universe is becoming conscious of itself, able to understand something of its past history and its possible future. This cosmic self-awareness is being realised in one tiny fragment of the universe—in a few of us human beings. Perhaps it is being realised elsewhere, too, through the evolution of conscious living creatures on the planets of other stars. . . .'

Logically I think that we cannot avoid the conclusion not only that this is so, but that this form of awareness has been realised by 'conscious living creatures' uncountable times on uncountable other planets. It is a phase of evolution, as we can gather from our own experience, and evolution is a continuous orderly sequence of cause and effect, which we can infer must proceed throughout the cosmos, not only in one infinitesimal part of it. Expanding knowledge and realisation of our place in the universal scheme makes the idea untenable—and ludicrous—that the minute speck of dust which we inhabit in an insignificant solar system in one of the uncountable galaxies (100,000 million similar to our own have been discovered already) in infinite space, should be the only planet on which consciousness, or self-consciousness, has developed, and is evolving in a form of life.

All that so far is known of natural law argues against such a proposition. Everything created has a function and a purpose; Nature has no use for playthings. If the role of at least a proportion of the unguessable proliferation of planets is not similar to that of this tiny globe—what is it? So far, we know next to nothing even of the other worlds in our own solar system. There may be no life on them now, but aeons ago they may have been inhabited, or in the next 'tick of the cosmic clock', another aeon, they may be.

It is only guesswork, but a guess made on a reasonable basis, to say that forms of life on planets at a stage of evolution similar to our own, would be recognisable as what we call human, animal and so on. Comparable patterns recur through all creation; the suns and planets we are able to observe seem to be built to the same model as our own. The atom's construction is the prototype of the solar system's; crystalline formations of all kinds are predictable.

So it is not straining reason to breaking-point to consider that there are in countless other worlds beings not too unlike ourselves who have reached a comparable state of conscious awareness. And since research has shown that nothing—neither space nor time, nor climatic nor atmospheric conditions—affects the power of thought, perhaps we may be receiving stimulus in our progress towards the next cosmic phase from them, and they from us. Nothing is impossible now that science has opened to us the world of the mind in which physical laws and limitations are transcended.

What science is saying today, we know that mysticism has affirmed through millennia. Now, at last, the point has been reached when the concepts of the scientist and those of the mystic are almost indistinguishable, though formulated in different terms. Materialism is becoming as out-of-date as the theory that the earth is flat. With each discovery fostered by the new awareness, we take another step into the Promised Land which visionaries and philosophers have glimpsed, but in which we have never dared to believe.

The Promised Land is a land of freedom from concepts which prevented most men in most ages from using more than a fraction of their powers and from experiencing more than a fraction of their possibilities. So long as we accept the teaching that the visible world and the laws which govern it are reality, at least while we are in the flesh, we are like the elephants in the story, who, corralled by a rope over which they could have stepped with the greatest ease, were efficiently encaged because they *thought* they could not get out.

Now that the axis of reality has shifted from the visible to invisible, we can step over the illusory boundaries to explore the almost uncharted territories of the paraphysical world. Dr J. B. Rhine sees this stepping outward as an adventure of tremendous possibilities. He says: '. . . the explorer who is properly prepared for such adventurous inquiry into the unknown of man's nature, into the problem of the unique driving influence in the universe men call the human spirit, will shed no tears if the uncertain shores on which he lands turn out to be, not Cipango with its teas, silks and spices, but a vast, an unexplored continent without as yet even a name. The new worlds of the past have *always* exceeded the wildest dreams of the adventurer.'

This is the charter of the Aquarian Age—the freedom to enter a world which exceeds 'the wildest dreams of the adventurer'; words which paraphrase the Biblical promise 'Eye has not seen . . .' and retell the parable of the prodigal son. The time came when he was weary of the husks—the outer forms, which cannot give lasting satisfaction—and returned to the place where he belonged.

And so it is with us. We are coming to realise that while material things are all very well in their way—toys to amuse and to be enjoyed—of themselves they are of as little value as the 'husks that the swine did eat'. They belong to the world of effect, and realisation of this opens for us the way to the world of cause, the 'place where we belong', the world of the mind.

In this world, man is being established, as Rhine says, as a 'spiritual being in a universe, which is, as we have seen, at least not devoid of spiritual forces'. Science, in fact is demonstrating by logic the truth of tenets which till now have ben a matter of blind faith. It is, in this way, doing religion a great service; far from destroying the churches' sphere of influence, it offers opportunities for consolidation unparalleled in ecclesiastical history.

But these opportunities are also a test. If orthodox religion is to survive as a force in the new world of the mind, major overhauls and reconstructions are unavoidable. As Professor Rhine says: '. . . even the most scholarly consecrated leadership in all the religious systems simply does not have answers that would satisfy the ordinary standards of evidence of everyday life in the bank, or in the court, or the market place, let alone in the sciences. In the face of that realisation, dogmatic religion comes to assume the shape and proportion of a gigantic group delusion, cutting itself off deliberately from the tests of reality by which its position could be verified, and by which its course towards greater positive knowledge could be directed. For in this old attitude is almost complete abandonment of realism, a surrender to a system of unverified fantasy, that in a single, isolated individual would be diagnosed as psychotic.'

The churches are not empty because people do not need religion but because they need it in a new form. Doctrines of today must take into account the possibilities of applying psychic or spiritual powers to the immediate problems of life and to its betterment, as did Christ himself. As T. C. Lethbridge points out, he was the greatest exponent of these powers in history. He healed the sick, he raised the dead, he fed the hungry, he turned water into wine. And he said that what he did, everyone else could do. 'And greater things than I do shall ye do.'

Dogmatic religion, which has never made much of a show of following its founder's example in dealing with the practical needs of its followers, is either unable to or at any rate does not so far take advantage of scientific discoveries which could do much to re-establish its leadership. Forms of orthodox faith and the ways in which they are presented have changed little through the centuries; the tremendous possibilities opened up by science's re-revelations seem to have made small impact on them. Professor Rhine comments: 'Would there be any more monstrous slavery in the world, no matter with what benignity it is practised, than that which confined people to a narrow, primitive religious belief through endless years of blind groping, a slavery of whole peoples that kept them forever missing the richer, more adequate life that might be theirs if they could only be liberated from a fear-inspired, horizon-lowering theory of the world in which they live.'

Slavery of whatever kind—mental, physical, economic—runs its longer or shorter course, then ends. It ends, as every phase of the human story ends, when a change of consciousness takes place which causes old forms and conditons to be discarded, as everything outgrown and outworn should be discarded. We are outgrowing and outwearing authoritarian dogma; unless orthodox religion finds means of re-stating truth in terms acceptable to modern needs, it will cease to exist.

The changes which are manifesting now are inescapable. To attempt to stem or to prevent them would have as much effect as King's Canute's struggle to control the tide. The changes are the out workings of evolution, the cosmic trend, the forward pressure of the universal motive power; or what some scientists today call the Supreme Mind; of what Einstein described as a 'superior reasoning power which is revealed in an incomprehensibie universe.' This, he said, was his idea of God, and his religion consisted 'of a humble admiration of the illimitable, superior spirit who reveals himself in the slight details we are able to perceive with our frail and feeble minds.'

Changed consciousness produces changed conditions. When we pass from one level of awareness to another, we are in a new world, the laws and values of which differ from those we leave behind; to cope with this new life new faculties must develop. When we evolved from the physical phase of existence, in which instinctive processes were dominant, to the next level, the reasoning, rational mind unfolded, through the urge to know and to learn. During this period the laws governing material phenomena were discovered. But as Alexis Carrel said: 'Despite its stupendous immensity, the world of matter is too narrow for him (man)'. So we struggle on to the next phase, and as we progress, again the faculties appear which enable us to establish relationships with conditions beyond the unknown frontiers at which we stand.

MELVIN POWERS SELF-IMPROVEMENT LIBRARY

___ HOW TO WIN AT CHECKERS *Fred Reinfeld* — 5.00
___ 1001 BRILLIANT WAYS TO CHECKMATE *Fred Reinfeld* — 7.00
___ 1001 WINNING CHESS SACRIFICES & COMBINATIONS *Fred Reinfeld* — 7.00

COOKERY & HERBS

___ CULPEPER'S HERBAL REMEDIES *Dr. Nicholas Culpeper* — 5.00
___ FAST GOURMET COOKBOOK *Poppy Cannon* — 2.50
___ HEALING POWER OF HERBS *May Bethel* — 5.00
___ HEALING POWER OF NATURAL FOODS *May Bethel* — 7.00
___ HERBS FOR HEALTH—HOW TO GROW & USE THEM *Louise Evans Doole* — 5.00
___ HOME GARDEN COOKBOOK—DELICIOUS NATURAL FOOD RECIPES *Ken Kraft* — 3.00
___ MEATLESS MEAL GUIDE *Tomi Ryan & James H. Ryan, M.D.* — 4.00
___ VEGETABLE GARDENING FOR BEGINNERS *Hugh Wiberg* — 2.00
___ VEGETABLES FOR TODAY'S GARDENS *R. Milton Carleton* — 2.00
___ VEGETARIAN COOKERY *Janet Walker* — 7.00
___ VEGETARIAN COOKING MADE EASY & DELECTABLE *Veronica Vezza* — 3.00
___ VEGETARIAN DELIGHTS—A HAPPY COOKBOOK FOR HEALTH *K. R. Mehta* — 2.00

GAMBLING & POKER

___ HOW TO WIN AT DICE GAMES *Skip Frey* — 3.00
___ HOW TO WIN AT POKER *Terence Reese & Anthony T. Watkins* — 7.00
___ SCARNE ON DICE *John Scarne* — 15.00
___ WINNING AT CRAPS *Dr. Lloyd T. Commins* — 5.00
___ WINNING AT GIN *Chester Wander & Cy Rice* — 3.00
___ WINNING AT POKER—AN EXPERT'S GUIDE *John Archer* — 5.00
___ WINNING AT 21—AN EXPERT'S GUIDE *John Archer* — 7.00
___ WINNING POKER SYSTEMS *Norman Zadeh* — 3.00

HEALTH

___ BEE POLLEN *Lynda Lyngheim & Jack Scagnetti* — 3.00
___ COPING WITH ALZHEIMER'S *Rose Oliver, Ph.D. & Francis Bock, Ph.D.* — 10.00
___ DR. LINDNER'S POINT SYSTEM FOOD PROGRAM *Peter G. Lindner, M.D.* — 2.00
___ HELP YOURSELF TO BETTER SIGHT *Margaret Darst Corbett* — 7.00
___ HOW YOU CAN STOP SMOKING PERMANENTLY *Ernest Caldwell* — 5.00
___ MIND OVER PLATTER *Peter G. Lindner, M.D.* — 5.00
___ NATURE'S WAY TO NUTRITION & VIBRANT HEALTH *Robert J. Scrutton* — 3.00
___ NEW CARBOHYDRATE DIET COUNTER *Patti Lopez-Pereira* — 2.00
___ REFLEXOLOGY *Dr. Maybelle Segal* — 5.00
___ REFLEXOLOGY FOR GOOD HEALTH *Anna Kaye & Don C. Matchan* — 7.00
___ 30 DAYS TO BEAUTIFUL LEGS *Dr. Marc Selner* — 3.00
___ YOU CAN LEARN TO RELAX *Dr. Samuel Gutwirth* — 3.00

HOBBIES

___ BEACHCOMBING FOR BEGINNERS *Norman Hickin* — 2.00
___ BLACKSTONE'S MODERN CARD TRICKS *Harry Blackstone* — 7.00
___ BLACKSTONE'S SECRETS OF MAGIC *Harry Blackstone* — 5.00
___ COIN COLLECTING FOR BEGINNERS *Burton Hobson & Fred Reinfeld* — 7.00
___ ENTERTAINING WITH ESP *Tony 'Doc' Shiels* — 2.00
___ 400 FASCINATING MAGIC TRICKS YOU CAN DO *Howard Thurston* — 7.00
___ HOW I TURN JUNK INTO FUN AND PROFIT *Sari* — 3.00
___ HOW TO WRITE A HIT SONG & SELL IT *Tommy Boyce* — 10.00
___ MAGIC FOR ALL AGES *Walter Gibson* — 4.00
___ STAMP COLLECTING FOR BEGINNERS *Burton Hobson* — 3.00

HORSE PLAYER'S WINNING GUIDES

___ BETTING HORSES TO WIN *Les Conklin* — 7.00
___ ELIMINATE THE LOSERS *Bob McKnight* — 5.00
___ HOW TO PICK WINNING HORSES *Bob McKnight* — 5.00

MARRIAGE, SEX & PARENTHOOD

_ ABILITY TO LOVE *Dr. Allan Fromme*	7.00
_ GUIDE TO SUCCESSFUL MARRIAGE *Drs. Albert Ellis & Robert Harper*	7.00
_ HOW TO RAISE AN EMOTIONALLY HEALTHY, HAPPY CHILD *Albert Ellis, Ph.D.*	7.00
_ PARENT SURVIVAL TRAINING *Marvin Silverman, Ed.D. & David Lustig, Ph.D.*	10.00
_ SEX WITHOUT GUILT *Albert Ellis, Ph.D.*	5.00
_ SEXUALLY ADEQUATE MALE *Frank S. Caprio, M.D.*	3.00
_ SEXUALLY FULFILLED MAN *Dr. Rachel Copelan*	5.00
_ STAYING IN LOVE *Dr. Norton F. Kristy*	7.00

MELVIN POWERS' MAIL ORDER LIBRARY

_ HOW TO GET RICH IN MAIL ORDER *Melvin Powers*	20.00
_ HOW TO SELF-PUBLISH YOUR BOOK & MAKE IT A BEST SELLER *Melvin Powers*	20.00
_ HOW TO WRITE A GOOD ADVERTISEMENT *Victor O. Schwab*	20.00
_ MAIL ORDER MADE EASY *J. Frank Brumbaugh*	20.00

METAPHYSICS & OCCULT

_ CONCENTRATION—A GUIDE TO MENTAL MASTERY *Mouni Sadhu*	7.00
_ EXTRA-TERRESTRIAL INTELLIGENCE—THE FIRST ENCOUNTER	6.00
_ FORTUNE TELLING WITH CARDS *P. Foli*	5.00
_ HOW TO INTERPRET DREAMS, OMENS & FORTUNE TELLING SIGNS *Gettings*	5.00
_ HOW TO UNDERSTAND YOUR DREAMS *Geoffrey A. Dudley*	5.00
_ IN DAYS OF GREAT PEACE *Mouni Sadhu*	3.00
_ MAGICIAN—HIS TRAINING AND WORK *W. E. Butler*	5.00
_ MEDITATION *Mouni Sadhu*	10.00
_ MODERN NUMEROLOGY *Morris C. Goodman*	5.00
_ NUMEROLOGY—ITS FACTS AND SECRETS *Ariel Yvon Taylor*	5.00
_ NUMEROLOGY MADE EASY *W. Mykian*	5.00
_ PALMISTRY MADE EASY *Fred Gettings*	5.00
_ PALMISTRY MADE PRACTICAL *Elizabeth Daniels Squire*	7.00
_ PALMISTRY SECRETS REVEALED *Henry Frith*	4.00
_ PROPHECY IN OUR TIME *Martin Ebon*	2.50
_ SUPERSTITION—ARE YOU SUPERSTITIOUS? *Eric Maple*	2.00
_ TAROT *Mouni Sadhu*	10.00
_ TAROT OF THE BOHEMIANS *Papus*	7.00
_ WAYS TO SELF-REALIZATION *Mouni Sadhu*	7.00
_ WITCHCRAFT, MAGIC & OCCULTISM—A FASCINATING HISTORY *W. B. Crow*	10.00
_ WITCHCRAFT—THE SIXTH SENSE *Justine Glass*	7.00

RECOVERY

_ KNIGHT IN RUSTY ARMOR *Robert Fisher*	5.00
_ KNIGHT IN RUSTY ARMOR *Robert Fisher (Hard cover edition)*	10.00

SELF-HELP & INSPIRATIONAL

_ CHARISMA—HOW TO GET "THAT SPECIAL MAGIC" *Marcia Grad*	7.00
_ DAILY POWER FOR JOYFUL LIVING *Dr. Donald Curtis*	7.00
_ DYNAMIC THINKING *Melvin Powers*	5.00
_ GREATEST POWER IN THE UNIVERSE *U. S. Andersen*	7.00
_ GROW RICH WHILE YOU SLEEP *Ben Sweetland*	8.00
_ GROW RICH WITH YOUR MILLION DOLLAR MIND *Brian Adams*	7.00
_ GROWTH THROUGH REASON *Albert Ellis, Ph.D.*	7.00
_ GUIDE TO PERSONAL HAPPINESS *Albert Ellis, Ph.D. & Irving Becker, Ed.D.*	7.00
_ HANDWRITING ANALYSIS MADE EASY *John Marley*	7.00
_ HANDWRITING TELLS *Nadya Olyanova*	7.00
_ HOW TO ATTRACT GOOD LUCK *A.H.Z. Carr*	7.00
_ HOW TO DEVELOP A WINNING PERSONALITY *Martin Panzer*	7.00
_ HOW TO DEVELOP AN EXCEPTIONAL MEMORY *Young & Gibson*	7.00
_ HOW TO LIVE WITH A NEUROTIC *Albert Ellis, Ph.D.*	7.00
_ HOW TO OVERCOME YOUR FEARS *M. P. Leahy, M.D.*	3.00
_ HOW TO SUCCEED *Brian Adams*	7.00

____ HUMAN PROBLEMS & HOW TO SOLVE THEM *Dr. Donald Curtis*
____ I CAN *Ben Sweetland*
____ I WILL *Ben Sweetland*
____ KNIGHT IN RUSTY ARMOR *Robert Fisher*
____ KNIGHT IN RUSTY ARMOR *Robert Fisher (Hard cover edition)*
____ LEFT-HANDED PEOPLE *Michael Barsley*
____ MAGIC IN YOUR MIND *U.S. Andersen*
____ MAGIC OF THINKING SUCCESS *Dr. David J. Schwartz*
____ MAGIC POWER OF YOUR MIND *Walter M. Germain*
____ MENTAL POWER THROUGH SLEEP SUGGESTION *Melvin Powers*
____ NEVER UNDERESTIMATE THE SELLING POWER OF A WOMAN *Dottie Walters*
____ NEW GUIDE TO RATIONAL LIVING *Albert Ellis, Ph.D. & R. Harper, Ph.D.*
____ PSYCHO-CYBERNETICS *Maxwell Maltz, M.D.*
____ PSYCHOLOGY OF HANDWRITING *Nadya Olyanova*
____ SALES CYBERNETICS *Brian Adams*
____ SCIENCE OF MIND IN DAILY LIVING *Dr. Donald Curtis*
____ SECRET OF SECRETS *U.S. Andersen*
____ SECRET POWER OF THE PYRAMIDS *U. S. Andersen*
____ SELF-THERAPY FOR THE STUTTERER *Malcolm Frazer*
____ SUCCESS-CYBERNETICS *U. S. Andersen*
____ 10 DAYS TO A GREAT NEW LIFE *William E. Edwards*
____ THINK AND GROW RICH *Napoleon Hill*
____ THREE MAGIC WORDS *U. S. Andersen*
____ TREASURY OF COMFORT *Edited by Rabbi Sidney Greenberg*
____ TREASURY OF THE ART OF LIVING *Sidney S. Greenberg*
____ WHAT YOUR HANDWRITING REVEALS *Albert E. Hughes*
____ YOUR SUBCONSCIOUS POWER *Charles M. Simmons*
____ YOUR THOUGHTS CAN CHANGE YOUR LIFE *Dr. Donald Curtis*

SPORTS

____ BILLIARDS—POCKET • CAROM • THREE CUSHION *Clive Cottingham, Jr.*
____ COMPLETE GUIDE TO FISHING *Vlad Evanoff*
____ HOW TO IMPROVE YOUR RACQUETBALL *Lubarsky, Kaufman & Scagnetti*
____ HOW TO WIN AT POCKET BILLIARDS *Edward D. Knuchell*
____ JOY OF WALKING *Jack Scagnetti*
____ LEARNING & TEACHING SOCCER SKILLS *Eric Worthington*
____ MOTORCYCLING FOR BEGINNERS *I.G. Edmonds*
____ RACQUETBALL FOR WOMEN *Toni Hudson, Jack Scagnetti & Vince Rondone*
____ RACQUETBALL MADE EASY *Steve Lubarsky, Rod Delson & Jack Scagnetti*
____ SECRET OF BOWLING STRIKES *Dawson Taylor*
____ SOCCER—THE GAME & HOW TO PLAY IT *Gary Rosenthal*
____ STARTING SOCCER *Edward F. Dolan, Jr.*

TENNIS LOVER'S LIBRARY

____ HOW TO BEAT BETTER TENNIS PLAYERS *Loring Fiske*
____ PSYCH YOURSELF TO BETTER TENNIS *Dr. Walter A. Luszki*
____ TENNIS FOR BEGINNERS *Dr. H. A. Murray*
____ TENNIS MADE EASY *Joel Brecheen*
____ WEEKEND TENNIS—HOW TO HAVE FUN & WIN AT THE SAME TIME *Bill Talbert*

WILSHIRE PET LIBRARY

____ DOG TRAINING MADE EASY & FUN *John W. Kellogg*
____ HOW TO BRING UP YOUR PET DOG *Kurt Unkelbach*
____ HOW TO RAISE & TRAIN YOUR PUPPY *Jeff Griffen*

The books listed above can be obtained from your book dealer or directly from Melvin Po
When ordering, please remit $2.00 postage for the first book and $1.00 for each additional k

Melvin Powers
12015 Sherman Road, No. Hollywood, California 91605